INDIA UNDER RIPON

A PRIVATE DIARY

WILFRID SCAWEN BLUNT

GYAN

Published by

Gyan Publishing House
5, Ansari Road
Daryaganj, New Delhi-110002
Phone: 011-47034999, 9811692060
E-mail: books@gyanbooks.com

Distribution Network
gyanbooks.com
India, USA, Canada, UK, Australia

ISBN: 978-93-7097-126-4 (PB)

First Published, 1909

2nd Impression 2025

Printed at: Gyan Press, Delhi.

INDIA UNDER RIPON

Arthur WILFRID SCAWEN BLUNT

INDIA UNDER RIPON

INDIA UNDER RIPON

A PRIVATE DIARY

BY

WILFRID SCAWEN BLUNT

CONTINUED FROM HIS

"SECRET HISTORY OF THE ENGLISH OCCUPATION OF EGYPT"

1909

CONTENTS

APPENDICES

INDIA UNDER RIPON

CHAPTER I

INTRODUCTORY

I OUGHT perhaps to have named this volume "The Awakening of India," because it describes the condition of Indian things at the time of Lord Ripon's viceroyalty, which was in truth the awakening hour of the new movement towards liberty in India, the dawn of that day of unrest which is the necessary prelude to full self-assertion in every subject land.

The journey it records was made under circumstances of exceptional interest at an exceptional moment, and should be instructive in view of what has happened since. It contains a foreshadowing of events which are under our eyes to-day, and suggests a solution of problems which, after long waiting and with a timid courage, is gradually being accepted as official.

The political situation in Lord Ripon's time was as follows: Mr. Gladstone, when he came into office in 1880, found himself at the head of an immense majority in the House of Commons, pledged to ideas of liberty in the East of which he had himself been the foremost preacher. With regard to India he had formulated the Liberal creed in a single sentence: "Our title to be in India," he had said, "depends on a first condition, that our being there is profitable to the Indian nations; and on a second condition, that we can make them see and understand it to be profitable." His predecessor's policy had proved a failure. It had been one of imperial expansion, of reckless finance, and of administrative coercion. It had resulted in a disastrous frontier war, in an immense financial deficit, and in the exasperation of the educated native community. There had been a terrible famine, the severest perhaps of the century. Many millions of the agricultural peasantry had died or were reduced to a condition of semi-starvation. Famine, to use the words of a popular Anglo-Indian writer of the time, had become "the horizon of the Indian villager; insufficient food the foreground." The forest laws, the salt tax, the ever increasing pressure of the revenue officers had driven some districts to the verge of revolt. The vernacular press, which would have denounced the Government as the cause of these evils, had been gagged in the towns; and disaffection, stifled in its expression but none the less real, was rife almost everywhere. The unrest was becoming, it was thought, dangerous. It was to remedy these evils, and to put the government of India on a footing of sounder economy, less war, and a closer confidence between rulers and ruled, that Lord Ripon was sent to India in the summer of 1880.

The choice of Lord Ripon as Queen Victoria's representative and Viceroy was, I believe, to a large degree Her Majesty's own. Little as she was in sympathy with Mr. Gladstone, she had this in common with the new programme, that the disaffection of her Indian subjects distressed her, and hardly less the arrogance with which they were treated by their fellow subjects of British origin. In the proclamation issued to the people of India after the Mutiny, her royal name had been appended to a promise of entire equality as between these and the others; and it touched her dignity that her promise should have remained so long unredeemed. She had, besides, a personal regard for Lord Ripon on account of his great integrity, and he seemed to her the man most reliable she could send to deliver a new message in her name to the people.

Lord Ripon landed in India in the late summer of the year of Mr. Gladstone's victory. He bore with him words of peace and hope which raised native imagination to a point of high expectancy. Mr. Gladstone's name, to those who understood English politics, seemed a guarantee of all reforms; his opinion about India had been proclaimed from the house-tops; and the Queen's personal interest in the matter of her proclamation was known, and gave additional assurance to the popular desire. Nor was Lord Ripon's individual attitude a disappointment to those who came in contact with him. Though possessed of no great personal gifts or graces, he was a transparently honest man, and it was felt that, as far as it lay with the Viceroy to affect the situation, he could be relied on as a friend to native India. He was seen from the first to be a serious man, but without the chill reserve which is so great a barrier between Englishmen and Orientals, and his manner had something paternal in it which inspired a full measure of native confidence. It was an advantage to him, I think, that he was not a member of the English Church, but a Roman Catholic of more than ordinary piety. Such was the impression made by Lord Ripon at the opening of his Indian career. It was noticed of him as a wonderful thing that, on landing at Bombay, his first visit was to the Roman Catholic Cathedral, and a little later that in the streets of Calcutta he would return the salutes of his native acquaintance, contrary to all viceregal custom, and to the point that it became the subject of private expostulation with him on the part of his official *entourage*. His first public acts were in character with the programme given him to carry out. The policy of enlarging British India at the expense of her Asiatic neighbours and of the native states was reversed; economy became the order of the day in finance; and, as a first measure of conciliation with educated native opinion, the gag of the press law was removed. It was made clear that under the new *régime* no native of India was to be persecuted for the expression of his political views.

Nevertheless it was not long before it began to be perceived that, however loyal Lord Ripon might be to his reforming principles, a change had come over the spirit of those at home, in whose hands the driving power of Indian reform really rested. In the early summer of 1882, Mr. Gladstone, to the scandal of the Eastern world and in contradiction of every principle he had professed two years before when out of office, allowed himself to be persuaded to take violent action in Egypt against the National Party of Reform, and, after bombarding Alexandria, to send an army of 30,000 men to put down the constitutional *régime* beginning to be established there, and restore, under pretext of repressing a rebellion, the forfeited authority of the Khedive. It was an act of brutal and stupid aggression, a war and an intrigue, undertaken in the interests of cosmopolitan finance and in defiance of both law and principle. Also, to make the matter worse for India, a large share of the burden and cost of the war was thrown on the Indian army and the Indian Exchequer. Against the gross injustice of this part of the transaction, Lord Ripon protested in vain. He was powerless to oppose the insistence of the Home

Government, and the financial iniquity was accomplished. From that moment it became evident to the Viceroy that his mission of reform in the entirety of its original scheme was doomed to failure. And so in truth it proved. The lapse from principle in Egypt entailed other lapses, and in India, and indeed throughout Asia, put back the clock of reform and self-government for at least a generation. The spirit of aggressive imperialism in the East, against which the Midlothian campaign had been a protest, was by Mr. Gladstone's own aggression revived and strengthened. His sermon of Indian economy, and his denunciation of unnecessary Indian wars were alike rendered ridiculous, and the whole position of those who had followed him as the Apostle of Eastern freedom, was abandoned to its enemies. Lord Ripon in the spring of 1883, when, after two years of unwearied labour in the attempt to gain over the Anglo-Indian officials to some practical measure in accordance with the Queen's proclamation, he decided at last to give battle on what is known as the Ilbert Bill of that year, knew himself already to be a beaten man; he felt that he was championing a lost cause.

The Ilbert Bill was in itself but a very poor instalment of that promised equality between her English and her Indian subjects which he had been sent to give. Its object was to put a stop to the impunity with which non-official Englishmen, principally of the planter class, ill treated and even on occasion did to death their native servants. It was to give for the first time jurisdiction over Englishmen in criminal cases to native judges—instead of to judges and juries only of their own countrymen. Trifling remedy, however, though it was, it roused at once the anger of the class aimed at, and a press campaign was opened against Lord Ripon of unusual violence in the Anglo-Indian journals. The Ilbert Bill was described as a revolutionary measure. which would put every Englishman and every Englishwoman at the mercy of native intrigue and native fanaticism. The attacks against Lord Ripon were certainly encouraged by the Anglo-Indian officials; and presently they were repeated in the press at home, and to the extent that the Bill became a question in which the whole battle of India's future was being fought over and embittered. The "Times" took up the attack; the Cabinet was alarmed for its popularity, and the Queen was shaken in her opinion of her Viceroy's judgement. Lord Ripon was left practically alone to his fate.

Those who have read my "Secret History of the English Occupation of Egypt" will understand in what way the cause Lord Ripon was still defending at Calcutta was likely to affect me. It will be remembered that, in the time of his predecessor, Lord Lytton, I had paid a flying visit to India where I had enjoyed the then Viceroy's hospitality during two months at Simla. It had been a visit solely of personal friendship, made at the close of a long journey in Arabia, Turkey, and Persia, and that, notwithstanding a Tory education and much prejudice in favour of my countrymen, and in spite, too, of the daily society of such high Anglo-Indian officials during my stay as Sir John Strachey, Sir Alfred Lyall, and Lord Lytton himself, who had been at special pains to instruct me in their ways and methods of administration, it had left me more than doubtful of the advantage to native India of our imperial rule. Strachey's policy of "forward finance" seemed to me one especially ruinous to India—a policy of ever-increasing expenditure, ever-increasing public debt, and ever-increasing taxation. Neither he nor Lytton had been able to convince me that the immense poverty of the agricultural peasantry was not connected with our extravagant English administration. This last Lytton, in his lighter moods, was fond of describing as "a despotism of office boxes tempered by an occasional loss of keys."

Still I knew nothing for certain about native India. At Simla I had had no opportunity of conversing with so much as a single representative of its thoughts in opposition to the official views, nor had I caught more than a glimpse of the skeleton figures of the starving ryots as I passed rapidly by railway through their plains. When I once more, four years later, turned my thoughts to Indian travel, the single advantage I had acquired was that in the interval my political education in regard to East and West had progressed, and I had graduated in the severe school of personal experience. The case of the Egyptian fellah is not very different from that of the Indian ryot, and the economical needs of both are closely parallel. I had witnessed the Egyptian revolution, which was a revolt of the peasantry against a burden of debt, with my own eyes and at close quarters, and I had found myself behind the scenes in its struggle with European intrigue, a struggle where I knew the right to be with the native reformers, the wrong with our obstinate officials. I was determined that this time it should not be under official chaperonage I would travel, but as far as was possible on a basis of free intercourse with whatever inhabitants of the land I could get access to. As a Home Ruler in the East, I wished to ascertain what the true feeling of the country was towards its English masters, and what the prospect of India's eventually gaining her freedom.

In this design I was of course greatly aided, as far as Mohammedan India went, by the common cause I had made with the Egyptians in their revolution, and the public advocacy of it I had undertaken. It had put me in communication with some of the liberal leaders of the Panislamic movement, and it is from them that I obtained, so to say, my passports to the confidence of their Indian co-religionists. To the Hindus I had no introduction. But here circumstances, at the outset adverse in appearance, aided me. My arch opponent in Egypt had been the Anglo-Indian Controller there of Finance, Sir Auckland Colvin, and he, having got wind of my intention, made an effort to frustrate it, by representing me to Lord Ripon as a person politically dangerous, whom it would be prudent to exclude from India, or place under official ban. Colvin's special service in Egypt had just come to a close and he was once more in active Indian employment, and his name carried weight. Nevertheless he found Lord Ripon irresponsive. Then, having failed at head-quarters, he had recourse to the Anglo-Indian press and, through an old standing connection with the "Pioneer" newspaper, denounced me in print, an ill-advised action which, more than any favourable introduction could have done, insured me a welcome with the Hindus. Thus it happened that wherever I went I was an object of pleased curiosity with the disaffected, as one who, having incurred the anger of the Anglo-Indians, was by that fact presumably their friend. If, in the sequel, my journey achieved its object, and indeed far more than its object, it was to the "Pioneer" and other organs of hostile official opinion that I mainly owe it.

At the moment of my leaving London I received, in connection with this and another matter, a message from Downing Street asking me to call there, and the first entry in my diary refers to this. The other matter was in regard to Egypt, where it had been suggested that I should stop on my way to India and see Sir Evelyn Baring, then newly appointed to the post he was so long to hold, and concert with him a plan of restoring there the National Party. The idea had been Mr. Gladstone's, and I reserve a full account of it for another occasion when I shall return to my Egyptian history, only premising here that it came to nothing at the time and was made a pretext later for excluding me from Egypt, reference to which exclusion will be found in the diary. The first entry of all refers to this, and to my then political connection with Lord Randolph Churchill, in concert with whom, more or less, my journey was undertaken. The Hamilton mentioned in the diary was Sir Edward Hamilton, Mr. Gladstone's chief private secretary; the Primrose, Sir Henry Primrose, then holding the same position with Lord Ripon. I omit in transcription nearly all that relates to Egypt, reserving that part of my diary for another occasion. As to Lord Randolph, it may not be unnecessary to explain that, in the battle in which I had been engaged during the past year in Egypt, by far the most effective ally I had found in Parliament had been the young leader of the Fourth Party. Churchill, though an imperialist of the Disraeli school, was a young man full of engaging qualities, with generous impulses and a large sympathy with the weak and oppressed. I had formed a close friendship with him, and had succeeded in interesting him in my Oriental ideas to the extent that besides taking up the cause of

Egyptian nationalism, he later visited India, and on his return in 1885 professed himself converted to Lord Ripon's policy. About this, and about his short career as Secretary of State for India, I had intended to include a chapter in this volume. But it has been decided that this, with much else of a later date than 1884, shall be reserved for another occasion. Churchill entered on his office with the best of intentions and ideas, and I am still of opinion that had he remained for a few years at the India Office he would have pushed on reform there as none of his successors have had the courage since to attempt it.

With this preliminary word I leave my diary to tell its own story.

CHAPTER II

CEYLON

"*12th Sept.*, 1883.

"LEFT home by the 10 o'clock train, and spent the day in London. A letter had come from Eddy Hamilton by the morning's post asking to see me before I went abroad, and I went to Downing Street at one o'clock. Mr. Gladstone is away yachting, and Eddy is acting Prime Minister, and a very great man. I had not been to Downing Street since last year—just upon a year ago—when I went to ask for Arabi's life. Eddy was extremely amiable this time, and asked me what I was going to do in the East. I told him my plans exactly—that I was going first to Egypt, and should call on Baring and, if I found him favourably disposed, should propose to him a restoration of the National Party, but if he would not listen I should go on to Ceylon and India; that I could not do anything in Egypt without Baring's countenance, for the people would not dare to come to speak to me; but, if Baring would help, I thought I could get the Nationalist leaders elected at the elections—all depended on the action of our officials. Also as to India—that I had no intention of exciting to rebellion; that I should go first to Lord Ripon, then to Lyall, and afterwards to the provinces; that the subjects I wished principally to study were the financial condition of the country, that is to say, to find out whether our administration was really ruining India, and to ascertain the views of the natives with regard to Home Rule. Of both these plans Eddy seemed to approve, said that Baring would be sure to wish to see me, and listen to all I had to say, and, though he did not commit himself to anything very definite about the rest, did not disapprove. With regard to India, he said he would write to Primrose, Lord Ripon's private secretary, to show me all attention; so on the whole I am highly satisfied with my visit. I had some talk with Eddy about Randolph Churchill. He said that my connection with him in Egyptian affairs did me harm, but I don't believe that, and I look upon Churchill as quite as serious a politician as the rest with whom I have had to deal. On Egypt I think he is sincere, because he has an American wife, and the Americans have always sympathized with freedom there. I believe, too, that he is at a turning point in his character, and means to have done with mere random fighting, and we both agreed that he has a career before him. For my own part I like Churchill. He does not affect any high principles, but he acts squarely."

The next day I left with my wife for Paris, where our principal interest was to see the small group of Egyptian exiles congregrated there.

"*13th Sept.*—We arrived by the night train at Paris, and alighted at the Hôtel S. Romain, a quiet place where we can see our friends. Presently Sabunji came in with Sheykh Jemal-ed-Din.[1] When I saw the Sheykh in London in the spring, he wore his Sheykh's dress. Now he has clothes of the Stambouli cut, which, however, sit not badly on him. He has learned a few words of French, but is otherwise unchanged. Our talk was of India, and of the possibility of my being able to get the real confidence

[1] A history of Seyyid Jemal-ed-Din Afghani, the well-known leader of Liberal Panislamism will be found in my "Secret History of the Occupation of Egypt," 1907. Mr. Sabunji had been employed by me in Egypt, and accompanied me there on the present occasion as my secretary as far as Ceylon.

of the Moslems there. He said that my being an Englishman would make this very difficult, for all who had any position to lose were in terror of the Government, which had its spies everywhere. He himself had been kept almost a prisoner in his house and had left India through fear of worse. Any Sheykh who gained notoriety in India was tracked and bullied, and if he persisted in an independent course he was sent on some charge or other to the Andaman Islands. People, he said, would not understand that I wished them well, and would be too prudent to talk. The poorer people might, not the Sheykhs or the Princes. He thought Hyderabad would be my best point, as there were refugees there from every province of India, and they were less afraid of the English Government. He said he would write me some private letters to explain my position, and to the editors of some Mohammedan newspapers. I told him what the political position was, and how necessary it seemed to me that the Moslems should show that they joined the Hindus in supporting the Ripon policy. All depended on the Indians showing a united front. He said they might have courage, if it could be proved to them that there were people in England who sympathized with them, but they only saw the officials, who *never smiled when they spoke to them*. I asked him about the language I should most prudently hold regarding the Sultan, and he advised me to say nothing against the Sultan in India, or about an Arabian Caliphate; it had been spread about that the English were going to set up a sham Caliphate in Arabia, under a child, whom they would use to make themselves masters of the holy places; the Sultan's name was now venerated in India as it had not formerly been.

"14*th Sept.*—Jemal-ed-Din and Sanua and Sabunji

came to breakfast, and we stayed talking all day. The Sheykh brought with him letters which he had written to the Nawab Abd-el-Latif of Calcutta, and the Nawab Rasul Yar Khan of Hyderabad, both of which I hope may be of great value. He told us some interesting particulars as to his own people and family, repudiates the idea of the Afghans being a Semitic people, says on the contrary that they are Aryans, like the inhabitants of Northern India, but his own family is Arabian, and they have always preserved in it the tradition of the Arabic language. He also discoursed on history. I read them my poem 'The Wind and the Whirlwind,' which Sabunji in part translated to the Sheykh. He said that, if he had been told there was in the world an Englishman who really sympathized with the misfortunes of India, he would not have believed it. Sanua exhorted me to have the poem translated into good Arabic verse by El-Rakkam, a pupil of Abdu's. I also went through with him a programme I have drawn up for the restoration of the National Party in Egypt, and talked over with the Sheykh a scheme of restoring the Azhar as a real university for all Islam, and he explained how it had been in old days."

The same evening we took train to Marseilles, and went on by Messageries steamer to Egypt, where we spent a fortnight. Our stay there was productive only of disappointment as far as the political situation went. I found Sir Evelyn Baring, when I called on him, willing enough to talk things over with me, but half-an-hour's conversation was sufficient to convince me that, whatever Mr. Gladstone might dream or pretend to dream about restoring the National Party and recalling the exiles, nothing was further from Sir Evelyn's mind. He had no intention whatever but that of supporting the Khedive and the party of reaction. We consequently turned our steps once more eastwards, and embarked at Suez on the 9th of October, in the British India ship "Ghoorkha," having so far altered our original plan of travel as to include in it Ceylon, where we desired to visit our exiled Egyptian friends, Arabi Pasha and his four companions. We intended to stay with them a few days only and pass on thence into Southern India.

We were delayed, however, longer than we thought. I had hardly got on board when I began to develop a malarious fever, which, before the end of the voyage had become serious. The "Ghoorkha" was a detestable conveyance, overcrowded, swarming with vermin, and miserably provided. There was no doctor on board, nor any means of comfort for a sick person. Driven out of my cabin by the heat and its discomforts, I was laid on a table in the saloon, and there passed my days in extreme wretchedness but nursed by my wife and her maid Cowie, who was devoted and admirable on such occasions. Our fellow passengers were a rough set of Colonial English and planters from India, Assam and Burmah. With these we had a constant battle for existence. In the early days of the voyage I still tried to write my journal, and I give such extracts from it as have anything of public interest.

"10*th Oct*.—The only persons on board we know anything of are the half-caste Russell going to Jeddah, and a young fellow, Mrs. Palmer's brother, who has been given a Government place worth £800 a year in the Mint at Calcutta. He is to stay there two years, and then to be transferred to the London Mint, this doubtless through Lord Northbrook."

This is a good instance of the way the Indian revenue is sometimes made use of to evade the difficulties of jobbery in England. Professor Palmer had been sent by Lord Northbrook, then at the Admiralty, on a secret mission connected with the intended invasion of Egypt, and had lost his life (see "Secret History of the English Occupation of Egypt"), and his widow had applied to his lordship for a pension. As the mission was a secret one, and could not be avowed, it was not found possible to include this in the English Navy Estimates, so Palmer's brother-in-law was jobbed into the Indian service in the way described, as part of the compensation due to his widow.

"The rest of the passengers are tea-planters, or English settlers in India, the class most angry at the Ilbert Bill, and we are not very amiably regarded by them. I have passed my time reading the 'Koran,' which is a great consolation in circumstances such as ours. There are moments when I could arise and proclaim a *jehad* on board.

"11*th Oct.*—I have had some conversation with an intelligent young tea-planter settled near the Burmese frontier. He seems to think a new rebellion is brewing in India. In his district within the last two years the villagers have taken to cursing the English when they pass, and even throwing stones. He has the usual arguments against the Ilbert Bill—the venality of native magistrates, prevalence of native false witness, and the rest. In another district the planters had sworn that they would not accept the bill if it became law, but would deal in their own way with the first native magistrate who presumed to try a European. He did not believe the bill would pass. If it did, India would be lost. The natives were already 'far too cheeky.' A sensible old lady who has lived twenty-five years in Burmah had something of the same opinion, but spoke very strongly against the opium trade. The Buddhist priests of Burmah have complained that our rule has demoralized the country, which before had no vices, but is now given up to opium eating and spirit drinking. She says this is quite true, and that the Government forced their opium on the people for the sake of the revenue. She likes Burmah, nevertheless, and is going out now with the whole of a very numerous family undismayed at possible dangers.

"12*th Oct.*—The Feast of Beiram. The waiters and crew, most of whom are Moslems, said their prayers together on the forecastle, having put on clean turbans. We are passing Socotra, which lies north of us, ranges of barren hills.

"13*th Oct.*—Last night an old indigo planter with a bottle nose entertained us with his views on the Ilbert Bill and kindred matters. He had been twenty years in Bengal; there were fewer planters now than before the Mutiny; the planters were the backbone of the Empire, and saved it in the Mutiny, and now were the backbone of its finance. I asked him to explain this, and he said that they advanced money to the Zemindars to enable them to pay the Government dues. They charged no interest, but took villages in exchange, their only advantage being that the villagers worked their indigo grounds for them. The planters would all leave India if the Ilbert Bill passed.

"There is a Mr. Y. on board who bought nine thousand acres of land last year from the Government, but the natives on it would only pay rent for sixteen acres, though they occupied it all. He was very indignant, and said the Indian Empire would go to ruin if they played any tricks with it. It was a conquered country, and the niggers were all rogues from the first to the last. The little tea-planter joined in, but assured us that no improvement was to be expected from making them Christians. Some of the planters in his neighbourhood had employed converted coolies, but found them far worse than the others; they used sometimes to go away all together and drink for a week at a time. Nobody became a Christian except for some underhand object, and as soon as he had got it he went back; he considered drinking part of the conversion. He mentioned how an Englishman of his district had been condemned to a year's imprisonment for manslaughter on false evidence, as the man he had injured had not died—though the Englishman beat him. They asked me what the English Government meant to do, what their idea was in upsetting things? I said I believed it was merely a question of economy; the Indian Government as it was did not pay its expenses; it was like sending away an expensive Scotch gardener from a poor garden; the country would be worse administered perhaps. I consoled Mr. Y., however, by assuring him that the people now in office, Lord Kimberley, Lord Northbrook, and Lord Granville, were as little likely to do anything really in the direction of freeing the Indians as any three Tories in the kingdom. In answer to a question, the tea-planter said: 'Of course it is impossible to get on without being bullies now and then, but it is a good rule never to touch the natives unless you mean it in earnest. If you strike a nigger and he thinks you are afraid to hit him hard, he runs you in to a certainty before the magistrate, but if you give it him well, he knows he deserves it. You must be careful, however, not to overdo it, for they are very soft, and four out of five have enlarged spleens, and they are capable without any exaggeration of dying to spite you.'

" 14*th Oct., Sunday.*—I am worse again to-day,

and can do nothing but sit up and lie down, and wish I was dead. The Moslem servants have found out we are different from the rest of their masters on board, and are very attentive. What irritates them particularly, they have told Sabunji, is that nobody speaks to them by name, but only as 'boy' here, and 'boy' there. There is a bitter hatred between them and the passengers, and no wonder. Not that there is any actual ill-treatment by these—that was put a stop to three years ago by a strike among the Bengalis, who refused any longer to be beaten on the British India boats—but brow-beating there is in plenty. Last night young Langa, Mrs. Palmer's brother, came to sit with us. He told us he had been given his place in the Indian Mint, although he was not even an Englishman. His father had been a Polish patriot, and he was indignant at the way the natives were treated on board. He is an amiable boy of about twenty-three, very like his sister in face and voice. A yellow butterfly was blown on board to-day.

"*15th to 18th Oct.*—Too ill to write. Last night, however, we cast anchor at Colombo just after sunset. We expected our friends to come to us on board, but I was too tired to care. Sabunji went forth like the raven from the Ark, and did not any more return!"

The next three weeks I spent grievously sick, and then beginning to be convalescent, at Colombo. On the morning of the nineteenth our friends Mahmud Sami and Arabi came on board to take us to a beautiful country house the former had prepared for us, and on landing we were received by a deputation from the Mohammedans of the town. The whole road we found had been decorated with flowers for our reception, and there was a triumphal arch at the entrance to the house, which was some miles from the landing-place. I was carried through it all, hardly conscious of what was going on, nor of the fireworks and illuminations which took place in my honour in the evening. My journal contains no record of these days until the 3rd of November, when I find a pleasant description of my daily life.

"*3rd Nov.*—I get up every morning as soon as it is light, and am carried to the verandah, where I sit and watch the rather curious view which is in front of the house. The house stands fronting a piece of fresh water, which is the river's mouth and is used by the fishing boats as a harbour. Beyond it there is a long strip of sand covered with green bushes, and beyond that again the sea. The fishing boats come in over the surf at daybreak, and then double back up the reach of still water, and just in front of the house are run up on the shore. It is astonishing how fast they sail, and how steady they are in the breakers. But they are of Catamaran build, and seem able to go where they like, and do what they like. They are quite light, too, for a man and a boy can pull them up high and dry without difficulty. When out at sea, those on board are half in the water, but they cannot upset, because as they heel over there is a spar resting on the water to which the boat is spliced. They are obliged, however, to run before the wind as they cannot easily tack. Then, soon after sunrise, boys come with goats which they turn out to graze on the green bushes; and then men with horses and oxen which they bathe in the river. None of the men swim, but they stand about in the shallow water, ducking up and down and splashing each other, so that with their long hair they look just like women. The oxen come in carts, and are taken out and bathed with pails which are poured over their backs, and the ponies are treated in the same way. It is a very pretty sight, and the same beasts and people come every morning, so that I seem to know them all. I sit there in a dreamy state drinking my coffee, and then go back to bed.

"Later in the day a sofa is put for me under the other verandah by the garden, and I have another kind of view. There is a grove of bananas with fruit nearly ripe, and all day long the little gray squirrels, which are hardly bigger than mice, run over them, jumping from branch to branch and looking into the bunches to see if there are any ripe enough to eat. They make a shrill cry when a kite or crow passes overhead, which is like a bird's. Then there are flowers, red and yellow and blue, which are visited by little birds like willow wrens, who get at the honey by pecking through the stalks. But in the middle of the day there are only butterflies, almost every day new ones, black and yellow, black and blue, and once one black and green; also small yellow butterflies, and black and white ones, and a butterfly like a large red Admiral, and that great russet-coloured one which one sees everywhere in Asia and North Africa, a link between the East and the West, *Chrysippus*. These sometimes come into the verandah, and are near getting caught in the great spiders' webs under the roof. The afternoons are generally rainy, but after the showers lizards come out and climb the bushes, and they have a favourite bush with dark leaves, in which one day I saw a chameleon. About four o'clock the sky becomes dark with hooded crows and jackdaws returning from the town to an island on the river where they roost. They raise a great clamour, and I have made a calculation that about seventy thousand pass every evening across the small bit of sky which I can see. They often stop on a banyan tree as they go by, or on the coco-nut palms. The other birds seem all afraid of them. At last, as it gets dark, they are gone, and then two little black and white robins come out and sit on a post and rail, and hiss at each other like blackcaps, and a pair of listless yellow-legged thrushes follow them and hop about among the grass. Then it gradually gets quite dark, and the fireflies come out chased by birds like nightjars, and the lamp is lit, and Cowie brings me my tea, and I am carried back to bed. This has been my life these twenty days."

During these three weeks, which in some ways were among the happiest of my life, for I always look back to the periods of recovery from a severe illness as being such, I was not without visits from our friends the Egyptian exiles and others of the Mohammedan community of Colombo. Arabi, especially, came daily to see me, and I found him of an extreme gentleness and kindness in a sick room. He was anxious to do all he could for me, and recommended me such remedies as are used by the fellahin in Egypt, and even took off from his arm, where he habitually wore it, a little leathern bag containing a charm or incantation and placed it upon mine. To this he attributed my recovery, and it may have been effective in this way, combined with the fresh milk which formed for the first fortnight my sole diet. I tried to believe it, and would have willingly believed too the other articles of his simple fellah faith. With Arabi and the other exiles I naturally had much talk about the past events of their country. But what they told me I need not here recapitulate, as I have already embodied it with much else in my Egyptian Memoirs.

I find in my diary that on the 6th of November I went out for my first drive, and that in the company of Arabi and Abd-el-Aal I went into Colombo, and that we saw Gregory's statue together in the Cinnamon Gardens, and three days later that I attended a public dinner given in my honour by the local Mohammedans. At this I made a public speech. Arabi had proposed the Queen's health in a few words of Arabic, and my own speech took the form of a return of thanks. From the date of their arrival at Colombo, the exiles had been exceedingly well treated by the Governor of the Island and his subordinates, and were in the habit of being invited to all the great receptions at Government House. And on the other hand, with their own co-religionists, they had attained a position of the highest consideration, Arabi being in the habit of leading the prayer in the principal mosque on Fridays.

The Mohammedans of Ceylon are known there as "Moors," a name given them originally by the Portuguese, which is applied also to the Mohammedans of the south-west coast of India. They belong to a far older Mohammedan settlement than the Moguls of the north, being, in fact, the descendants of Arab traders who in the first centuries of Islam came not as conquerors, but as commercial settlers from Oman and Yemen. Unlike the Mohammedans of the north, they are a pushing and prosperous community, having most of the shopkeeping trade in their hands, especially that of jewel merchants. There is also a comparatively small Mohammedan community of Malays, the descendants of a force of Malay soldiers formerly maintained by the Dutch. With them I found living on terms of friendly intercourse the Brahminical Tamils, who consider themselves to be of Dravidian race, originally from Southern India, though they have probably mixed much with the Aryans in past times. They, too, are a pushing race, commercial and combative, and had driven the Cingalese out of half the island before the arrival of the Portuguese in Ceylon. The Dravidians number here and in Southern India some seventeen millions, and the Tamils are considered their leading branch. Their form of Brahminism is of a purer type than in the north, as they hold closer to the Vedas, so much so that the Brahma Suraj reformers make no way with them; their doctrines have been forestalled. They are also more particular about the consecration of their idols, and the performance of their religious ceremonies. The head of their community at Colombo, Ramanatha, told me that he had been shocked in Northern India at the rough and ready idols even the princes worshipped, unconsecrated, in their own houses. He says there is a good feeling between all the members of the Asiatic creeds at Colombo, but the Catholics, Methodists, and Wesleyans are on bad terms with these. The Catholic population is large along the coast. On the 9th the Tamils entertained me at a banquet, to which the Egyptian Pashas and several Europeans were also invited. These were Mohammedan Tamils, of whom there were about one hundred present. Though unfit for it, for I was very tired, I made a long speech, or rather sermon, to them on the subject of Mohammedan reform, and reform in their political life. It was rather a venturesome attempt, but was well received by them. I spoke, of course, in English, which all understood.

We also made acquaintance, while in Colombo, with the Governor, Sir Arthur Gordon, a very excellent man, who was on the best of terms with the various native communities. There was in Ceylon a good tradition of this kind, dating, I believe, from Sir William Gregory's governorship some years back, and contrasting in a very marked manner with the relations I afterwards found in India between the rulers and the ruled. Ceylon's position as a Crown colony, with institutions of a semi-representative kind, puts the natives of the island in a position of comparative equality with the Europeans, and is answerable, doubtless, for the better feeling displayed towards them by these, at least in public. There is none of that extreme and open arrogance we find in Northern India. Nor was there on the part of the natives I came in contact with any expression of that race bitterness which in India is universal. On Sunday, the 11th November, my journal, interrupted by my illness, begins again to be regularly kept.

"*11th Nov.*—We bade good-bye to our friends, and took steamer for Tuticorin, the southernmost point of the Indian peninsula. The night before I had a serious talk with Mahmud Sami. He is a man of a very superior education, and has behaved to us throughout as our host with the most consummate courtesy. Immediately after breakfast came some other chief friends among the Moors, with them Haj Ibrahim Didi, the Sultan of Maldive's nephew, who is also Consul for him, though the Maldive Islands are so cut off from the mainland that he has had no communication with head-quarters for years. The Pashas came on board to see us off, and I embraced each one of them as they went over the ship's side, and, last of all, Arabi, for whom I feel a true affection. In spite of faults and failings, there is something great about him which compels one's respect. His faults are all the faults of his race, his virtues are his own.

"Looking back on the last three weeks spent in Ceylon, I recognize in them perhaps the happiest of my life. When I arrived I was so weak I could have died happily. But, though I did not die, I have had such satisfaction as seldom comes on earth, that of seeing the bread one has cast on the waters return to one a hundredfold, a feeling that at last the power to do good has been won, and more than one's wishes granted. This is true pleasure and true happiness. I regret the quiet life at Mahmud Sami's as I regret a home. We could see the banyan tree in the garden, and the boats on the shore, and the columns of the verandah as we steamed away. I doubt whether I shall ever be happier than I have been there."

CHAPTER III

MADRAS

"*12th Nov.*

"AFTER a good passage of about fifteen hours we sighted the Indian coast, first the western hills, and then the low shore off Tuticorin. We have been carrying four hundred and thirty-five Indian labourers coming home after working in Ceylon. The captain says they carry 15,000 every year each way. They are fat and merry, so I judge that they thrive during their absence from home—all I believe Hindu Tamils. On the pier we were met by twenty or thirty Moslems, representing the local Mohammedan population of two hundred families. They had been telegraphed to about us by Ibrahim Didi. A Moor from Galle, Kasim Biak, did the honours, entertaining us at breakfast with a friend, Bawa Sahib, also from Ceylon. The native Moslems seem very poor. I asked them about their condition, and they complained of having no school. Their Imam had work enough to do leading the prayers five times a day, and had no leisure to teach. They also complained of being subject to annoyance from the Hindus, who came with drums outside their mosque, and that the magistrate, being a Hindu, would not prevent it. They all wear a turban here, as do the Hindu Tamils. There seemed to be no English resident in Tuticorin at all. We only stayed two hours, and then went on by train, accompanied by our Mohammedan friends, now increased to about fifty.

"The country for a mile or two inland is pure sand, and very pretty with its desert vegetation, thorn acacias and groves of dom palms. The heavy rains had brought up beautiful bright green grass, on which flocks of long-legged goats were led to feed. By the side of the railroad I noticed several birds well known to me, the turtle dove of Egypt, the kite, the hen-harrier, the bee-bird, and the roller, also birds unknown to me, a little magpie, a long-tailed blackbird and others—butterflies, too, in some variety, and flowers, yellow and blue, one like the convolvulus minor. Later, the country opened into a vast cultivated plain, perfectly level, but with fine mountain ranges to the west, a very light soil, but improving as we got further from the coast, though nowhere good on this day's journey. It is easy to understand a drought causing general famine. The cultivation is much as in the rest of Central Asia, lightly ploughed lands, without fences or boundaries, scattered trees, acacias or banyans, and at great distances villages; no sign anywhere of 'gentlemen's seats,' or of any habitation better than the poorest, herds of lean sheep or goats, the only cattle a few buffaloes. The whole country has been recently under water, and this year at least there ought to be crops, but they are not yet out of the ground.

"At Kumara Puran we came to some low hills, which I think were of red granite, and here the country was greener, with millet and rice crops, and more trees. I noticed mulberry trees as well as banyans, and near the station, Australian gums. Much water about in the pools. After these hills the land improved, growing more beautiful; but night came on, and though there was a full moon we saw little more. About half-past seven the train came to a stop, and we were made to get out and walk some two or three hundred yards, as the rails had been washed away by a flood. All around the frogs were croaking in thousands. In another place was a fine old stone bridge broken down, with a great stoppage of bullock carts, and we arrived about nine o'clock at Madura. I was almost dead with fatigue. Two Mohammedans, Abd-el-Aziz Sahib and another, were awaiting us at the station, but I could do nothing but get to bed.

"13*th Nov.*—Madura is a pretty place, with palm trees and flocks of parrots. In the early morning we watched them flying overhead, talking as they went. At nine the Mohammedans came again, accompanied by an *alem* of Arab descent, a *sayyid*, who spoke good Arabic, but with a peculiar old-fashioned accent. We had a long talk, principally about the misfortunes of their community. The Moslems throughout Southern India have always been a very small minority—descendants of the former Mogul rulers of the country—for the mass of the population never conformed to Islam. In those days they occupied the chief posts under Government and in the army, but these have now passed away from them to the Hindus, who are preferred to them for Government employment because of their better knowledge of English and better schooling. Their cry then is for schools, that they, too, may be employed. Unlike the Moors of Ceylon, none of them are engaged in trade, nor have they any means of embarking in commerce. Only a few are shop-keepers. About a dozen have lands, on which they live, and the rest work for wages for their daily bread. Many died in the famine seven years ago. They are decreasing in numbers and wealth, and are overridden, they say, by the '*kafrs*.' It is difficult to see any way out of this state of things, and I doubt even if schools would help them much. The *alem* had heard of course of Arabi, and also of me; and they all took great interest in the affairs of Islam beyond the seas. But their ideas are vague. They asked us several times if we were not relations of the Queen, and I had some difficulty in explaining our system of government. They enquired with great interest whether it was true that the Russian Emperor had sent troops to Afghanistan, and their faces brightened when I told them that, though I knew nothing of troops, I had seen in the papers that a Russian Envoy had appeared at Kabul. I fancy they look forward to a restoration some day of Mohammedan Government under Russian protection as a way out of their difficulties. Here, however, it is not easy to imagine any such event, for Hinduism is clearly all-powerful, and the Mohammedans are few, and they are strangers in the land."

Madura is indeed the most interesting Hindu city in India, the place where the ancient Brahminical religion has been least touched by foreign conquest, Mogul, or French, or English. There is absolutely no sign in the city of anything alien. We did not see a European face, or a trace of Saracenic architecture. A festival was going on and an immense crowd thronged the streets, thousands and thousands of men dressed in white, with ochre patches on their foreheads, and of women in their beautiful gauze drapery, and carrying flowers. Fortunately I had never heard of Madura and its famous temple, and it was by accident that we came upon it as we wandered without guide through the streets. I find the following very inadequate description of it:

"In the afternoon we drove about the town, the most interesting I ever saw, and went over the Palace and the Temple. The Palace is a fine thing, but is being pitilessly restored at great expense by the Madras Government. Its proportions, however, remain, and it may be hoped that the damp air will tone down some of the raw plaster work quickly. We found it the home of squirrels and parrots and other birds. The view of the Blue Mountains from its roof is one of the loveliest imaginable. The Temple, however, is quite another thing. It is the supreme sight of Madura, and indeed, one might profitably travel from England and return only to have seen this. It is not only unmatched, but is beyond all comparison with the rest of the buildings I have seen in the East, as far beyond them as St. Mark's at Venice is beyond Spurgeon's Tabernacle. In shape it is a vast square composed of courts and halls, and corridors, deep in shade, with open spaces where the sun pours down. At the corners are four structures, like great Towers of Babel, covered, or rather encrusted, with sculptured gods, monsters, and devils, the whole enclosed with an immense stone wall, where there are no apertures. The door by which we entered from the street gave little idea of what was within. It might have been the entrance to a bazaar, and its comparative meanness enhanced the quite unexpected wonder we were about to see. It opened on to a kind of covered way, whose roof was supported by rows of figures carved in stone, grotesque and monstrous, but still finely sculptured, the lower parts of them black with the elbow polish of many generations of worshippers. This corridor was perhaps three hundred yards in length, and at its entrance were a number of open shops, where goods connected with the worship were being sold—'the buyers and sellers of the Temple'—always thronged with worshippers grotesque as their gods, with painted foreheads, and sometimes painted bodies.

"We passed through the crowd unquestioning

and unquestioned. There was no one to explain the meaning of anything we saw. I walked on as in a dream, being still weak with my late fever, and because of the hot sun outside. Presently the shut street widened, and we came to elephants, painted, too, with gilded tusks, which might have been statues, so quietly they stood, but for the flapping of their ears and the swaying of their trunks. Beyond them the street once more narrowed, and was crossed by the framework of a pair of huge gates of brass, carved also with innumerable gods. Through this we stepped and at last came out upon an open square tank, surrounded with galleries, carved and painted, and surmounted with the palm trees which grow inside the Temple, and at the extreme corner by one of the Babylonian Towers. Here naked men were washing in the green water, and we turned aside attracted by a distant sound of chaunting. We were once more in the gloom, and passed through halls and corridors of growing obscurity towards what seemed to be the Temple itself, 'The Holy of Holies.' Men here were sitting in a ring upon the floor, and there were arches of palm trees wreathed with flowers, and we smelt the smell of incense. It was from these the chaunting came, but no one took notice of us as we passed. Then we came on to another open court, where there were more elephants, and we saw one led away with brass bells upon it, ringing as it went. Then on through other corridors and still through thousands of sculptured gods, where worshippers were offering flowers, and so back once more to the open street of the town. I cannot describe it more. It is a temple, the home of a worship living still, as it lived three thousand years ago, and still the resort of a nation of worshippers. A temple, not a mere house of prayer, and one where the ancient gods of wood and stone and bronze and gold are still propitiated with offerings and adorned with wreaths of flowers. I was thoroughly tired out with what I had seen, but perhaps for this the better pleased."

The same night we went on our way northwards, by train, and stopped while it was still dark at Trichinopoly.

"14*th Nov.*—We were awakened this morning in the rest house where we had slept by a sound of martial music, military noises, 'and the shouting of the captains,' or rather by the hoarse voice of an old English general giving the word of command to two thousand Madras Infantry on the parade ground close by. This was the first sign of anything English since landing in India, for not so much as a white official had been visible on the railway, and these sounds were like the breaking of a spell, though still we came in contact with no Englishmen. We drove after breakfast to another celebrated temple, passing through the town and under the fort. In the streets we met a pretty marriage procession, the bride mounted on a pony, and covered with golden ornaments, and again, a young married pair similarly decked out in an open carriage. The Temple of Trichinopoly is at a considerable distance beyond the town, as large, but less interesting than that of Madura, the roofed portion being smaller, nor are there the same carved gods, nor the same appearance of ancient and daily use. We saw it, too, under less perfect circumstances, for the guides of the place had found us out, and insisted on explaining all we did not want to know, and making the elephants salute us, an incongruous thing. It is hateful to be here as members of the alien ruling caste, reverenced and feared, and secretly detested. We paid our guides and the *mahouts* with open hands. It was all we could do to make them amends for our presence.

"As the day wore on, returning from the temple, we once more found the roads alive with men and women, most of the men wearing the Brahminical paint. There are two clearly distinct types of countenance among the people, one with narrow retreating forehead, thick overhanging eyebrows, and coarse features, the other refined and handsome, with here and there a head (for all go uncovered) which might have belonged to a Roman senator, yet distinctly not European. These last are, I suppose, of Aryan descent, the other of Dravidian. The common peasants here have all the appearance of savages, so much so that one expects to see bows and arrows in their hands. They go naked to the waist, and bareheaded, shaving the front part of the skull, but wearing their hair long behind. Nearly all the townsmen are painted with white dabs and streaks, but the Brahmins have a coloured stripe down the forehead, with a stripe of white on either side. Some of the young Brahmins are very handsome, and in their clean white clothes, with books under their arms, are in striking contrast with the peasantry.

"At Tanjore we saw yet another temple, with its colossal bull under a stone canopy. It is said to be a monolith, but is painted to imitate bronze. What interested us most was a series of portraits of Siwaji and his descendants, once rulers of the country, in a little shrine, the whole enclosure surrounded by a deep moat, and fortified, but without worshippers, and all deserted. The palace near it is still occupied by Siwaji's descendants, dispossessed and pensioned. They are only women now who live on in this rambling place, shut up, sad remains of state greatly out at elbows. The rooms are fine. In the library they showed us some interesting Indian paintings of the last century, and an illustrated book of Chinese tortures, which we may imagine the last Rajah consoling himself with after his loss of power. It was a festival day, and we saw the pomp and glory of the little court turned out, two elephants and two camels, a dozen poor led horses, one mounted officer and twenty soldiers, aged retainers most of these, put into cast-off English uniforms." The dispossessed Princes of India always reminded me of captive wild beasts shut up in cages, lame and diseased, and dying of their lack of moral exercise.

The last two days of our journey to Madras we were without any native communication, as we had got beyond our recommendations from Ceylon, and on the other hand had come in contact as yet with no Europeans. My journal deals principally with the natural features of the country, which had become now flat and monotonous, with crops of rice, mostly under irrigation. I find a list of birds seen from the train: egret, pied bittern, little bittern, snipe, pied kingfisher, whiteheaded kite, kite, hoopoe, a variety of roller, bee-bird, lark, parrot, hen-harrier, shrike, long-tailed blackbird, myna, partridge, a variety of pheasant, dove, crow, sandpiper, small cormorant, kestrel, sea-gull, magpie, robin, besides many small birds I did not see near enough to identify. I also saw tracks of wild boars in one place. At Chingleput hills began, and a pretty country with large lakes and tracts of jungle, the formation granite with red earth and boulders.

"*17th Nov.*—Madras. A horrible place. We are at Lippert's Hotel, facing the sea, with a broad esplanade in front, down which the red dust drives.

We wrote our names down at Government House. They took us at first by mistake to the Government Office in the Fort, where I was invited to sign my name in a book as 'an officer returning from furlough, and demanding an extension of leave.' Government House, when we got there, was a white pillared edifice standing in a dreary park. There was a sentry at the door, but no other living soul, not even a footman out of livery, or a charwoman, to tell us that 'the family was out of town,' but the doors were open and a book was there. Mr. and Mrs. Grant Duff are at Guindi, another residence seven miles off."

We stayed a week in Madras, which was longer than I had intended, but as soon as it became known that I had arrived I began to receive visits from the more prominent natives, Hindus as well as Mohammedans, which interested me.

My first visitors at Madras were a couple of Hindu gentlemen, editors of the local newspaper, the "Hindu"; their names, Subramania Ayer and Vira Raghava Chaya; intelligent, clear-headed men, contrasting by no means unfavourably with men of their profession in London. Their manners were good, and their conversation brilliant. The matters principally discussed between us were the heavy pressure of the Land Revenue on the Madras peasantry, the burden of the salt tax, the abuses connected with the Civil courts, the ruin of the cotton manufacture and industry by the enforced free trade with England, the unreality of the so-called "productive work," especially as to roads, and the conservative opposition of the covenanted Civil Service to all reform—neither viceroys nor governors were able to oppose them. I asked what was thought of Lord Ripon by the mass of the people. "He is the first Viceroy," my visitor said, "who has been known to them by name in this Presidency. Hitherto the people have only known the local collector, but Lord Ripon's name is known. Indeed he is looked upon by the ignorant, especially since the recent agitation on the Ilbert Bill, as a new incarnation of God." "And Mr. Grant Duff?" I asked. "We consider him," he said, "a failure. He came out as Governor of Madras with great expectations, and we find him feeble, sickly, unable to do his work himself, and wholly in the hands of the permanent officials. The Duke of Buckingham, of whom we expected less, did much more, and much better."

I found this opinion of Grant Duff a very general one among the natives. Though a clever man, he had spent all his life in the confined atmosphere of the House of Commons, and was quite unable to deal with a state of society so strange to him as that which he found in India. I was constantly asked by them what line they should take, and what hope there was for them of any kind of self government or real reform. And I explained to them frankly what the position of parties was in England, that the Radicals, of whom Lord Ripon was in some degree one, would be glad enough to see India governed for the Indians; that the Tories made no pretence of governing India except in English interests, and by the sword; and that between them stood the Whigs, who talked about progress, but always left things standing as they were. My advice was that they should press their grievances now while Lord Ripon was in power, as there was some chance of their being listened to, avoiding only anything like disorder, which would be a pretext with the Home Government, which was purely Whig, to stop such few reforms as Lord Ripon had begun. I encouraged them, however, to continue the agitation for representative Government in the Councils, and thought they might get it in twenty or twenty-five years time. Their general answer was, they would be satisfied if they got it in a hundred years.

These first visitors sent others to me, and a clever young Brahmin, Varada Rao, constituted himself my cicerone with those who were afraid to come to me openly. The most interesting of those he took me to visit, though it was not timidity but advanced age which had prevented him calling, was the old Mahratta Brahmin, Ragunath Rao, some time minister of Holkar and brother of the still better known Madhava Rao, a man of the highest distinction, much wit, and the widest possible intelligence. Indeed, his conversation might have been that of a Socrates, whom in person he much resembled, being a little rugged man whom I found very simply clad in a shirt, a blue head-dress, and with no shoes or stockings to his feet, but who at his first word impressed me with a sense of his integrity and his vast intellectual superiority. On the high politics of India his discourse was most instructive, and, like Socrates, he had the habit of illustrating each point of his discourse with a story always good and often extremely amusing. He dwelt especially on the difference there was between the old-fashioned personal rule of the Indian Princes, with whom there was always the possibility of a personal appeal to the head of the State, and the blank seclusion of the English rulers, who were walled off from all knowledge of what was going on by their ignorance of native life and their complete severance from native society. In old times it had not been thus. Under the East India Company, when communication with England was rare and difficult, the English officials and even the Governors and Governors-General were thrown to a large extent for their society on the Indians of rank and position, whose language they had been obliged to learn and with whom they lived on a footing of something like equality. Now they lived wholly among themselves, and were almost without intercourse with natives of any class, except perhaps the lowest, whom they treated at best with good-humoured contempt. Thus they heard nothing and knew nothing and cared nothing for the feelings and opinions of the people, and the abyss between the rulers and the ruled was every year increasing.

He described with great humour the position of a modern Viceroy, who comes to Calcutta, or rather to Simla, with the idea of understanding the native case and doing good, and who finds himself with a crowd of permanent English officials always surrounding him and pulling him by the coat tail whenever he approaches what they consider a dangerous subject. His term of years as Viceroy is at most five. The first two are occupied in getting used to the climate and way of life, in learning how to behave and what to say to the native princes, in studying the history of past affairs, and learning the official view of the larger questions he has to deal with. The next two years, if he is an honest man and man of energy, he begins to propound his policy, only to find that he is everywhere defeated in detail by officials who bow to him and pretend to agree with him, but who go away and raise obstacles which defeat his ends, or at any rate delay them till his power to enforce them is nearly over. Usually he swims with the official stream, saves what money he can out of his immense salary, shoots tigers, and amuses himself with viceregal tours and visits and durbars to the native princes, spending half his years always away from native India in the Himalayas, and giving balls and entertainments to the Anglo-Indian ladies. The last year of his term he is looked upon as already defunct and of no importance, and he packs up his things and goes home satisfied with having done no worse than his predecessors.

I wish I had recorded a tithe of his wonderful talk in my journal. I heard from his friends that his plain speaking had constantly brought him into collision with the officials, but it had ended by their being a little afraid of him, so keenly did he understand their weaknesses, and so bitter was his wit in exposing them. Sir Charles Trevelyan, who is the only Governor who had left a really good impression on the natives I came in contact with, had given him much of his confidence, and an official position with a pretty good salary, but his successors had done their best to suppress him. He has, however, too high a social position to be wholly put down, and private means which enables him so far to hold his own against them.

We called also on Judge Muteswami Ayar, to whom I had letters from Ramanatha, but both he and Ranganatha of the Presidency College made excuse. Being in the Government Service, Varada Rao explained, they had probably consulted the English officials about the introductions I had sent them, and were advised to be ill or not at home. The natives in the public service are completely under the thumb of the Government, and unless they have means of their own dare not offend their English superiors. Their promotions, if not their places, are at stake, and the Covenanted Civil Service neither forgets nor forgives. A native is only admitted into the higher ranks of employment on the understanding that he pulls with the crew. So the Judge, after some mysterious discussion with the servants and goings to and fro, was discovered to be "not at home."

The same day, 21st November, I received a visit from Mir Humayum Jah Bahadur, the head of the Mohammedan community at Madras, a fine old gentleman, with a courtly manner, very formal, and very cautious of committing himself to opinions on any subject. As member of a family descended from Tippu Sultan, famous in old days for its diplomatic talent, he is the leader of the Mohammedan world here, and presides over all associations and charities, and I laid before him the school difficulties of his people at Madura. This rather alarmed him, as he thought I wanted him to move in the matter with the Government, and recommended me to speak about it myself to the Governor, Grant Duff. Although he evidently intended his visit to be one of compliment, his manner throughout was a defensive one. Every now and then a little gleam of sunshine would pass over his face, but only to be carefully suppressed. Later, however, he sent a young Bengalese Mohammedan, Seyd Abd-el-Rahman, to see me, an intelligent young lawyer of the modern type, who had married a Eurasian, and visited Europe. His Eurasian wife had become a Mohammedan, but still dressed as a European, her father having been English, and we went with him to his house, where she appeared without a veil to give us tea. We were the first English people who had shown her any civility since her marriage.

Other visitors that afternoon were the Brahmin head master of the Hindu middle school, and Rangiar Naidu, a Hindu Zemindar, a landowner on a large scale. "He complained much of the ill conditions of the peasantry, who were habitually underfed, and especially of their sufferings from the salt tax. The land taxation is more severe now than it ever was, amounting to one half the gross produce. All are in debt because the Government insists upon having its due in advance of the harvest, and in money. This obliges the peasantry to borrow from usurers,—just as in Egypt. He assures me the Madras ryots are not unthrifty, and if they could they would lay by their money for an unrainy day. They do not invest in savings banks, not trusting them, but hoard in coin or in silver ornaments for their women. But there is no margin now left them by the land tax. All this is precisely as in Egypt. He promises to take us over some villages to see how things are on Friday or Saturday at Tirupati, where we have been invited to a Hindu festival. Rangiar Naidu is rich and independent of the Government, which cannot interfere with his position, an hereditary one. He says the new forest laws are very hard on the people, whose cattle used to have free pasturage and are dying fast now owing to the restrictions.

"*22nd Nov.*—Young Varada Rao came before I was dressed this morning to take me to call once more on Muteswami, who now expresses a great wish to see me privately; and we were just driving off when we met Ragunath Rao coming on foot to our hotel. The old man was dressed with more care to-day, having a cashmere gown on and a handsomer head-dress, but still no shoes or stockings. He looked the distinguished and polite gentleman he is. His conversation was even more amusing and admirable than yesterday, and he speaks quite without reserve about the Government and its ways. He told us that he and his cousin, who is also a very rich man, have hereditary estates near Tanjore, and it had always been their intention some day to retire from Government employment, and settle down at home.

They had been too long absentees, and wished to look after their estates in quiet. But they had been obliged to abandon their plan, owing to the little protection given them against the impertinences of the English district officers, and even their persecution. He gave us three or four instances of this. One was of a friend of his, a former magistrate and most respected official, who had retired, as he himself had intended to retire, to spend his last days in his own town. He was a man of independent character, and not wishing to be troubled any longer with etiquette, neglected to pay any special court to the Resident Collector. This brought him into official disrepute, and one day he found himself arrested on a charge of conspiracy, a charge absolutely unfounded, and involved in legal proceedings, which, besides endless annoyance, cost him some thirty thousand rupees. I asked him 'What kind of conspiracy?' 'You don't suppose,' he said, 'I mean a political conspiracy. We are far too frightened here for anything like that. No, this was a vulgar charge of conspiracy to cheat and defraud a neighbour. My friend disproved the charge, but it has left him a broken man. He is now the humble servant of the Government, and bows to the ground when he sees the smallest Government officer.' I wish I could recall all his good stories, all his wise opinions and illustrations. There are not a dozen men in the House of Commons who could hold their own with him in talk.[1]

"I have been urging him to come to England, but Varada tells me it is all a question of caste. If Ragunath would go, many of his fellow Brahmins

[1] When Robert Bourke, Lord Connemara, was sent as Governor to Madras in 1886, I recommended Ragunath Rao to him, and he gave him once more a post as Minister to one of the Native Princes.

would follow his example, for he is leader in Madras on questions of this sort. The difficulty is this, that according to Brahminical teaching India is the one land of a holy life, therefore none who lead holy lives can leave it. It is not permitted to cross the sea. Twenty years ago it was not permitted even to go from Madras to Calcutta by steamer. Now it is allowed, but on condition that no meal is taken on board. All agree that this strict caste rule must sooner or later be relaxed, but nobody likes to be the first to break it. Talking of the arrogance of the English officials, Seyd Abd-el-Rahman's Eurasian wife, who is a sensible young woman, tells us that she remembered in her home in Bengal a collector who used to make people passing down the street by his house take off their shoes and put down their umbrellas in his honour.

"Our single English caller, and he was the first Englishman we had spoken to since landing in India, was a Mr. Laffan, acting secretary to the Government, curious to know whom among the Mohammedans I had seen. He affected liberal ideas about India, and said that the native members of the Legislative Council would certainly soon be elected by popular vote. I fancy he had come to find out what I was doing. At last, in the twilight like Nicodemus, came the Judge, Muteswami, looking rather ashamed of himself, and with confused explanation of why he had not seen me yesterday. He is a tall dark Tamil, almost black, a self made man, who began life as a servant and learnt English from his master's children. This may account for his timidity, for he seems a man of worth and integrity. He explained the Ilbert Bill to me with great lucidity, especially as to its effects upon English planters in their relations with the natives. He said that with few exceptions the planters were very lawless people, that hitherto they had been for all small offences practically out of reach of the law, because the distance to the High Courts, where alone they could be tried, was too great for natives to resort to them. As to the contemplated change making them amenable to the ordinary Courts, the only fear was that the native Judges would be too lenient to them for fear of being thought partial."

The same night we dined at Guindi with the Governor, Mr. Grant Duff, "a thin, sickly, querulous man" is my comment on him, "out of temper with everything around him, yet paid ten thousand a year by the Madras Indians for ruling them." I find no record of his conversation, but remember that his manner to me was somewhat reserved and suspicious. We did not get back to Lippert's Hotel till midnight.

"*23rd Nov.*—Our night's rest was short, for our train started at six forty-five. Young Varada Rao was waiting for us at the station to say good-bye. He has sent his servant with us to Tirupati, where we are to meet his father Rama Rao, who has gone there with other native big-wigs and a number of Pundits to open a Sanskrit College. We are invited to take part in the doings there, but shall be too late for the actual ceremony, which begins at ten. Our visit to Madras has been on the whole successful. Though we began without much introduction, we have established capital relations with all the leading Hindus of the place. The Mohammedans we have seen less of. They are of little energy or importance in the Presidency. Their social leaders are pensioned by, and so dependent on, the Government. The rest are poor and unprogressive."

It may here be said that we left Madras accompanied by a very excellent servant, a native Christian named Solomon, who had been provided for us by our friend Ragunath Rao. Solomon was a dignified and altogether worthy old man, absolutely honest and faithful in his service, and with but a slight knowledge of English. As he was the only native Christian with whom we came in contact in India, I am glad to be able to give him this high character.

"Tirupati is a very beautiful place, surrounded by high hills, and is a celebrated resort of Brahmin pilgrims from all parts of India. The temple, though not very large, has a splendid pagoda at the entrance, and stands in the middle of the town, and there are other pagodas at a distance, leading up to a sacred hill not very far away. The ceremony was over when we arrived at the bungalow, which had been fitted up at great expense for the expected guests. It was very hot, and the drive from the station had been tiring, in country bullock carts drawn by ponies, and we were glad to rest in the shade, though we had missed the expedition to the sacred hill which had followed the ceremony. A good luncheon had been prepared for us, and soon after Rangiar Naidu arrived and took us over the temple and the town. The gala preparations, he informed us, were in honour of Mr. T., an English official who had come to represent the Governor on the occasion. He was away with the rest on the sacred hill, and would not be back till after dark. Rangiar Naidu besought us not to let him, or any of those with him, know of our intended visit to the villages, as he would certainly prevent it. This T., he said, has a reputation of being a friend of the natives on the ground of his knowing something of Sanskrit, and patronizing their educational institutions, but Rangiar and all our friends are suspicious of him;—old Ragunath Rao spoke of him yesterday very plainly as a humbug.

About nine o'clock, after great lighting of lamps in a kiosk, the party from the hill returned, escorting the Government officials in all state—T. a dry, stiff-looking civilian, very much on his dignity, and surprised and rather disgusted to find us here. It was evident that Rama Rao had not told him how we had been invited by his son, and I let the cat out of the bag, without intending it, by telling Rama Rao in the official hearing that Varada had come to see us off at the station, and Rama looked confused and began to talk of other things. It was painful to see the fear everybody was in of this very ordinary Englishman, but I suppose he has the power to ruin them, and that he and his like do ruin those that cross them. With him was another Englishman, the head of a school department, a more genial man, and one other. A dinner for a hundred had been prepared, but no more English had come than these three, and so we five sat down and ate what we could of it.

T. was not communicative, but nevertheless we made conversation on various more or less political subjects, the school inspector, who liked talking, helping us not a little. Afterwards I had some conversation apart with Rama, but both he and the Pundits were too frightened to say much so near the 'presence.' They, poor people, had brought a piece of gold or silver plate to give to the great man, an offering which he received without a word of thanks, and had put in his carriage; only to two or three did he vouchsafe a few words, remaining seated while they stood to listen. It is inconceivable why these Indians should put themselves to the trouble of entertaining at such expense and to so little profit. The kiosk alone cost £30 they told us, and the whole entertainment cannot have cost far short of £100, which would have better gone in helping to endow the

College. Government gives nothing, and the thing is to be supported by the funds of the Temple, which are large. It was amusing to see the relief which came over everybody when the officials had left, as they did as soon as the fireworks were over, about eleven. We, too, were not sorry. As there were no beds, we slept on the floor, on which, also, the servants and the poor people from outside soon after rolled themselves up—it was a large place—very happily with Mr. T.'s cushions and carpets.

"I have forgotten to say what was to me the most interesting part of the day's proceedings. While waiting in the shade of a grove that afternoon we had seen a procession come to a little shrine with offerings close by—a beautiful pagan rite, with drums and pipes leading the way, and behind a number of women walking with large copper dishes on their heads filled with rice and flowers as offerings to the god. They stopped under the grove near us, and there lit fires and cooked their rice—a merry party sitting on all the afternoon. Towards evening the women approached the altar, which was an oblong table of stone supported by a dozen upright slabs carved with curious devices. Each woman chose her slab, and painted it with ochre, yellow and red, and then crowned it with flowers. I asked what it signified. They told me it was Friday, one of the fortunate days, and that the women had come to pray for fertility. The rice, after being offered, they will eat, and count it as a feast. It is seldom the peasants get so good a meal, for their usual food is only a cake made of a kind of rape. Rice is held to be too good for common fare." This was an interesting day spent in beautiful surroundings, and remains in my mind as one typical of Southern India.

"*24th Nov.*—In the morning Rangiar Naidu came

according to promise with two pony carts, and took us to see the villages. On the way he explained to us the history of the Sanskrit College and yesterday's festivities. Some years ago the English Government, in pursuance of its policy of non-interference with religious affairs, gave up its inherited guardianship of the Hindu temples to native trustees, known locally as 'churchwardens.' But the transfer was made with so little care that in many instances the trustees had been able to evade the law, and make themselves to all intents and purposes owners of the estates. In the case of Tirupati, the income is very large, several *lakhs* of rupees, and has become vested in the hands of a single man, R. S., known by his official title of Mohunt. The abuse of trust in the Madras Presidency had become, however, so notorious that last year an attempt was made in Council to pass a bill in remedy of the evil. But this had been strongly opposed by Mr. T., and so defeated, to the anger of pious Hindus towards T., but the gratitude of the Temple wardens. It is by these, or rather by the single Mohunt, that yesterday's festivities were arranged. The Sanskrit College is an act of expiation to cover a misappropriation of the funds, since these are not for education but for the maintenance of the Temple. As for Rama Rao, his timidity is explained by his being a member of the Council, and so revocable at the will of the Government after his three years term of office. Rama Rao's family came from Hyderabad four generations back, where they were servants of the Nizam, but on the occasion of a marriage they had followed the Nawab of Arcot to Madras. Their language at home is Telegu, which is that of the Hindus of the Deccan."

Our visit to the villages occupied us the whole

day, and was most successful. Knowing Egypt as well as I did, I had little difficulty in ascertaining the facts I was in search of, that is to say, the proportion of land tax to the gross produce, the local indebtedness, the effect of the famine of seven years before, the oppressive incidents of the salt tax which especially affects the cattle, and the new forest restrictions. The common food of the ryots I found to be *raghi*, a small grain like rape, which they make into a cake, or mix into gruel, making it palatable with red pepper. Few of them have milk to drink, and their lack of sufficient nourishment is plainly visible in their emaciated appearance. Their houses, though of mud like those in Egypt, consist of only one room each, but are kept very clean. It is part of their religion to wash everything daily. My diary contains several pages of details regarding the villages we examined, but these are hardly worth reproducing here. I omit them as I do similar village inquiries made elsewhere, reserving the results for a separate chapter.

"Rangiar Naidu accompanied us to the railway station in the evening, and gave me letters to friends farther on. He is a highly educated man, was at school with Ragunath Rao, and maintains close friendship with him. He is of the Khastriah or military caste, which is not common in the Madras Presidency. His type of face is distinctly Egyptian, and he might well be a village sheykh of the Delta. He is a rich man and member of the Municipal Council of Madras, an elective post which leaves him independent.

"*25th Nov.*—By night train to Bellari, the headquarters of the famine district, and so of great interest. There were five hours of daylight before arriving, and we found the country much changed from yesterday. This part of India is a high plateau, a thousand or fifteen hundred feet above the sea, with occasional hills of gneiss or granite, five or six hundred feet higher. The soil is light, and there is no irrigation, and, in spite of a rather unusually wet season, the crops looked scanty and poor. No rice is grown, only *raghi* and millet, but in some parts cotton makes a fair crop. Architecturally, there is nothing worth seeing at Bellari, but we had letters to the leading Hindus and a rich Eurasian, and have found our visit so profitable that we have decided to stay on another day. First, however, we were hospitably entertained at luncheon by the English railway superintendent, Mr. Hanna, an intelligent man who has been twelve years in the country and likes it. But of course we learnt nothing much from him, as the English live in a world of their own.

"In the afternoon, however, eight or nine Hindu gentlemen came to see us, as highly educated as those at Madras, and even more free spoken. Among them was a Brahmin of high caste, who had broken his rule by visiting England, and had even become a Christian there, losing thereby his caste but not altogether his social position at Bellari. He spoke about the absurdity of the reason commonly given by English officials for having no social intercourse with the natives, namely, that the laws of caste prevent it. 'Here you see me,' he said. 'A few years ago my caste laws were so strict that I could not eat with any of these gentlemen'—turning to the rest who sat round—'I was obliged to throw away my meals if one of them happened to look at me while I was eating. Yet it did not prevent us being the best of friends. Neither, now that my caste is gone, am I less intimate with them, although they in their turn cannot now eat with me. Is it then necessary that men should eat together to be friends? The Europeans receive me no better to-day, though I could eat and drink with them all day long. The difficulty is entirely of their making.' He said this with as little embarrassment as there might be in England between one who on religious grounds only eats fish on a Friday, and others who eat meat. The manner of the speaker, too, was so good, and with so much conversational charm, that the refusal of the English officials to associate with him sounded to us particularly ludicrous. These Hindus are no wit inferior to Italians or Spaniards in their address, and are very little darker of skin.

"The Eurasian to whom we had the letter was with them, also a municipal councillor and clearly on excellent terms with the rest. He assured us it was quite untrue that the mass of the Eurasians sided with the English in their quarrel with the natives. On the contrary, their social sympathies were with the latter, and it was only the richer ones and those in Government employment who affected English ways. There was no real sympathy anywhere, as the English despised the Eurasians even more than they did the true natives, and the Eurasians were under greater disabilities as to the public service. He himself owns a cotton mill in partnership with an Englishman here, but they do not mix socially together. Our talk was principally on these matters. The Brahmin who had been in England had been received by Bright, Fawcett, Dilke, and other notabilities, had stayed in country houses, and been fêted everywhere. Here the collector's wife is too proud to call upon his wife. They expressed themselves much disappointed with the Gladstone Ministry, of which they had had great hopes. Lord Ripon was the best Governor-General India had ever had, but he had been thwarted throughout in his work, and had not been properly supported at home; he had been able to achieve nothing. Mr. Grant Duff had been the worst disappointment of all. He had come with a flourish of Liberal trumpets, but had proved a mere windbag, good at making speeches on generalities, but useless at administration. He had left all work to the permanent officials, who had thwarted Lord Ripon's good intentions everywhere.

"*26th Nov.*—Called on Mr. Abraham the Eurasian, and found him full of information. The pressure of the salt tax here is incredible, but true. In the time of the Mahrattas and the East India Company there was a simple tax of five per cent. Salt was allowed to be made, and the tax was on consumption. Now it is a Government monopoly, and at the present moment the Government manufactures its salt at the seaside at eight rupees the *garce*, a measure of six hundredweight, and sells it at Bellari for two hundred and eight rupees. Moreover, within the last three years, a new law has made matters worse, for the use of earth salt has been forbidden, and whereas before that time thirty *sears* (the *sear* is a measure of two lb.) could be purchased for a rupee, now the peasant can get only eight. Rough brown salt sells here for one and a half rupee a lb., although it is a common product of the country. The police are empowered to enter houses night or day, and, on their accusation of there being a measure of earth salt in it, the owner of the house may be fined fifteen rupees, or imprisoned for a month. Many false accusations are thus brought, and pressure put by the police on the ryots. If the villagers send their cattle to graze anywhere where there is natural salt on the ground, the owner is fined or imprisoned, and the salt is thrown in heaps and burned. The cattle are dying for want of it, and the people are suffering seriously.

"They talked also much of the extraordinary waste of money on public works, especially the State railways. The station here at Bellari cost R100,000, and two others R200,000 and R400,000 a piece. In the evening we went with Abraham to see his cotton mill, which has been open for more than a year, and was begun before the abolition of the cotton duty, and it shows some public spirit that they have gone on with it notwithstanding. The manufacture is of cotton thread, which is sold in the town to be made up by hand weavers. He took us later to see a village where we heard much the same stories as at Tirupati. We were told many tales of the famine, the relief of which was so badly managed that no less than forty persons belonging to the village, though so close to the railway station, died of hunger. In good times a man could live here for three half-pence a day, all included. They eat nothing but *gholum* and red peppers. During the famine, money was distributed instead of grain by the Government, so that some died with the coins in their hands. The million and a half spent in this district of public money was, according to Abraham, almost entirely wasted. One officer sent from the north had three thousand rupees as his travelling allowance for only twenty-two days, and then returned saying he could not understand the language. The Mansion House Fund, distributed by the municipality, was better managed, and saved many lives. Abraham insisted that it was not the want of railroads that caused the deaths in the district. The Bellari railroad was in full working order at the time. Neither was it over population, for there were two million acres uncultivated. The true reason was the severity of the taxation, and the extinction of the larger landowners, who used to keep grain in store for bad years. The remedy should be lighter taxation, and the maintenance of public stores of *gholum* and *raghi* at all the central stations. Corn will keep well in this dry district underground for years, and always used to be so kept, but the land is rack-rented now, and no provision made. The taxes lately have been gathered in advance of the harvest. Baring, he said, was responsible for much of this as Finance secretary.

"We dined with Sebapathy Ayar and his wife. It was he who had become a Christian, having been converted by Dean Stanley and Miss Carpenter about twelve years ago. The dinner was as English as possible, and they drank wine. But she wore her Indian dress and jewels—a nice woman. Afterwards a number of friends came in, and we had a very pretty nautch with Telegu singers, and all chewed Betel leaves, which, it appears, can be done in common without injury to caste. There was one Mohammedan among them from Bombay. The Hindus here are very courageous and outspoken. They all discussed the advantages, or rather the lack of advantages of British rule, without any reticence, and agreed that, while good had been done in the past, evil was being done now. They were loud in their praise of Ripon as an honest man, who meant well by them. But they said that in fact he had been able to do nothing for them. The officials had made it impossible. No real reform could be begun till the Covenanted Service was abolished. They did not fancy the idea which has been put forward of the Duke of Connaught succeeding to the Viceroyalty. He was young and without experience, and would be entirely dry-nursed by the officials.

Nothing could be worse than a Viceroy who should only be a figure-head.

" *27th Nov.*—By train to Hyderabad, though not yet arrived. But we are in the Nizam's territory. I am surprised and pleased to notice that ever since crossing the Krishna River, which is the boundary, the cultivation has appeared more flourishing, less waste land and better crops, sheep instead of goats, and farmers riding about on horseback, a thing I have not seen since landing in India. The land, however, is light, and must be very dry and hot at some seasons of the year. It is a great plain with picturesque granite rocks here and there, some of them fortified. The Hyderabad territory is a high plateau situated about the centre of the Indian peninsula."

CHAPTER IV

HYDERABAD

"*28th Nov.*

"ARRIVED at Hyderabad at daybreak. We found Seymour Keay's carriage waiting for us, and a very amiable note from Mr. Cordery, inviting us to stay at the Residency. The note was forwarded by Keay, so we accepted both the carriage and invitation, and are now at the residency. I am glad of this, for when we were in England we had made a kind of half promise to stay with Keay and his wife, but since then Keay has brought forward several charges against the Indian Government, which, though they may be true, I do not wish to identify myself with, and I wrote from Madras to tell him so, and that I could not, under the circumstances, just now stay with him, all my movements being reported in the papers. I was advised, too, at Bellari, to go to the Residency, as it would give me a better position with the Hyderabad authorities. Now it would seem that Keay has squared his difference with Cordery, and is not offended at our declining his own invitation. So all has happened for the best.

"This is a splendid house, built early in the century in the Palladian style, extremely handsome and extremely comfortable. We have a wing of it to ourselves, and could not be better lodged. The grounds, too, are fine, with great banyan trees, on one of which there is a large rookery of flying foxes. In the afternoon we called on the Keays, and Cordery has been good enough to invite them to dinner. Their position is rather a doubtful one at

Hyderabad. Keay is a banker, and made himself useful in many ways (being a very clever fellow) to Salar Jung, helping him to draft his political claims on the British Government, especially in respect to the Berar Provinces. But he quarrelled with the late resident, Sir Richard Meade, and accused him openly of receiving bribes. Now the Government at Simla is a bit afraid of him, and he has been received back into favour. Keay's presence at dinner has served to break the ice of politics, for he brought up all the most burning public questions." *N.B.* Keay's connection with Salar Jung had made him acquainted with all the ins and outs of the scandalous persecution to which that great native statesman had been subjected by the Indian Government, nor did he scruple to make use of his knowledge as occasion served in native interests. This made him a thorn in the side of the Calcutta Foreign Office. In 1885, having made a considerable fortune, he returned to England, and was elected to Parliament by a Scotch borough as an extreme radical. I had made his acquaintance in England in connection with a very able pamphlet he had published, called "Spoiling the Egyptians."

"*29th Nov.*—Our host here, Mr. Cordery, is a man of about fifty-five, who distinguished himself, I believe, as a young man at Oxford, and is considered one of the lights of the Indian Civil Service. He is agreeable, and easy going, and fond of the good things of life. At first he was very official and reserved, but, as I have spoken my own views with very little disguise, he has now become more natural, and I find him a man of considerable information, some wit, and by no means unsympathetic. As our host, he is all that a man should be, but it is evident we are under surveillance here, and I suspect our entertainment at the Residency is designed to keep us out of mischief. It reminds me of our hospitable entertainment by the excellent Huseyn Pasha at Deyr, when we wanted so hard to make acquaintance with the Bedouins. I have made up my mind, however, to talk quite freely to every one I meet, whether my speech is reported or not. We have received two visits to-day at Mr. Cordery's invitation, for such is the etiquette, the first from Ghaleb Jung, an official of Arab descent, who came accompanied by the Munshi of the Residency, deputed, I suspect, to listen to our conversation. But we talked Arabic, of which the Munshi knew little, and told the whole history of the Egyptian War, and our hope of Arabi's return to power. Ghaleb is by origin related to the Sultans of Lahaj near Aden, but his family has been settled here for some generations, and he did not speak Arabic with any ease.

"A more interesting visitor was Laik Ali, the young Salar Jung, who has succeeded to his father's title. He is only twenty-two, but has already an extremely dignified and at the same time quite natural manner, just the manner, in fact, of our best bred Englishmen. This, and his height, which is considerably over six feet, remind me vaguely of Pembroke, though Salar Jung has no remarkable good looks to recommend him, and seems likely to grow fat, which Pembroke never will. He talked well, and with very little reserve, said he thought the English Government had made a great mistake in Egypt, and seemed delighted at the prospect of Arabi's return. I told him about the letter I had from Sheykh Jemal-ed-Din for the Nawab Rasul Yar Khan, and he said that the Sheykh had been a friend of his father's, and invited us to breakfast with him for Saturday, promising also to invite the Nawab, so that we might talk without official listeners. I am immensely taken with this young man, and it consoles me for not having found his father still alive here. Salar Jung, the father, was a standing reproach to our Government, and, according to Lytton, a standing menace. Salar Jung, the younger, ought to play a leading part in the history of Indian emancipation.

"With Cordery at the Residency there is one Trevor, a younger, but, according to my friends at Bellari, a more dangerous, man. He is a good type of Indian civilian, decidedly clever, and a good talker, and under him again Melville. They looked on me at first with great suspicion, but since I have told them plainly that I should like to see the Covenanted Civil Service, to which they belong, abolished, we have got on friendly terms.

"After luncheon Major Clerk, the Nizam's tutor, came to take us through the town on elephants, which pleased us much. The town is most interesting, being after Cairo the most gay and busy in the Mohammedan East. Compared with Madras, it is as Paris to a decayed watering-place. Instead of the squalid back streets and the pauper population of native Madras, Hyderabad is like a great flower bed, crowded with men and women in bright dresses and with a fine cheerful air of independence, more Arab than Indian. Many of the men carry swords in their hands, as they do in Nejd, and one sees elephants and camels in the streets, besides carriages, and men on horseback. It is impossible they should not be happier here than in the mournful towns under English rule. And so I am sure it is. We went to-day to the Palace of the Bushir-ed-Dowlah, from the roof of which there is one of the most beautiful views in the world. Hyderabad lies in a sort of elevated basin, surrounded by low granite hills, picturesque and bare, the town half hidden in green trees. It has thus something of the effect of towns in Arabia, of which it in other ways reminds us. It covers a very large space on account of the gardens inside the walls, and is in truth an immense city, containing, with its suburbs, 250,000 inhabitants. From the Palace we went on to Salar Jung's tank, a beautiful sheet of water of a thousand acres, with a dam, which seems at first sight too weak for the mass it sustains as it is very high, and only a foot and a half thick at the edge, and the water brims over, so that as you sail about on it, you look down upon the city. But the dam is really a strong one, being constructed on the principle of an arch, the better to uphold the water. Passing on, we were taken to what had been the French barracks a hundred years ago when the French garrisoned the city.

"30*th Nov.*—Out before breakfast to see the Nizam's stables, a number of ungainly Walers, and another stable full of Arabs. These last were very nearly all small horses, and may likely enough have been bred in Nejd. Mohammed Ali Bey, the Nizam's master of the horse, is of Persian descent, an admirable horseman and a good fellow.

"After breakfast another Arab visitor called, brother of the El Kaeti who made himself Sultan of Makala in Hadramaut with English help, also Seyd Ali Bilgrami, a Mohammedan from Delhi, one of those brought here by Salar Jung—'a great pity' in Cordery's opinion—to wake up public opinion. He has had a partly English education, and has an appointment as civil engineer. His brother, Seyd Huseyn,[1] was old Salar Jung's private secretary. He

[1] Seyd Huseyn Bilgrami, now member of the Indian Council in London.

explained to us the state of parties here. At Salar Jung's death the Minister's son, Laik Ali, was appointed with the Peishkar, a local Hindu nobleman, to a joint commission of Government, the Nizam being a minor. The Peishkar paid little attention to business, and young Salar Jung was kept as far as possible in the background, the principal influence being exercised by a third official, Shems-el-Omra, an enemy of Salar Jung's. And thus affairs had got into a bad state. This was encouraged by the Residency, whose policy it was to show that the native Government was unfit to keep order in the country. Under old Salar Jung the Hyderabad State had been as secure as any part of India.

"We drove in the afternoon through Secunderabad and the English cantonments to Bellarum, where the Resident has a country house.

"*1st Dec.*—To breakfast with Salar Jung. He showed us his late father's horses. Among them two Arabs, the finest I ever saw, one an old white Hamdani Simri from Ibn Saoud's stud in Nejd, the other also white, a Kehailan from Ibn Haddal, fifteen one in height, and the most perfect large Arab possible. The particulars of their breeding were given us by one Ali Abdallah, a man of Arab origin himself, he assured us, connected with the Ibn Haddal tribe. I sat next to Salar Jung at breakfast, on the other side of me being Seyd Ali Bilgrami already mentioned. With him I discussed the whole question of the future of Islam. He had read my book, but took what he called a more pessimistic view than I do. He agreed, however, with me that if we could get Arabi and the Azhar Liberals restored to Egypt, and so a religious basis for reform, the effect in India would be great. 'We look,' he said, 'to Egypt and Mecca, far more than to Constantinople

(Seyd Ali is a Shiah), but we are all very backward in India. A religious basis is indispensable.' He then talked of the pilgrimage, and said he had been consulted by the English Government as to what should be done to improve the arrangements for it. He had referred them to my book. As a Shiah, he does not love the Sultan. The English Government would do far better to break that connection and protect the Arabs instead, but he was far from hopeful. Here at Hyderabad Salar Jung's death had been an immense misfortune. Of Sheykh Jemal-ed-Din, whom he had known here, he said he was too much of a socialist and firebrand to carry through a reformation. He talked, too, of the Mahdi, wishing him success. He said that if he succeeded it would be repeating the history of Abdillah in the sixth century of the Hejra. On the whole, a very pleasant breakfast.

"In the evening Nawab Rasul Yar Khan, who after all had not been at the breakfast, came to see me, a good little *alem* of the Azhar type one knows so well in Egypt, liberal, socialistic, and an enthusiastic disciple of Jemal-ed-Din's. He knows no English, but is learned in Persian, and to some extent in Arabic. In this last we conversed. He tells me the majority of the Mohammedans here are Sunnis, but there is little difference between them and the Shiahs, and no ill-feeling. The mass of the people are quite ignorant of all that goes on outside the Deccan, but they had heard of the Egyptian War, and had sympathized with Arabi. Of Lord Ripon and the disputes in India only those who knew English and could read the English papers had heard anything. He himself knew very little. There was no religious learning here, nor any body of learned men. In all India you would not find a teacher like

Jemal-ed-Din. He produced with reverence out of his pocket a photograph of the Afghan Sheykh, and also a copy of the 'Abu Nadara,' in which my portrait had appeared, and he read out to us the poetry written under it. I asked him if there was no Mohammedan newspaper published here, and he said there was one. But when I gave him a copy of my Colombo speech for it, he was frightened, and asked whether the English Government would not be very angry. I like this little man extremely. He promised to call again on Monday.

"*2nd Dec.*—Ik Balet Dowlah (Vikar-el-Omra) called; he is of Salar Jung's party, and a liberal, opposed to his brother Kurshid Jah (Shems-el-Omra), a conservative, and the directing spirit of the Peishkar party. The Residency, of course, supports the Peishkar party, as they get more power by working through the reactionaries opposed to reform,—precisely as in Egypt. Cordery is doing what he can to get rid of the clever young Mohammedans introduced from the north by the late Salar Jung. The ablest of these is Seyd Huseyn Bilgrami. Cordery sent for him this morning to tell him that he should leave Hyderabad as soon as possible, such was the Resident's will. The arbitrary power of the Resident here is beyond belief. I notice that Ik Balet Dowlah trembled before the little red-faced Cordery like a boy. Seyd Huseyn does not tremble, but he will be obliged to go all the same. We had luncheon with him and his brothers to-day, all very clever men, as also with Mulvi Cheragh Ali, who is looked upon here as a member of the sect nicknamed 'of nature' by the old-fashioned Mohammedans, because they advocate a reformation political, social, and religious, on the lines described in my 'Future of Islam' three years ago. Only he thinks the present Sultan and Caliph might carry it into operation. This is because he has never visited Constantinople, and so does not know how hopeless that hope is. With these young men—and we discussed all these questions—one can talk as freely as with Englishmen. And I am not surprised at Cordery's being afraid of them. The excuse for getting rid of them is that they are strangers here, which is true, for they are Delhi men. I doubt if Cordery is pleased at our going to their house.

"We went this evening at sundown to see the flying fox rookery in the Residency grounds. It was the most curious sight imaginable. All day long they hang, many hundreds of them together, head downwards from the branches, making the whole of the great tree look as if it were infected with some horrible blight. They are very large, having a spread of nearly three feet across the wings, but in the day time these are folded up. As the sun goes down and it begins to darken, they one by one awaken and stretch and scratch themselves, and at last one lets down a wing and a leg, and drops from his perch, and flaps away just like a great crow, and is followed by another and another, till there are thousands in the air, all going off in the same direction to some fruit garden which they know, and which they spend the night in pillaging.

"We dined with Major Clerk, already mentioned as the Nizam's tutor. Cordery is trying to get rid of him, too, as he is an independent man, and is honest in looking to the Nizam's interests instead of those of the Calcutta Foreign Office.

"*3rd Dec.*—Breakfast in the city with Sultan Nawaiz Jung, another of the Arabs resident here, who is, I find, actual Prince of Shehr Makalla in Hadramaut. Nearly all the Arabs at Hyderabad have come originally from the south-east coast of

Arabia. He received us with great pomp, having soldiers of his own in chocolate uniforms, and sent a smart carriage with an escort of lancers to fetch us from the Residency. His house is in the City, a very pretty one, with palm trees growing in an inner court, painted carving, and a fountain. The dinner, however, was disappointing, being in the Anglo-Indian style, which is one of the worst schools of cookery in the world. Sultan Nawaiz is known in Arabia as El Kaiti, and has a poor reputation there, having gained his wealth and present principality with British aid by money-lending. Here, too, he is a money-lender, and at the Residency they say that the Hyderabad Government owes him thirty lakhs of rupees. He belongs to the Peishkar party, and talked at breakfast in terms of great 'loyalty' to the British Empire. This he may well do, as our Government supported his claims at Makalla, deporting his rival and victim to Zanzibar. He is not a pure bred Arab, and talks Arabic with some difficulty.

"In the afternoon we were taken by Cordery to the races, where we were presented to the Nizam, a shy little young man of sixteen, with a rather awkward manner. Salar Jung, who is twenty-two and over six feet high, stood imposingly beside him. The races were of a gymkhana sort, elephant, camel and pony races, over which Salar Jung's younger brother presided with the master of the horse, Mohammed Ali Bey.

"Dined with the Keays. A young man Vincent, brother to Howard and Edgar, has arrived at the Residency from Madras. Like all these 'politicals' he is clever, and affects liberal ideas.

"*4th Dec.*—At half-past seven we went to the Palace, and saw all the Nizam's horses. There were several good Arabs among them. They gave us an exhibition of tent-pegging, in which the Nizam, who is a good rider, distinguished himself considerably. Mohammed Ali Bey, however, who is a really splendid horseman, surpassed all the rest, and performed the feat a cutting a sheep in two with a single stroke, using a Japanese sword. We found the Peishkar there, and were introduced to him, a very old man, bent nearly double, whom we were surprised to find, for he is a Hindu, able to talk Arabic. Salar Jung and his brother and many others were there. We breakfasted in a kiosk out of doors. After the entertainment in the afternoon, Vikar-el-Omra showed us his horses, and Anne paid a visit to his Zenana. He has two handsome Arabs, besides others of less note. He also had an exhibition of tent-pegging, and a performance of Deccan horsemanship. The Deccan horses are very like the old-fashioned Spanish horses, and are trained much in the same way.

"Coming home Mrs. Clerk gave us an interesting account of Hyderabad politics. She says the young Nizam's extreme shyness and frightened manner are due to an accident which happened in his Zenana. While playing with a pistol he accidentally shot a child, and he has been made to believe that the English Resident has power at any time to imprison him for this. He is, however, she says, talkative enough with her, and declares his intention of managing everything at Hyderabad himself as soon as he gets on the throne. He likes young Salar Jung, and respects him because he speaks frankly to him, but is afraid of Cordery, who supports Kurshid Jah and has placed one of Kurshid Jah's sons to be always with him. Cordery is under Trevor's influence. Cordery is angry with Major Clerk because he has opposed a guarantee of the Northern Railway which the Indian Government for strategical reasons supports. Cordery wants to get rid of Clerk and Gough and all the former friends of the late Salar Jung, and to isolate young Salar Jung from such liberal advisers as Seyd Huseyn Bilgrami. The policy seems to be to keep the Hyderabad nobles in ignorance of modern thought, and it also looks as if the Indian Government encourages the bad administration purposely. It is precisely what they are doing in Egypt.

"*5th Dec.*—We received from our friend Rasul Yar Khan this morning a little compliment, consisting of thirty 'cups of sweetness,' that is to say of that number of dishes of whipped cream. In acknowledgement, Anne wrote in Arabic, 'The sweetness of your gifts delights us, but we are grieved at the absence of the giver.' This seems to have been much appreciated, and he now sends to ask us to dinner, calling me in his note, 'The defender of the Moslems.' Rasul Yar Khan is the chief of the Ulema here, and is, moreover, a magistrate, and much respected.

"We breakfasted with Ali Abdullah, the Arab superintendent of the Nizam's breeding establishment, and met there Salar Jung and his brother, Seyd Huseyn Bilgrami and others, and went on to drink tea with them at Salar Jung's country house at Serinagar. They talked freely about social and political matters. We discussed the drinking of wine, which is common among the Mohammedans of Hyderabad, where there are drinking shops even in the City. I told them that in England we did not respect Mohammedans who drank wine, and that very few drank in Egypt, and none in Arabia. I begged Seyd Huseyn to advise Salar Jung most strongly to speak to Lord Ripon when he is at

Calcutta, and tell him the whole state of things here.

"Dined with Bushir-ed-Dowlah, a rather dull entertainment of about forty people, mostly English, our only new native acquaintance being the chief of the Shiah Ulema, Seyd Ali, a native of Shustar, with whom we conversed in Arabic. He, too, is a friend of Jemal-ed-Din's, he says, but has the name of being 'a great fanatic.' He is a thorough Iraki, and I confess I do not like him. He remembers Layard at Mosul, when he was a boy. Bushir-ed-Dowlah speaks very little English. After dinner we were entertained rather lugubriously with a magic lantern representing the Afghan War.

"*6th Dec.*—Anne went with the rest on a long expedition to Golconda, but I stayed at home, being tired with the constant gaieties, going only to Seymour Keay's.

"Dined at Vikar-el-Omra's, a handsome house—gold plate, nautch, and illuminations, but no native guests. Vikar-el-Omra is out of favour with the Residency on account of the quarrel with his brother Kurshid Jah. Cordery, however, was there and about twenty English. Major Gough, who is one of the Nizam's people, was among them, and begged me to speak to Lord Ripon in support of Salar Jung when I see him at Calcutta, which I most certainly will do.

"*7th Dec.*—Received a visit from a native teacher at the Moslem school, and we had some interesting talk. He told me the Mohammedans here were far from happy. They were isolated and without knowledge of what happened in the outer world. They wanted knowledge and education; schools there were, but no superior instruction. They had had a great Minister in Salar Jung, but he was dead. The men now in power had never left the walls of Hyderabad. They were in the hands of the English, who were destroying all the good work that Salar Jung had done. His son was a good and able young man, who had large ideas because he had travelled. But the Peishkar knew nothing, and he made a circle on the table with his finger, signifying the walls of the city. I asked him about Kurshid Jah, and he made the same sign. The Government, he said, is in the hands of two or three ignorant men. Men of learning are being driven from the country. The teacher had with him a friend who knew Persian. They were both much pleased to hear that Anne had read the Koran through three times. This is an old-fashioned man, who evidently hates the English heartily, but I am struck with his liberality as between Mohammedans; and Mohammedan Hyderabad, whether Sunni or Shiah, seems ripe for reform. I had a talk later with Cheragh Ali, mostly about his book. His book contains nothing more than Mohammed Abdu, or any of the Liberal Ulema of Cairo, would subscribe to. Indeed, the reforms it suggests have all been advocated by them, and are defended with much the same reasoning. I showed him, however, that he was leaning on a broken reed if he trusted to Constantinople for a reformation.

"We dined at Salar Jung's, a very beautiful fête, and Anne had much conversation with him as he took her in to dinner. He has promised her to entrust me with his father's correspondence as to the disputes of recent years. And he has asked us to a private breakfast for Sunday, when he will tell me everything, and consult me fully. At these big dinners, unless you sit next any one, there is no opportunity of talking to him. Every one is afraid, even if there are no Europeans present, of being overheard by the Residency retainers. Seyd Ali Shustari was there, and Rasul Yar Khan, and we talked in Arabic, and thus we had no such fears. The old Shiah is a poet and a wag, and as such, licensed to be free in his discourse, even a little *mejnun*, and made great game of the Resident's hilarity in his cups. He was outspoken, too, about the Peishkar. The Hindus, he says, are pleased at the new *régime*, but the Mohammedans are all angry. The Peishkar was of the party, but, being a Hindu, he did not dine. He has asked us to a dinner he gives on Monday, but we shall by that time have left Hyderabad. He does not dine at table even in his own house with his guests, but superintends the feast. We cannot stay here longer than until Monday.

"*8th Dec.*—Saw a Mekkawi, one Seyd Abdullah, a merchant, who gave us a great deal of information both about Meccan and Hyderabad politics. He is a great admirer of the Sherif Abd-el-Mutalleb, whom he remembered as a boy at Mecca, for he has been here thirty years without going home. He told us of the rebellions of Abd-el-Mutalleb against the Turks, and how, when they fired at him in the street, he used to throw his cloak open so as to show he had no fear. The Sherifs used to keep the Arabs in rebellion for fear they should join the Turks against them. In his old age Abd-el-Mutalleb had taken to opium and spent his days in sleep, and so had been deposed. My visitor is himself a pure Arab, and his language is easy to understand. His chief lamentation was at living away from home, and that it was impossible to get Arab wives here. They would not leave Arabia, and the Arabs of Hyderabad, of whom there are a large number, were obliged to marry the women of the place.

" With regard to Hyderabad politics, he spoke with the greatest enthusiasm of the late Salar Jung, who was himself of Arab descent. He described the state of things when he first came here thirty years ago, how people killed each other openly in the streets, and how the great Minister had established peace everywhere. I asked him about the Shiahs, and he said there was no quarrel here between them and the Sunnis. He himself was a Sunni, but they all prayed together. They were on good terms, too, with the Hindus. The Hindus did not eat with them, but that was all. Of Laik Ali he spoke very highly, said he was a young man of good thought and good language, and would become a great Minister like his father. All the people loved him. As to the Peishkar he neglected public business. He had no energy, and letters of importance were put aside. It was very different from old Salar Jung's time. I asked him about the Nizam, whom he spoke of as the 'Pasha,' and he said he was good, not at all dull, but that he was young, and the nobles about him taught him to be silent in public, and so he seemed lacking in intelligence, but with his own people he talked and was merry enough. I like this Meccan merchant much, and doubt if there are many shop-keepers in London who could give me as sensible an account of their local politics as he has given me. The Hindus in the Deccan are mostly men of the lower castes. There are few nobles or Brahmins among them, and their only rich men are the money-lenders. The rest are shop-keepers, and out of the town peasants. The Peishkar is their only great man.

" The Nizam came to dinner at the Residency, and took Anne in. There was also a large party of Nawabs and dignitaries, the Peishkar, Salar Jung,

Kurshid Jah, Bushir-ed-Dowlah, Vikar-el-Omra, and the rest, as well as the Roman Catholic bishop and some English. Kurshid Jah has asked us to dinner for Tuesday, but neither to him, nor to the Peishkar can we go, as we leave on Monday. The Nizam was as usual very silent, but this is etiquette. Trevor tells me the Nizam's father never spoke at all to the English officials, or even looked at them.

"*9th Dec.*—The schoolmaster called again. He asked me what the Mohammedans ought to do to better their condition. Every year they were becoming poorer in India. The Government ruined them where they had land with taxes, and they had no employment in the towns. I suggested they should take to trade, learn English, and compete with the Hindus, and he agreed with me that that might be best. He said, however, that in many parts a Mohammedan who learned English was still called a *kafr* by his fellows. Here at Hyderabad the taxes were not excessive, but the English system surrounded them, and English goods were killing the native industries. He said if nothing were done to help them, the English Government would have every Mohammedan in the country against them.

"He also complained terribly of the tyranny of the English officials and their brutal manners. He asked how it was that I was different from them, that I made him sit down on the same sofa with myself, that I addressed him politely, and did not treat him as a slave. The officials, he said, sit without moving in their chairs and talk to us, while they leave us standing, abruptly in words of command, without any salutation or words of friendship. You treat me, a poor man, as your equal. Why is this? I explained to him there were degrees of good breeding amongst us, and that the better the breeding the greater the politeness. That the men who came out to India as Government servants were, many of them, taken from a comparatively low rank in life, and that, being unused to refined society, or to being treated with much consideration at home, they lost their heads when they found themselves in India in a position of power. I hoped, however, that this might soon be changed. He said the officials made their nation hated by the people; many who were willing to think the English Government was good were estranged by the manners of its officials. He asked me again why I travelled so far to see them, and why I cared to help them, and I explained that in youth I had led a life of folly, and that I wished to do some good before I died, and that I had received much kindness from the Moslems, and learned from them to believe in God, and so I spent a portion of every year among them. I like the man much.

"At ten we went to breakfast with Salar Jung, a farewell visit. We had bargained to have no English with us, and the party consisted of himself, his brother, and his sister's governess Mdlle. Gaignaud, of Seyd Huseyn Bilgrami, and of our two selves. We talked very freely of the political situation, which is this. In a few weeks the Nizam will come of age, and an attempt is going to be made by the Residency to get his signature to a treaty which, in renewing the alliance existing between the Nizam and the Government of India, contains an article abrogating all previous treaties, thus putting the Berar provinces permanently into English hands."

The question of the Berars was this. Many years ago, before the time of old Salar Jung, the Hyderabad State was badly governed, and its finances became so involved that the Nizam was obliged to borrow several millions sterling from the Calcutta Government. The Government took in pledge for the debt the provinces in question, which were the richest he possessed, it being agreed that they should be administered by the Government of India until the loan was repaid. This arrangement naturally gave much employment to Englishmen and many highly paid posts to members of the Covenanted Civil Service, and it has consequently been their settled policy to make the resumption of the provinces by the Nizam impossible. In this view the provinces have been exceptionally well administered; the taxation has been light, and everything has been done to make the peasantry satisfied with English rule, so that they form a striking contrast with most parts of British India. It was never expected that the Nizam would be able to repay his debt, but, in case he could, the prosperity of the provinces would then, it was thought, be a reason for refusing. This is precisely what happened. Salar Jung, being a man of great ability, not only restored order in the Deccan, but brought the Hyderabad finances into so prosperous a condition that he was able to come forward with the borrowed millions in his hand, and claimed their repayment and the restitution of the provinces. It was for his insistence on this point that his persecution at the hands of the Imperial Government began, and was carried on relentlessly until his death. The claim, however, still remained, and could not be contested, as it was embodied in a public treaty between the two States, and advantage was being taken of the Nizam's minority and the death of his powerful Minister to get it annulled.

"Seyd Huseyn is positive that the draft of the proposed new treaty is already at the Residency. He has been shown a copy or *précis* of it, and believes it will either be forced on the young Nizam as soon as he comes of age, as a condition of his ascending the throne, or that the signature of the Peishkar will be taken before that event. This he thinks could be done legally, as the Council of Regency has sovereign powers. The Council consists of the Peishkar, old and infirm, of Kurshid Jah, the presumptive heir to the throne, both men under the influence of the Residency, and of Bushir-ed-Dowlah, who is without colour or strong character. Young Salar Jung so far is only secretary to the Council, and so without voice in its decisions. I find it difficult, however, to believe that Lord Ripon's Government would venture to rush so important a treaty through in the last days of the Regency; and I think it far more likely that pressure will be put on the young Nizam, partly by flattery, partly by threats at Calcutta, to get a signature from him simultaneously with his installation. On the other hand, the other important matter insisted upon by the Indian Government, the Railway Convention, has been carried through precisely in this way with the Peishkar, for Cordery told us so himself, and it is possible that Seyd Huseyn may be right, and the attempt on the Berars will be made at once, rather than trust its execution to the Nizam's subserviency. This decides me to hasten my journey to Calcutta, where I shall lay the whole case before Lord Ripon, and protest against the sharp practice of the Foreign Office diplomacy.

"The existence of the draft treaty at the Residency explains to me what has hitherto seemed inexplicable, the strong support given to the Peishkar, in spite of his misgovernment; the isolation in which Salar Jung is being placed by the dismissal of so many of his father's best servants; the stories circulated against the character of all those who have advocated the retrocession of the Berar Provinces; Cordery's words about Laik Ali's 'headstrong character' and that his only chance was to make common cause with the Peishkar; the favour shown to Kurshid Jah as heir to the throne and substitute in case it should be found necessary to get rid of the young Nizam, along with the bad character Cordery attributes to the latter; and the tales of his childishness, of his early corruption with women and other scandals. Cordery at dinner has talked a great deal to Anne on all these matters. It also perhaps explains how the other day, when he had been speaking more severely than usual to Laik Ali, he put his arm paternally on his shoulder and said Laik Ali must forgive him, for he was only following his instructions. He made a sort of apology to Seyd Huseyn, too, when he sent for him the other day. He told him he must leave Hyderabad for six months, but added 'I am doing you an injustice, but it is necessary in the public interest.' I exhorted Laik Ali to talk openly of all these things to Lord Ripon when he sees him at Calcutta, and I have promised to urge Lord Ripon to pay full attention to him. As soon as he arrives with the Nizam's party at Calcutta I will see him and advise him, for none of Laik Ali's friends are to be allowed to go with him. He has given me printed copies of his father's private correspondence relating to the Berars and other matters, and will send to me at Bombay a copy of the minute written by his father on the case. It is a curious comment on the little trust placed by the native Government in English administration that he does not send me the minute by post, but will forward it through an agent to be delivered by hand.

"Talking on general matters of government, Laik

Ali said that he did not think that the Nizam would be fit to govern the country by himself, as he has thought of doing, but neither is the country fit for self-government. The custom has been that it should be governed by a Minister, and doubtless he intends to be that Minister. I shall do what I can to help him, as he possesses his father's traditions, and there is no question he is very popular at Hyderabad. His age is his only drawback, as he is little more than twenty-one. I asked him about this particularly, and he said he was born in August, 1862. But he is far older than his years. He has invited us to come back for the Nizam's installation. The Peishkar's administration seems to have been signalized by a general round of plunder as in the old time. It is not only from Laik Ali that I know this, but from everybody I have spoken to. When Salar Jung died, Sir Stewart Bailey was sent from Calcutta to settle matters here, and Laik Ali was appointed Co-Administrator with the Peishkar, and as such he ought now to be taking his share in the administration, but this has been prevented. There is no public office at which business is transacted, and the Peishkar will not consult him or let him into his house with any regularity for the discussion of affairs; nor will he send him, as he ought to do, the documents for his signature. The consequence is he is powerless to do or to prevent anything, and he says he will throw up his office if after he has been to Calcutta the position is not altered. He now has the responsibility without the power, and this he refuses to go on with.

"We are beginning to be out of favour at the Residency. Cordery is alarmed at our independent visits to the City. He made a remark two days ago about it to Salar Jung. Perhaps his sudden announcement that he is going to Calcutta may be connected with a suspicion that we know his plans. At four, Rasul Yar Khan came to fetch us to dine with him in the City, a final breach of discipline, as English people going to the City are expected to be bear-led by some one from the Residency. Rasul Yar Khan lives in a little old-fashioned house, with a pretty court surrounded by arches, and we were glad of the opportunity of seeing a *bourgeois* Hyderabad establishment. He had invited several friends to meet us, Nawaiz Jung, Cheragh Ali, Seyd Huseyn Bilgrami, and Mulvi Mehdy Hassan; and we had some good talk. They told us when Lord Beaconsfield came into office ten years ago, every Mohammedan in India looked to the Conservative party as friendly to them. But Lord Lytton's policy had undeceived them. The Afghan War had been most displeasing and had estranged every mind, and they had entirely lost confidence in any English party. They talked, too, of a letter Lytton had written to Lord Salisbury, which had been published, explaining how Mohammedans would be excluded from the public service.

"Mehdy Hassan sat next me. He is a native of Lucknow, and told me I should be well received by the Mohammedans there, for they knew my name well, and he has promised to give me letters for some of them. They would be glad to learn the truth about the Egyptian War, for until a few months ago they had all been deceived about it, thinking that the English had really gone to Egypt as the Sultan's allies. They said I should do well to give a lecture at Calcutta on the subject, but that it would be difficult to get up a public protest against future wars waged with Mohammedans, because, although the thing would be popular, it would be too dangerous for the leaders in it, who would from that moment become marked men. They told me I had no conception of the despotism under which India was held, nor of the danger there was for them in meddling with politics; Jemal-ed-Din's stories about the deportation of religious Sheykhs to the Andaman Islands were perfectly true. The dinner was a good one, partly European, partly Indian, but we left early in order to appease Mr. Cordery.

"10*th Dec.*—Left Hyderabad by the early train, many of our friends coming to see us off. The Meccan brought us provisions for the road, and the schoolmaster was there, and Sultan Nawaiz's son. I made them all three sit down on a bench with me, on which Trevor was also seated, a proceeding English officials are not used to. Then Seyd Huseyn Bilgrami and others of the Northern Mohammedans came, and our good little Rasul Yar Khan with his brother insisted on going with us two hours' journey on our road. He had gone that distance, he said, with Jemal-ed-Din, and would go with us. He sent us some splendid presents last night, including the finest cashmere shawl I ever saw, which we had some difficulty in sending back, as also a box of ostrich feathers from Sultan Nawaiz, which his son brought to the station. But it would never do for us to take presents, though other English travellers it seems do. The Keays and several English also came to the station, and Trevor, who I suspect wanted to know the names of our native friends.

"The country near Hyderabad is very curious, wild, uncultivated hills, trees and boulders, but beyond there is a rich plain at a lower level, bearing good crops of *gholum*, flax, and *raghi*, cotton also, I believe, but I could not distinguish the crop. The villages in this district have all the remains of fine stone walls, with round towers, each a little fortress against the raiding bands which once drew black-mail from them. The largest town, Kalbarga, seemed to have fine buildings. We travelled on through the night, and arrived early at Poona the next morning.

"11*th Dec.*—Poona is an uninteresting place, without a vestige of Eastern colour. It stands in a bare plain, feebly relieved by a river bordered with acacia trees, and some shapeless hills of trappe formation. Great macadamized roads run everywhere, and modern buildings of debased Gothic with meaningless belfries and inscriptions to Sir Bartle Frere dot the landscape. Barracks, of course, and factory chimneys abound, and institutions of all sorts. The climate, however, is a healthy one. Poona is 2,000 feet above the sea, and at one time it was proposed to remove the seat of Supreme Government here from Calcutta.

"We were taken by Miss Dillon, with whom we are staying, to see the Deccan College, an absurd building, from the tower of which we viewed the scene described. It contains a hundred and twenty boarders, all Hindus but half a dozen, only one Mohammedan. Ninety of the Hindus are Brahmins. I talked to some of the pupils in the reading rooms. They told me they read the 'Bombay Gazette,' which represented their views better than any other English paper, but the best native one was the 'Hindu Prakash.' The English Director struck us as being rather a weak vessel, contrasting unfavourably in the point of intelligence and knowledge with a learned Brahmin who explained to us the connection of Hindi, Mahratta, and Hindustani with Sanskrit. On the other hand, I noticed this learned man thumbing without ceremony palm leaf manuscripts of the eleventh century in a way which would have made a book collector's blood run cold. In these two incidents the difference between the East and the West is exemplified."

In the afternoon a friend of Rangiar Naidu came to see us, and gave us a number of interesting statistics as to the state of agriculture in the Bombay Presidency. It is hardly worth, however, transcribing them here, as they do not differ essentially from those we received elsewhere, and I have incorporated the result of all my agricultural inquiries omitted from my diary in the chapter on "The Agricultural Danger" given at the end of this volume.

On the 12th we went on to Bombay, where we spent a couple of days in the society principally of a Europeanized Mohammedan to whom we had brought letters, Mr. Mohammed Rogay, a wealthy man, advanced and liberal, and the head of the Moslem community. His ideas were all of the most modern type, far too modern on some points quite to please me. "He drove us through the native town, which is most picturesque and cheerful, very unlike Madras. Rogay would like it all pulled down, and built up again in rows of sham Gothic houses." A more interesting personage was Mr. Malabari, editor of the "Indian Spectator," a friend of Colonel Osborne's. "He is a Parsi, but says his sympathies are rather Hindu than of his own people. He is an intelligent, active little man, going about constantly from place to place on philanthropic and political business. He confirms everything we have heard elsewhere as to the agricultural misery, and promises to take us a round of inspection on our return, as well as to get up meetings at which I can express my views, and agrees that there will be no improvement until India has gone bankrupt—bankruptcy or revolution, as Gordon suggested.[1] He also described how such English officials as dared to protest against the over taxation were persecuted. If any of them espoused the wrongs of the natives he was bullied out of the service, and then his evidence was scouted on the plea that he was only 'a man with a grievance.' Such had been Colonel Osborne's case. Malabari is only thirty, though he looks eighty. He has written, among other things, certain loyal poems which are sad trash. He is, however, a great admirer of Lord Ripon, and he exhorted me to support him with prudence."

The rest of our time at Bombay was spent principally in the Arab stables looking at horses, but of this more on the occasion of our second visit.

"15*th Dec.*—Started for Calcutta, and found Gorst[2] in the same train, and had a long talk with him. Randolph Churchill is as keen as ever about Egypt, and is going to make a speech about it at Edinburgh. Gorst has come to India professionally 'to advise the Nizam as to the retrocession of the Berar Provinces,' but I was in doubt which side he and Churchill took in Indian matters. He told me, however, that up to the present moment the Fourth Party had not committed themselves on the Ilbert Bill, and I advised him strongly to take up the cause of the people. It was going a-begging among statesmen, for the natives trusted neither the Conserva-

[1] This refers to a talk I had had with General C. G. Gordon at the end of 1882 in which he had assured me emphatically that "no reform would ever be achieved in India without a Revolution." Gordon, it will be remembered, accompanied Ripon, as his private secretary, to India in 1880, but soon after their landing at Bombay had resigned his place. The opposition of the covenanted civil service to any real reform had convinced him that he would be useless to Lord Ripon in an impossible task.

[2] Sir John Gorst.

tives nor Mr. Gladstone, and though they were grateful to Lord Ripon personally for his sympathy they quite understood he had been able to do next to nothing for them. There was no reason why Churchill should not raise the cry of 'The Queen and the natives of India,' as against the official class. It seems that Gorst formerly brought the matter of Berar before Lord Salisbury, and interested him the right way, but Lytton was adverse, and afterwards it was Gorst who prosecuted the 'Statesman' newspaper on the part of the Government for its publication of the facts relating to Salar Jung's attempted arrest, and the bribe taken by Sir Richard Meade. He told me the prosecution was dropped in consequence of representations from the Calcutta Foreign Office that a scandal would be created, and he himself was of opinion that Sir Richard Meade would have come badly out of the affair. I warned him how difficult he would find it to get speech of the Nizam, or to do anything at Hyderabad if staying at the Residency. But I did not tell him all I knew of the politics of the place, or about the Draft Treaty, for I mean to set the facts first before Lord Ripon.

"16*th Dec.*—Still in the train. Read up the Hyderabad Blue Books (those given me by Laik Ali). They are very instructive."

CHAPTER V

CALCUTTA

"*17th Dec.*

"ARRIVED at Calcutta, and were met by Walter Pollen [an aide-de-camp of Lord Ripon, and a private friend of ours], who has taken capital rooms for us at 2, Russell Street. Wrote our names down at Government House, and arranged with Primrose, the private secretary, that I am to have an interview with Lord Ripon on Wednesday afternoon. Sent several letters of introduction which had been given us to Hindus of the place. There is notice of a meeting of a thousand persons held under Rangiàr Naidu at Madras to protest against the Address presented to T.; I have telegraphed to congratulate him.

"*18th Dec.*—A very busy day, as I had to write a vast number of letters for the English mail. In the morning Norendro Nath Sen, the editor of the 'Indian Mirror,' called, a well-informed man. I asked him about Lord Ripon, and he said he was supporting him all he could in public, but privately he feared Lord Ripon was weak. In point of fact he had done nothing for the Indians though he had shown his sympathy and taken their part in their quarrels with the English. 'We are thankful,' he said, 'for small mercies. If the Ilbert Bill had been given in its original integrity it would have been worth something. Now it is worth nothing except as the recognition of a principle. Still we are thankful.' 'As to the local self-government bill,' he said, 'people are very suspicious. There are many who looked upon it as likely to be made use of by the officials to impose heavier local rates in the people's name than they would venture to do in their own.' I think this very likely, as it is exactly what Ismaïl did with his Chamber of Notables in Egypt. Increased taxation is the aim of all these despotic governments, of the Indian more than any. Nor were they satisfied with regard to the Bengal Rent Bill. I asked him about the Mohammedan community here, and he said they were very timid and time-serving. He had proposed to them to get up a demonstration on my arrival, but they had been afraid of the Government. Amir Ali, the head of the advanced party, was like an Englishman, and he and his followers played into the hands of the Government. He himself had more sympathy with Abd-el-Latif, and the old-fashioned Mohammedans who kept themselves independent, but these were afraid to express their opinions. They looked on Amir Ali as a renegade. I have, fortunately, letters to both these leaders, and one from Jemal-ed-Din to Abd-el-Latif, so I hope I shall be able to gain their confidence.

"Later Sir Jotendro Mohun Tagore called, a Hindu of rank as he has the title of Maharajah. He confirmed much of what Norendro said about Lord Ripon, and was clean against the Rent Bill, but, as he explained, he was prejudiced on this point, being himself a Zemindar. The point of the bill is to break the agreement made by Lord Cornwallis in 1793, by which the absolute ownership of the land was recognized in the Zemindars. The present tenure is briefly this: the Zemindars are the proprietors, and cannot be assessed at more than one-fifth of the gross produce of their estate. They generally let their land to middlemen or farmers, who employ the ryots or labourers, just as we do in

England. The effect of the bill will be to transfer the ownership to these occupants, who will then hold them directly from the Government. At present no increasing of the assessment is announced, but the agreement made by Lord Cornwallis being once broken, it seems probable that this will follow. The Zemindars will be reduced to the ownership only of such lands as they occupy. The contention of the Government would seem to be that the land will then be better cultivated and produce more, and their fifth be proportionately increased. But Sir Jotendro is of opinion that the old system of husbandry was safer than any new system is likely to be. The land might be made to produce more by steam ploughing and high farming, but in the end the fertility would be exhausted. Here, again, precisely the same thing has happened in Egypt. He has promised, however, to put us in the way of seeing some villages here and there that we may study the question on the spot, and we are to make him a return call in a day or two.

"Last came Schomberg Kerr, Lord Ripon's chaplain, who knew my brother and sister so well years ago. He is a very nice fellow, and not unlike his cousin, the other Schomberg Kerr.[1] But he was wary of talking politics, as befits a Jesuit and a private chaplain. I fancy he makes it a rule to confine himself strictly to spiritual advice, but I don't know.

"19*th Dec.*—Seyd Amir Ali called, and we talked about Arabi. I taxed him at once with having written that letter to the 'Times' just before the war saying that all the Indian Mohammedans supported the action of the English Government, and he said he was sorry for it now, but the Mohammedans had

[1] The late Lord Lothian.

been deceived as to the true state of the case. They now recognized Arabi as an honest man, fighting in defence of his religion. I noticed, however, that he looked rather confused when I charged him with this, but I think we shall get on well together in spite of the pot hat he wears. I told him that Gladstone wanted to restore Arabi, and urged him to protest against any further wars against Mohammedans, whatever the pretext might be. I told him that the only way to get attention paid to the wishes of the Mohammedan community was to inspire a certain amount of fear. By holding their tongues in a crisis like the Egyptian War, or pretending to sympathize with the Government, they threw away their advantages. I trusted that if there should be any serious talk of sending Indian troops to suppress the Mahdi he would call a general meeting of his party to protest against it. Amir Ali is a young man not much over thirty, and evidently very clever, and if he has the courage to take an independent line, may play a great part. But they say his ambition is to be made Chief Justice.

"While we were talking, arrived a dignified old man, Manockji Rustemji, the Parsi Consul-General for Persia, with his son. We talked about the Bengal Rent Bill, to which, like everybody else I have talked with, they are opposed. Sir Jamsetji Jijibhoy is staying with him, and he promises to send him to see us. I like this old man very much. He is a friend of Ragunath Rao's, and spoke very warmly of him, saying that he was a far cleverer man than his cousin, Sir Madhava Rao, who has more celebrity but less courage. We are to call on his wife next week.

"At a quarter to three I paid my visit to Lord Ripon, feeling rather nervous about it beforehand, but I have every reason to be satisfied with the result. I had a good hour's conversation, first about the state of the agricultural districts which I described, and afterwards about the really important business of Hyderabad. I set the whole state of the case before him, the reversal by the Peishkar and Kurshid Jah of all Sir Salar Jung's policy; the dismissal of the skilled administrators; the consequent break-down of the administration; the return to old practices of corruption and the rest of it; and, lastly, 'what would seem incredible but for which I could nevertheless vouch' that the Peishkar's misgovernment was strongly supported at the Residency. I made no charge against Mr. Cordery, who I considered was merely the responsible person representing the several interests of the official class. But I could only explain the matter to myself by supposing that these officials feared a retrocession of Berar, and so purposely abetted the misgovernment of the State. This had been done without doubt in former years for similar reasons, and I had had sufficient experience of official ways in Egypt to make me very distrustful. Lord Ripon smiled at this and said that official ways were always a little the same everywhere, but he did not commit himself to any opinion as to whether I was correct or not. He said, however, that I must know well how great a difficulty there was in Hyderabad in finding any one competent to carry on Sir Salar Jung's administration. He had considered Sir Salar's death a great misfortune, though others, and he believed Lord Lytton, had thought otherwise. It was the more deplorable to himself because he had just had the satisfaction of restoring the good relations which had so long existed between Sir Salar and the Indian Government, but which had latterly been interrupted, and he had personally a high opinion of Sir Salar's integrity and good faith. But who was there to fill his place?

"I then told him my high opinion of young Salar Jung, both as a good young man, and one with statesmanlike qualities, which only wanted practice to develop into a capacity equal, perhaps, to his father's. He said that he was glad to hear me say this, for such had also been Sir Stewart Bailey's opinion. But Laik Ali was very young for so responsible a position. I said that he was twenty-one, and he asked me whether that meant twenty-one according to the Mohammedan or the English reckoning. I said: 'According to the English, as he was born in August, 1862,' and so was very nearly as old as his father had been when he first became Prime Minister, for Sir Salar had been only twenty-four according to the Mohammedan reckoning, and, if one considered how troubled and disorganized a State Hyderabad then was and compared it with what it is now, it would be seen that Laik Ali's position, if he were made Minister to-morrow, would be a more favourable one by a great deal than his father's had been. Now all the machinery of government was there, and it only required to be kept going, instead of having to be created. I also begged him to see the young man himself privately when he came to Calcutta, and he said he would certainly do so, and as Laik Ali could speak English, they would not want an interpreter, and he would give him every encouragement to explain his position and ideas thoroughly. All Lord Ripon's manner showed a thorough good will towards young Salar Jung, and I have little doubt that he will give him his support. He then asked me about the character of the Nizam, and I told him I could say nothing for certain, because he had been so silent in our interviews that I had not been able to judge, but it was my opinion that he was far from being without ideas of his own, and very likely a will of his own too. He asked me whether the people of Hyderabad wished him to be proclaimed of age this year or not till two years later, and I said it was not a case of their wishing. They all expected it to be at once, and would be grievously disappointed if it was deferred. There was a strong feeling of loyalty and affection towards the Nizam among the people, and they would resent his being kept out of his right. He also asked about Bushir-ed-Dowlah and to which faction he belonged. I said I could not answer certainly, but I believed Laik Ali considered him to be among his friends. Bushir-ed-Dowlah seemed to be without strong political colour. Lord Ripon remarked, however, that he, Bushir-ed-Dowlah, had been on bad terms with Laik Ali's father. Of this I knew nothing.

"Then, with some apologies, I mentioned the report about the draft treaty. At this Lord Ripon laughed, and said it was the first he had heard of it. He certainly would never consent to taking any such treaty from the young Nizam. It would be a fraud, and I might dismiss it from my mind; all that might possibly be asked of him would be some limitation of his absolute power for a couple of years or so until they saw how he got on with his Government. As to a treaty concerning the Berar claim, he, Lord Ripon, was incapable of proposing it.[1] I said I was sure it was so, and would dismiss it from my mind. Lord Ripon's manner, though re-

[1] *N.B.* Precisely this leonine treaty in the form of a perpetual lease was imposed on the Nizam twenty years later by Lord Curzon under circumstances of extreme compulsion.

served at first, was very cordial to me in the latter part of this conversation, and he shook hands warmly with me and said he was glad I had spoken to him on these matters, and hoped to see me again. Since my famous interview with Mr. Gladstone in March, 1882, I have not been so favourably impressed by any statesman that I have conversed with. *Absit omen.*

"*20th Dec.*—Looked in on Knight, Editor of the 'Statesman,' who gave me his views on the decadence of English morality, which he dates from the first Afghan war. He has been useful as exposing many of the official iniquities here, and takes, as it seems to me, generally just views. He would not, however, admit that the finances were in any danger, but looks rather to a revolution to end the present system.

"From him I went to Sir Stewart Bailey, and, as the conversation led up to it, told him something of the state of things at Hyderabad. He seemed surprised that Cordery was actually supporting the Peishkar and Kurshid Jah; said he thought he had been weak in letting things go on so far unchecked; repudiated all idea of its being done on policy; did not think that Trevor really influenced Cordery; Trevor was not nearly as clever a man, but very likely he had been too long at Hyderabad. Sir Stewart, however, spoke with great sympathy of Laik Ali, and said his was a waiting game, and it was only a matter of time his becoming Minister. We discussed his age, and he asked me, as Lord Ripon had done, whether I thought him capable of being now at the head of affairs. I said of course it was a very responsible position for a youth of twenty-one, but I believed him capable of it if really supported and rightly advised at the Residency.

He was very popular in Hyderabad on his father's account and his own, and would find no opposition except from the old Mogul nobles.

"We then discussed the north-west men. Sir Stewart does not like Seyd Huseyn Bilgrami, says his letters are flippant, but agreed with me that Salar Jung's system, to be carried out at all, must be so through people who had received a modern education. Of Gough he spoke highly, but not of Clerk. On the whole I am satisfied with our conversation. It is evident Sir Stewart meant to have Laik Ali supported when he made the arrangement which left him co-administrator, and will do what he can for him now. At leaving he said it was a question whether it might not be better to let things go on a little longer and then interfere, or to interfere now on the Nizam's coming of age. I said I considered they had gone quite far enough. In any case he promised to talk the whole matter over with Laik Ali, and I shall be surprised if Trevor is not removed and a change of attitude insisted on with Cordery. Talking of past affairs at Hyderabad, Bailey said that Sir Richard Meade's alliance with the late Emir el Kebir against Sir Salar Jung had been most unfortunate, and had 'dragged the Indian Government through a deal of mud.' He did not wish to be quoted in this opinion, but such was the fact.

"*21st Dec.*—Mulvi Seyd Amir Huseyn, deputy collector and magistrate at court, a friend of Amir Ali's, came. We discussed the Bengal Rent Bill, and he told me he had been one of the original supporters of a scheme to relieve the ryots, and had sent in a memorandum on the subject to the Government, but now the Bill had been drafted he had changed his mind about it. He considered that it would not really relieve the ryots, and would most certainly be made a precedent for further spoliation of landlords by the Government, and eventually for increased assessments. The breach of faith with the Zemindars was glaring, and it was not proposed to compensate them in any way. [I remember Lytton complaining to me at Simla in 1879 of the Bengal Land Settlement as an injustice to Indian Finance, and saying that it would be necessary to break it.] With regard to the condition of the Bengali Mohammedans, the Mulvi explained that they were an oppressed community, the Hindus having it all their own way, and there was very little courage among them, though the antiquated Mohammedans and Hindus lived on excellent terms. They dared not take any prominent part against the Government. He himself was a magistrate and deputy collector, but he had five English superiors, one above the other over him from the Collector to the Lieutenant-Governor, who, on the complaint of any one of them, would be down on him if he expressed his opinions. I told him India needed martyrs, and until they learned to have the courage of their convictions nothing would be done for them; reforms were only granted to the importunate, and on compulsion.

"Next came Kristo Das Pal, a member of the Legislative Council, and editor of the 'Hindu Patriot.' He is looked up to as the most prudent, yet independent of the Bengali Hindus, and I found him sensible, and with a very accurate knowledge of the forces with which he had to deal, both here and in England. He, too, opposed the Rent Bill, on the ground that it is not a *bona fide* measure of relief to the ryot, but the thin end of the revenue wedge which grudges the comparative immunity of Bengal from rack-renting. 'If they were in earnest,' he said, 'they would first relieve their own ryots, who are starving in Madras and Bombay, instead of doing so out of the pockets of the Zemindars here. It was robbing Peter to pay Paul.' The ryots of Bengal, though poor, were rich compared with those of the other two Presidencies, and needed far less relief. That this is so would seem to be proved from the fact that they do not here complain of the salt tax. They are rich enough not to feel the burden, for it is only hard upon the *very* poor. Talking about Lord Ripon, he said Lord Ripon had wished the Indians well, but with very little practical result, though he was the best viceroy they had ever had. He was of opinion that, before anything could be done, the Civil Service must be thrown open and reorganized. The present civilians had no sympathy with India or its people. They came and went like birds of passage. They must also have representation of some sort. At present they had none except through chance travellers like myself: I promised to do what I could to make the matter known. He asked me whether I was in Parliament and could ask questions, and I explained to him my position and promised, though I could not do it personally, to get his questions asked in proper form if he would provide me with the materials. This he agreed to do, and I gave him my address, and the necessary instructions. But the more I see and hear of the state of things in India, the more convinced I am that Gordon is right. 'Nothing will be done without a revolution.'

"In the afternoon we called on Mr. Manockji Rustemji, and found Sir Jamsetji Jijibhoy with him. He being rich and an old man talks very freely. It is absurd to suppose that the Parsis do not sympathize with the rest of the natives. He has known every viceroy since Lord William Bentinck, and likes Canning the best. Canning stood up bravely after the mutiny, and prevented innocent blood being shed. The English wanted martial law proclaimed in Calcutta, and he refused. Where it was proclaimed, any man who had a grudge could write an anonymous letter to his neighbour of a treasonable character. The letter was opened by the police, and the man to whom such might be addressed would be brought up, condemned without trial, and hanged. A good old man.

"Called also on Sir Jotendro, who lamented Mr. Gladstone's apostasy from the principles he had proclaimed in Midlothian. He said his speech on the question of making India pay the expense of the Egyptian campaign had destroyed all confidence in him in India, and he wondered that any man should be so base. I told him that in England words said out of office bind no statesman in office, an explanation which seemed to surprise him. We afterwards talked poetry, Byron, Moore, Tennyson. He did not understand Tennyson, preferred Moore infinitely. Sir Jotendro has a handsome old-fashioned house in the centre of the town, one of the first houses, he says, that were built in Calcutta; the city had grown up round it.

"*22nd Dec.*—The 'Englishman' announces a concordat on the Ilbert Bill, which Seyd Amir Ali who called this morning declares is ten times worse than withdrawing the Bill. The English are to be tried by a jury composed in majority of their own countrymen. This will make them quite independent of the law, and he talks of getting up meetings to protest. Mr. Rustemji also called, and Mrs. Ilbert to ask condolence. She says her husband has been abandoned by every one, and now by Lord Ripon. She blames Lord Ripon for his weakness, not the people at home. Lord Kimberley had written to her husband urging him to stand firm, but the members of council were frightened out of their wits, and Lord Ripon has followed them. Her husband is broken-hearted at it all, and they are going away for a week to hide in some country district. It is all very disgraceful. I told her I could not understand any one paying a moment's attention to the Anglo-Indians. The Viceroy should have been absolutely indifferent to them and their noise. She said 'If you had been Viceroy, I have no doubt it would have been so,' which I take as a compliment.

"At last Mulvi Abd-el-Latif, the head of the older-fashioned Mohammedans, has called. I had a letter for him from Sheykh Jemal-ed-Din, but I feared he would not come. He is a judge, and much occupied or would have called before. I found him all, and more than all I could have expected. He began by telling me people were afraid here of coming to see me, partly because I was looked ill on by the Government, partly because they knew I was taking notes on all I saw or heard, and they were not sure but what I might compromise them, or compromise their cause by telling too much. He knew, however, that I had the Mohammedan cause at heart, for he had heard from Sheykh Jemal-ed-Din what I had done, and he thought it best to tell me all frankly, and put me on my guard. Also it would explain to me why the Mohammedans had not come forward to welcome me. He then sketched the position of the two parties among the Mohammedans. Amir Ali and his friends had broken with the mass of the community by affecting English dress and ways, and posing as reformers, although they were in no way qualified in a religious sense for such a position. Amir Huseyn they even considered to be an unbeliever. In any case, Amir Ali did not represent the Mussulman community in Bengal, for he was a Shiah, and they were Sunnis. He, Abd-el-Latif, was a reformer too, though working on other lines. He wished to improve the religious education of the people, and had been labouring for the last twenty years to get the Government to establish proper schools. Reform must be introduced by religious, not irreligious persons, or it would take no hold on the people. These young men were out of all sympathy with the mass of the Mohammedans. They knew nothing even of the religious language, Arabic, or Persian which was the language of good society. How could they serve as a medium between the English Government and them?

"In all this I sympathized, but discouraged him from hoping that the Government would do much to help Mohammedan education as such, for the tendency was towards merely secular education, and would hardly be reversed. I hoped, however, that they might be able to found something in the way of a University which should be within their means, a University where, as in the Azhar at Cairo, the students lived on their own resources, and merely attended lectures. He promised to introduce me to some of the Ulema to talk these matters over, but he was afraid to have the meeting at his own house. In fact, he had already arranged that it should be at that of Dr. Hörnli, the Swiss director of the Madrasa, so that the Government should not take umbrage. We also talked about Amir Ali's letter repudiating Arabi during the war, which Abd-el-Latif was very angry at. It did not represent their opinions. Now, with the Afghan War, he said, it was different. They had approved of that, because they looked on it as an attack on Russia, which was the greatest of all the enemies of Islam. Thus, I suppose, it had been explained to them. I told him, however, that I hoped in future the Mohammedans of India would set their faces against all wars waged against Mohammedans on whatever pretext.

"I like this man much. He is of the sort I like far better than Amir Ali and Seyd Huseyn, and yet I fear the others are more likely to succeed. They represent the future, he the past. He himself has a son who wears coats and hats and boots to his father's great grief, but he said the son complained that in Indian dress he could not enter the Anglo-Indian houses, such are the difficulties put in the way of social intercourse. Abd-el-Latif wears eastern robes and head-dress. It appears that he did not personally know Jemal-ed-Din, for he was afraid of compromising himself with one under Government ban. 'I refrained purposely,' he said, 'from asking any official about you, for I should have found it impossible to see you if they had spoken ill of you. Fortunately they have said nothing yet, at least not to me.' This visit has been a pleasing and a valuable one.

"We dined with Dr. Johnstone the Bishop, a good specimen of his class, with more liberal views than nearly any Englishman I have talked to in India. He does not want to convert anybody or Anglicize them. He was interested in Mohammedan education, wished them to study their own language, and described a college he had seen at Lahore. I shall put him into communication with Abd-el-Latif, as he may be able to help him, having, I suppose, some interest in official quarters.

"*23rd Dec.*—The Nizam arrived yesterday with his suite, and I went to see Salar Jung and tell him the result of my interview with Lord Ripon. He seemed very grateful for what I have done, and I gave him some advice about his relations with the ultra liberal party among the Mohammedans here. I recommended him to conciliate Abd-el-Latif and not to be too intimate with Amir Ali, as, though Amir Ali might be right in the line he took, he, Salar Jung, would run the risk of sharing his unpopularity with old-fashioned people. If he was to be minister of a Mohammedan State, he must show himself truly a Mohammedan. Any suspicion of impiety would diminish his influence. This was a mere matter of prudence. I think he is sensible enough to see this. He is coming again this evening to talk further. I left cards on the Nizam, Peishkar, and the rest.

" In the course of the morning Seyd Nur-el-Huda, a Mohammedan from Patna, called with his friend, a Christian Brahmin. Nur-el-Huda is one of the new school, having been educated at Cambridge, but seems a good sort of fellow. The Hindu, Dr. Sandwal, or, as he writes it, 'Sandel,' is a doctor. He, the doctor, was born a Christian, as his father was converted many years ago, and I asked him how it affected his social position. He said it cut him off from all Hindus, and the English would not receive him either. He had studied medicine in England, hoping to get practice here on his return, but it was impossible for a native doctor to compete with the English official doctors, and though he had had the highest recommendations from Sir Ashley Eden and others, he could get no Government appointment either here or in the Mofussil on account of his race. They are both very angry at the Ilbert Bill compromise, and the doctor gave me particulars about the pressure which had been put lately on native officials respecting it. A friend of his, holding a minor post under Government, had received a 'demi-official' letter from his English superior, warning him that if he attended meetings in favour of the Bill he should suffer for it. This I can well believe, when I remember the pressure that was put on officials, even in England, to prevent them from subscribing to the Arabi Defence Fund last year.

"At 11 o'clock we started driving for Uttarpara, a village some eight miles up the Hugli, where we spent the afternoon most profitably with our Zemindar. He is the son of one of the greatest landholders in the district. His father's rent roll amounts to about £50,000 a year. Of this, however, he touches but a small portion, for the real owner of two-fifths of the property is the Maharajah to whom he pays £15,000, while he pays another £15,000 in round figures to the Government for the rest. Considerable reductions on account of bad debts, and the cost of collection must again be made. Still it leaves him a very rich man as things go here. Nor has he at all neglected his duties as a landlord. He lives on his estate, and is the father of the municipality of Uttarpara. He received us in a public library he built some years ago, a handsome Palladian house, well supplied with books and newspapers. They take in the 'Illustrated,' 'Saturday Review,' and all the Calcutta newspapers; and he intends now to use the upper part of the building as a college for fifty young men. The Government has given him nothing in this matter up to now, but offers £100 a year towards the college. The father is a venerable old man, reminding me vaguely of Cardinal Newman. He is blind and very infirm—but talks with vigour. He lamented the growing ill feeling between the English and themselves, and confirmed what all old men declare, that the new class of civilian officers is inferior in every quality, except cleverness, to the old Haileybury men. With regard to the Ilbert Bill, he said it was an attempt to reform justice in the country, which greatly needed reforming. The administration of the criminal as well as the civil law was very bad. The English did not now understand the ways of the natives; and those natives, who owed their position to competition, did not inspire respect from their countrymen, being mostly chosen from the lower castes. He talked with great feeling, and evidently sincere regret for the better days which were gone.

"We then drove to some villages with the son, and put our usual series of questions. It is very evident from the answers that the Bengal ryots, at least in this district, are far better off than those of Madras. Our Zemindar estimated the cost of living for them at about three rupees a month, instead of two as at Bellari, and they eat rice and fish instead of only *raghi*. I have promised to attend a meeting on the 29th respecting the Rent Bill, when the whole question of the state of the peasantry will be threshed out. Next we saw a village school for boys and a genteel school for little girls, at which some of the family were learning with the rest. All this is due to the care of the landlord, and far different from anything that can be seen in the whole Madras Presidency, where the Government is the universal absentee proprietor. On the village green, when we came back from our inspection, we found an awning put up, and a meeting being held of the municipality and others—perhaps a hundred people—to protest against the Ilbert compromise. The proceedings were quite up to the level of such things in England; resolutions were passed and speeches made. Surendra Nath Banerji, a Calcutta orator, had been expected, but did not turn up. But the local speechifying was not bad, part in English, for our benefit I suppose, and part in Bengali.

"We did not get home till late.

"*24th Dec.*—Mail day, so stayed at home writing letters. To our great pleasure the Mulvi Sami Ullah of Aligarh (Hamid Ullah's father) called with two of his nephews. He arrived here two days ago to see the exhibition, but will be back at Aligarh to receive us by the time we get there. We had an animated discussion about the 'Concordat,' the old man explaining that the proper conduct for the Mohammedans here was being debated, some being for expressing themselves satisfied, others for making common cause with the Hindus. All, however, were at heart vexed and angry at what had been done, and recognized in the Ilbert Bill a matter of common interest. He had seen Amir Ali yesterday, who had changed his mind and was now on the Government side. He wants, the Mulvi explained naïvely, to get promotion, and that is why he supports the compromise. He himself was for a moderate attitude. I spoke my mind very plainly, and told them that, if they deserted the Hindus in this instance, they would never have any reform given or justice done them for another twenty years. They must sink their differences and their little private interests if they wanted to force the Government's hand. The Bill was the battle-ground on which the whole principle of legislation for India was being fought; and the Mohammedans could turn the scale by their attitude one way or the other. The young men warmly applauded this, and I think, too, the Mulvi was partly convinced. I told them, if the Mohammedans only knew their power they would not be neglected and ill-treated by the Government as they now were. In England we were perpetually scared at the idea of a Mohammedan rising in India, and any word uttered by a Mohammedan was paid more attention to than that of twenty Hindus. But, if they sat still, thanking Providence for the favours which were denied them, the English public would be only too happy to leave them as they were. The Mulvi promised to make my opinion known at a Conference which had been summoned for this evening to consider the action of the Mohammedans, and so I trust I may have done some good, at least with the Liberal party. Of Abd-el-Latif I feel more doubtful, for there is great ill-feeling in Calcutta between the old-fashioned Mohammedans and the Hindus.

"They were hardly gone when another Mohammedan called, Mulvi A. M., to whom I had had a letter from Seyd Abd-el-Rahman. This is a man of the type I like best, of the school, in fact, of Jemal-ed-Din, who here, as elsewhere, laid the foundation of a liberal religious movement. He gave me a clearer account of the parties in Calcutta than I have yet received. Amir Ali and his friends have put themselves out of the pale of Mohammedan society by their English dress and ways, while Abd-el-Latif and the body of the Mulvis (Ulema) are too strictly conservative. He had been converted to the large idea of a Mohammedan reform and Mohammedan unity by Jemal-ed-Din, and there were many now of his way of thinking who held a middle position between the rival parties. I urged him too to join the Hindus in their protest against the compromise, and he said that if one of the prominent leaders would call a meeting, he could promise to bring a hundred men to it, but he was only translator to the High Court, and could not commence the movement. He then spoke with great sympathy of the work I had done in Egypt, and of my writings. He speaks good English, but in no other way affects European manners, wearing his own dress, a little white skull cap and a long frock. (Sami Ullah and his nephews wear the fez.) I like A. M. greatly, and have promised to dine with him on Thursday, and meet the men of his way of thinking. He reminds me of Rasul Yar Khan, and looks like an Arab of the South, though he assures me he is a pure Bengali, as far as he knows his genealogy. He has all the signs of breeding an Arab should have, his thumb going well beyond the forefinger joint, his complexion clear and dark and his features regular. Also he is thin and has the eager frank manner of an Arab, and the lack of reserve. He told me Jemal-ed-Din had been disappointed with the Mohammedans of Calcutta, who were afraid of listening to him on account of the Government. He had found them selfish and unpatriotic. Of Amir Ali he has a poor opinion. Abd-el-Latif he thinks timid, and the rest of the Mulvis are intensely ignorant.

"Then I called on Dr. Hörnli, a Swiss, who showed me the Madrasa, an institution which educates eight hundred boys and young men from eight to twenty-two years old. There are five hundred English and Persian students, three hundred Arabic. They pay twelve annas a month, and most find even that too expensive. There are rooms for about sixty, who have bedsteads, chairs, and tables, while the rest board in town. He did not know what became of the students in after life. He believed the Arabic scholars became Mulvis in the country towns. There were twenty professors, at from thirty to one hundred and fifty rupees a month; the head master got three hundred. It was holiday time unfortunately, and only half a dozen boarders were left in college.

"Walter Pollen tells us the Viceroy told the Nizam at his reception that he hoped to see him soon assume the duties of his rank. This looks well.

"*25th Dec., Christmas Day.*—The 'Indian Mirror' has a leading article exhorting all classes to receive us with honour, and to show their gratitude for our sympathy with the Egyptians and with themselves. I think we have come at the right time.

"We have had three visits to-day, first from Sambhu Chandra Mukerji, formerly Minister to the Rajah of Tippara, an independent prince on the Assam frontier, a very superior Hindu, handsomely dressed in shawls and a huge shawl turban. He asked me many questions about Arabia and the Mohammedans in various parts of the world, and seemed to know their history well, as also the state of modern affairs everywhere. We discussed Mr. Gladstone's character. He had followed his career closely from the day of his article on 'Church and State' downwards, and was of opinion that he had always been shifty and insincere. He had not been surprised at his repudiation of the Midlothian doctrines, nor at his conduct in Egypt. He has evidently a poor opinion of morality as an element in English statecraft, and rates our party professions exactly at their worth. How absurd it is to talk of the Hindus as intellectually inferior to ourselves—indeed as anything but far our superiors.

"Secondly, Kebir-ed-Din, the joint editor of the one Mohammedan journal published in Calcutta, a Jewish looking person with a turban and dyed beard. He said he belonged to the Amir Ali faction, but except that he talks English, he has nothing of the modern school about him. I tried to impress upon him the necessity of supporting the Hindus in the matter of the Ilbert Bill, but found him exceedingly pigheaded. He seemed quite unable to get beyond the idea that there were no Mohammedans in the Civil Service who would benefit by the Bill, or to see that the principle of legislating in native interests was at stake. I think this was as much from stupidity as ill will.

"After this we paid a round of visits, but only saw the Lyalls, who are staying at Belvidere, the Lieutenant-Governor's official residence, a really beautiful place. I had some political sparring with Lyall, which was amusing, as he is very light in hand. Rivers Thompson, the Lieutenant-Governor, we did not see, he being seriously ill.

"Ate our Christmas dinner in absolute silence at the *table d'hôte*, feeling rather 'like Jews at a christening,' but received an agreeable note from Mr. Ghose, the President or Secretary of the Indian National Association, recording a vote addressing us a welcome on our arrival, and a hope that our stay in Calcutta would be for the advantage of India.

"*26th Dec.*—A busy morning. Our earliest visitor was Mulvi A. M., with whom I talked over the whole range of Mohammedan prospects. He asked me what I thought of the ultimate fate of India, and I explained my view that it should be put on the same footing as Australia, that is to say, that each province should have its English Government, supported by English troops, but that the whole civil administration, legislation, and finance should be left to native hands; that the effect of this would be to put Northern India practically under Mohammedan, Southern India under Hindu Government, a solution which pleased him much. He said that none of the Mohammedans wished to do away altogether with English government, as it would only lead to fighting, as there was no chance of Mohammedans and Hindus agreeing for a century to come, but of course they did not like English administration. It favoured the Hindus unduly. But, left to themselves, they should be able to hold their own in all Northern India. The English policy, however, had been to suppress them, and throw obstacles in the way of their educating themselves and learning their own power. The Mulvis of Calcutta were terribly ignorant of politics, and of all that was going on in the world. At the time of the Egyptian War they had not known whether Egypt lay North or South or East or West. I am to dine with him to-morrow, to meet Jemal-ed-Din's disciples.

"We then talked about education, and discussed the possibility of getting up a University. The difficulty, of course, is money. All the great Mohammedan landlords were ruined at the time of the Permanent Settlement, when their lands were confiscated; and the other rich men who lived on Government employment were ousted from it in 1862 by the change of the language of the Courts. Now there are hardly any rich Mohammedans in Bengal. The masses are living on daily wages, and cannot even afford the rupee a month necessary for their sons' education. While we were talking, Nawab Mir Mohammed Ali was announced, one of the few remaining Zemindars, a little old man, very small and wizened, wearing a handsome dress, with a fine emerald in his cap. We continued our conversation, and I rather took his breath away by suggesting him as a possible contributor to the University. A more congenial subject to him was the Bengal Rent Bill, on which he was eloquent, and he invited me to attend the meeting on Saturday. Then Abd-el-Latif's son, in European clothes, joined us, and we got on the Ilbert Bill, as to which I exhorted them all strongly to make a concordat with the Hindus, helping them this time on a promise of help from them when their own interests were at stake. The old man was rather frightened at this and went away. I had it out, however, with Abd-el-Rahman, and hope he will influence his father. Unless the Mohammedans show their teeth on an occasion of this sort, they will never get attention paid to their wrongs.

"When they had gone Salar Jung looked in to thank us for all we had done for him and for the Nizam, and I showed him the memorandum of my conversation with Lord Ripon. He also invited us on the Nizam's part to dine with him on Sunday. It is certainly something worth doing to have upset the Cordery-Peishkar conspiracy, and got the Nizam installed; for Salar Jung tells us that Lord Ripon has announced to the Nizam that he shall come of age in February. He has also invited us to assist at the installation ceremonies at Hyderabad, which we will do if possible. Then, if Salar Jung is named Dewan, our triumph will be complete. Salar Jung has seen Stuart Bailey, and been very well received by him.

"Next came Surendra Nath Bannerji, the Hindu editor who was put in prison for questioning Judge Norman's conduct on the bench. He is evidently a man of energy, and having been a martyr and survived it, shows more courage than most of them. He is very angry at the Ilbert Bill compromise, and let slip the *gros mot* of 'revolution' in regard to it. He was very urgent with me to get the Mohammedans to join them in protesting, and I promised to do my best this evening at Amir Ali's dinner. It is high time certainly they should sink differences, but the Mohammedans are hard to move. Their position was well explained a little later by our last visitor this morning, Mulvi Ahmed, Municipal Councillor and an independent man. He explained that there was hardly a leading man among the Calcutta Mohammedans who had any means apart from his Government pay. Neither Amir Ali nor Abd-el-Latif could afford to come forward as a champion, as all their prospects depended on the Government. Mulvi Ahmed drew a most gloomy picture of Mohammedan prospects. They were all, he said, in despair here in Bengal. It was impossible for them to do anything, impossible to combine with the Hindus who were so selfish, they wanted every post for themselves. Out of forty-eight Municipal Councillors there were only five Mohammedans, and as more power was given to the natives the Mohammedan position would get worse and worse. It was their poverty which stood in their way. They could not pay for the education necessary to pass the competitive examinations, so they were left behind. I tried to convert him to my view of energetic action, but in vain. There was no one to take the lead, and it would result in no good.

"At last all were gone and we went to the races just in time to see Sherwood beat Euphrates, a very fine race. Sherwood, when moving, has all the appearance of an Arab, so I reverse the opinion formed of him in the stable. Euphrates is a great tall animal with a fine head; but neither he nor Sherwood are horses to breed from. They lack quality. There was a great gathering of Mohammedans in front of the race stand, and I saw Abd-el-Latif in close conversation with Kurshid Jah. The Nizam was there, looking more comfortable and at ease than I had seen him before. He was full of smiles, and even talked a little to us.

"We dined at Amir Ali's, a dinner entirely of Mohammedans, with the single exception of a Mohammedanized Hindu, a very clever man, who had been in England, and knew everything and everybody. There were about fifteen at dinner, and we talked very freely on all matters of Mohammedan interest, and after dinner some fifty more arrived, in fact all the leading Mohammedans in Calcutta, Abd-el-Latif among them, wonderful to relate, and one of his sons—I believe he had never been inside Amir Ali's house before—and a cousin of the King of Oude, and many learned men in turbans and every variety of dress, and strangers from Bussora and Nejd, all assembled to do us honour. So I think we may congratulate ourselves upon having made a successful visit to India. I never expected to be received so cordially, but the moment has been a favourable one. I do not find any of that blind devotion to the Sultan which Jemal-ed-Din led me to expect, but things have doubtless changed since he was here, and the weakness of Constantinople is producing its natural effect, contempt. Only for the Sultan personally, as head of the Mohammedan nation, there is of course a certain loyalty. Still, my opinions are generally approved, and that is significant.

"I had an opportunity of saying a few words to Abd-el-Latif about the attitude Mohammedans should take in this Ilbert quarrel, and he agreed with me that it might be well if they showed their teeth a little. But he is a cautious man and would promise nothing. With Amir Ali and Amir Huseyn I was able to do more, and I shall be surprised if, at the meeting of the National Mohammedan Society to-morrow, they do not take my view. I proposed that they should address a dignified and moderate protest to the Viceroy, admitting that the Ilbert Bill did not immediately affect the Mohammedan community, but taking their stand on the principle that the proposed compromise affected the rule of equality before the law. At the same time I advised Amir Ali to come to a regular concordat with the Hindus for their mutual benefit.

"The only visits we had this morning were from two Mohammedan doctors, one a surgeon of the 9th Bengal Cavalry and a native of Assam, the other a Lucknow man who had been educated at Lahore and had a grievance about which he had come from Gaya to consult me.

"We dined at Mulvi A. M.'s, an entertainment of a very different sort from last night's. He lives in a poor little house in the old quarter of the town, and we dined in his one room with eight or nine fellow students, all looking as if they were starved, but brimful of intelligence. They were most eager to hear what we had to tell them of Arabi and the Egyptian War, and Jemal-ed-Din and our hopes for the future of Islam. They talked very freely, and did not conceal their hatred of England, and their hope that the Mahdi would drive us out of Egypt. 'During the Egyptian War,' they said, 'we all looked to Arabi to restore our fortunes, for we are in a desperate state and need a deliverer.' I told them of my hopes in Egypt, which pleased them much. They had some of them read my 'Future of Islam,' and the rest were waiting to read it in Hindustani. For Jemal-ed-Din they professed something like worship, and they were readers of 'Abu Nadara' and the 'Bee.' These young men had very pleasant faces, but their starved bodies were mere skeletons. They spend all their money on their education, and I fear the dinner he gave us will cost our host several months' income. I had no notion he was so poor. Only one of them was well dressed, a very nice young man, who told us he had been at the National Mohammedan Association meeting to-day, where, though the sense of the meeting was hostile to the Ilbert compromise, no resolution was come to. Amir Ali, who presided, seems to have contented himself with a neutral attitude, but they are to have another meeting later—too late probably. The dinner reminded me a little of some of our visits to the Azhar quarter at Cairo, only I was never in so poor a house there. The food was cooked in the Indian way, and we drank water. Our host would not eat, but served us. They all had excellent manners, and though they spoke without any reserve, nothing was said which should not have been said. This visit has given me more insight into Mohammedan ideas in India than all I have yet seen and heard. It is clear that they would welcome any deliverer here, Russian or French, or from the Devil. One of them had read a poem by Victor Hugo in praise of Arabi, and argued therefrom that the French must sympathize with them. Also the Government of Chandanagore they say is a model Government.

"*28th Dec.*—It appears that the author of the famous 'Concordat' is none other than Colvin; so here I find myself once more fighting him as in Egypt. I have little doubt that he is working the English newspapers as he did two years ago at Cairo.

"Keay called in the morning, and, as he is going to speak to Lord Ripon about Hyderabad, I told him briefly of my own conversation, so as to give him a line. He is writing a full account of the Hyderabad intrigues for the 'Statesman.' Then

Abd-el-Latif came, and we discussed his rivals, Amir Ali and Amir Huseyn, whom he calls worshippers of Nature. He asked me to attend a meeting of his society, the Anjuman i Islam, and give them my views on Mohammedan education; and I think I will do this, though it will be rather an experiment. Kurshid Jah paid us a visit, but he came with an English Secretary, and is a dull talker, so I got nothing out of him. Our short conversation was through an interpreter.

"Then, at twelve, I went to the first meeting of the National Conference, a really important occasion, as there were delegates from most of the great towns —and, as Bose in his opening speech remarked, it was the first stage towards a National Parliament. The discussion began with a scheme for sending boys to France for industrial education, but the real feature of the meeting was an attack on the Covenanted Civil Service by Surendra Nath Bannerji. His speech was quite as good a one as ever I heard in my life, and entirely fell in with my own views on the matter. The other speakers were less brilliant, though they showed fair ability, and one old fellow made a very amusing oration which was much applauded. I was asked to speak, but declined, as I don't wish to make any public expression of opinion till my journey is over. But at Bombay I shall speak my mind. I was the only European there, and am very glad to have been present at so important an event. The proceedings would have been more shipshape if a little more arrangement had been made beforehand as to the speakers. But on the whole it went off very creditably. Both Bannerji and Bose are speakers of a high order. The meeting took place upstairs in the Albert Hall, and about one hundred persons were present. Before the speaking commenced, a national hymn was sung by a man with a strong voice, who played also on an instrument of the guitar type.

"Walter Pollen dined with us, and after dinner I went to an evening party at the India Club. This was started a year ago with the view of amalgamating Englishmen with Indians, but the bitterness of feeling is now so great that, with the exception of two or three secretaries in attendance on Indian princes, I believe I was the only Englishman present. The Catholic Archbishop, however, and Father Lafont were there, and I had some conversation with them about Cardinals Manning and Howard. Abd-el-Latif introduced me to a good many notables, the King of Oude's brother, the Rajahs of Cutch Bahar and Tippara, and the Diwan of the Rajput Rajah of Ulwar. Tippara is a regular Chinaman in feature, and it needed no large amount of candour in him to repudiate the flattery of his courtiers when they told him he was a pure-bred Aryan. Cutch Bahar is a young man with an English education, who appears at race courses in a white hat, and is popular with the Anglo-Indians. He wore his own clothes here, but is uninteresting. The Diwan invited us to stay with him at Ulwar, and I shall certainly do so, as it will be a good opportunity of seeing a Rajput court. There were also an uncle of Nebbi-Ullah's from Cawnpore and about two hundred other gentlemen of distinction from Calcutta and the provinces, all in their best clothes.

"*29th Dec.*—The only visit this morning was from Delawar Huseyn, a deputy-magistrate and a sensible man, who gave the same melancholy account of the poverty of the Mohammedans in Bengal. I fear their case is nearly hopeless. In spite of their large population, they are without influence. The mass of them are extremely poor, mere peasants, or, in the town, day labourers. They have no commercial connection, and the sons of the few rich men are obliged to look to Government employment for a living, whereas the Hindus are rich and pushing. It is a struggle for existence, in which the Mohammedans are the weakest, and so are going to the wall. In the north-west, he tells me, it is not so.

"At twelve I went to the second meeting of the Conference, at which the Civil Service was again discussed; and I made a short speech, in answer to some complimentary remarks made with regard to my presence, in which I said that I was glad to have had the opportunity of being present at these the first meetings which had a national character in India, and which prefigured the parliament which they were all doubtless looking forward to. I said that I, too, looked forward to this, and to their complete self-government. I believed *all* nations were fit for self-government, and few more so than the Indian, and I described the condition of Greece when it was first set to manage its own affairs, a conglomeration of robber chieftains, piratical seafarers and an absolutely uneducated peasant population. Yet, after fifty years, they had an orderly Government, with universal education, commercial prosperity, and a shipping which had driven every competitor out of the Levant. In view of such results, who should say that any nation was unfit for its own rule? This produced much cheering, and they all expressed themselves highly delighted with my sympathy. To-morrow Keay is to come to the meeting, and will speak about the rural distress.

"Then, at three, I went with Anne to another meeting, that of the Zemindars at the Town Hall.

It was a public meeting, and much more numerous, but the room is badly constructed, and it was difficult to hear the speakers. They passed resolutions against the Rent Bill, being all interested in the matter. Our friends from Uttarpara were there, and Sir Jotendro, and many princes and Nawabs, and Gorst. We dined at Sir Stuart Bailey's, Salar Jung and his brother being there, also Lyall, and Durand, the Foreign Office Secretary. We discussed the necessity of lying in politics, and I fear I made some rather uncomplimentary observations, not knowing that Durand held the position he did.

"Abd-el-Rahman, the son of Abd-el-Latif, with a brother-in-law, called, and we discussed Seyd Ahmed's ideas of education and ideas of religion. They, of course, disapprove. Seyd Ahmed originally intended to teach everything in Urdu, but has abandoned that for English, and now the education at Aligarh is wholly English. Religion is not taught there, they say. Seyd Ahmed began as a Sunni, then adopted Wahhabism, but is now a Deist. We also discussed the idea of a university on a religious basis, which is what it ought to have, and they agreed with me that Calcutta would not be a good place on account of sectarian differences, expensive living, and the poverty of the Bengal Mohammedans. My own idea, an idea which struck me last night as I lay awake, is Hyderabad. It is central, it is cheap, and it is a seat of Mohammedan Government. Religious thought would there be free from English and Hindu interference. With this notion I called on Salar Jung, and found him delighted at the prospect, and he is sure the Nizam, too, would be delighted, and he will speak to him and let me know. He is really grateful to me for what I did for him with Lord Ripon.

"Then I went to the last meeting of the National Delegates, in which they discussed the National Fund. There was some rather spirited conversation, and I suggested to Bose, the secretary, that he should send the hat round, but he said if he did that they would never come again. However, offers of fifty and one hundred rupees began to be made, and one rich Zemindar came down for one thousand. I myself contributed one hundred, and I believe the subscription ended with a considerable sum. I then offered to give my assistance in managing their telegrams, and expounded to them the necessity of publicity as to their meetings and resolutions. I also suggested that they should raise a fund among those of their number who held official positions, as an insurance against persecution. This would give them courage. Also that they should take up especially the cause of the ryots in Madras and Bombay. That would give a wide extension to their influence. It was Arabi's advocacy of the cause of the poor that brought all Egypt to him.

"Keay then came in and delivered an address about the cause of the ryots, which was well received. But I notice that the Conference is very provincial in its interests, as quite three parts of the delegates are Bengalis. Afterwards there was a discussion on Parliamentary government in which Bose was eloquent, and I made a second speech, giving my ideas on what might be looked forward to—first, elections to the legislative council, secondly, representation in the English Parliament, and thirdly, home Parliaments of their own in the different provinces on the Colonial system. Not many speakers joined in this discussion, which was restricted to generalities even by Bose. The proceedings terminated with votes of thanks to Keay and me—and so ended the first session of the Indian Parliament. May it be memorable in history.

"We dined with the Nizam, but I did not consider it advisable to talk to him myself about the university scheme, though I shall urge on him, through Salar Jung, to propose it to the Viceroy on the occasion of his installation. The moment would be opportune, and he could not well be refused.

"31*st Dec.*—This morning we had a flood of visitors whom I will name in order.

"Ferid-ed-Din Ahmed, Nebbi-Ullah's uncle, with Akbar Huseyn, the translator of my book, the 'Future of Islam.' We talked a good deal about this, and I have promised to write a new short preface, in which I will say something complimentary about the Sultan—this rather to conciliate Constantinople than the people here, for, in reality, they have lost most of their respect for the Ottoman Caliphate since the Egyptian War. Ferid-ed-Din is not one of the new school, and he told me he had met the book accidentally, and had been struck by the Arabic motto on the cover. This had induced him to read it in spite of some one's having told him that it was anti-Mohammedan. It had converted him to believe in an Arabian Caliphate, and he said it would convert others, for very few Mohammedans here know how, or why, Abd-el-Hamid claimed to be Caliph. This is very satisfactory. He then introduced some half a dozen merchants and chief persons from Allahabad, who came as a deputation to announce their intention of doing me some honour when I came to their city. We discussed the foundation of a university, to which they heartily agreed, condemning the Aligarh College as irreligious, and they said Hyderabad would be the very best place, if it was possible to get the Nizam's patronage. On this point

I reassured them, and doubted only the English Government's conduct, and counselled them to treat the matter for a while as a secret.

"Prince Jehan Kadur, brother of the King of Oude, and Prince Suleyman Kadur, his nephew, called, a visit of compliment, but the former invited us to stay with him at Lucknow, which will be pleasant. The King of Oude lives here and keeps a menagerie, which we are to see.

"Rasbihari Mukerji from Uttarpara came to wish us good-bye, a very nice youth, grandson of the old man, and an ardent patriot of the best sort.

"Rajah Siva Prasad, with a note of introduction from Lyall. Mukerji knew him by name, and warned me that he was a friend of the English, and had been recently burned in effigy in his native town, Benares. I found him, nevertheless, a very well educated and clever man. He contended that the country was continuously increasing in prosperity, compared it with the state of things a hundred years ago, and said that within his recollection more land had been taken under cultivation. I asked him whether the ryots ate more rice than forty years ago, and he answered 'The size of a man's belly does not increase.' He is a friend of the Maharajah of Benares, and invited us, on his part, to stay with the Maharajah for a week. This man has, of course, been sent by Lyall to show us that there are some natives who support the Government; but that is all fair. We will go to him at Benares, and hear what he has to say.

"Abd-el-Rahman Mazhar, of Samaria, and a Cadi of Bagdad, with a friend. They had just come *via* Colombo, and had seen Mahmud Sami, whom he extolled for his learning.[1] He himself had been

[1] Compare Lord Cromer's book, "Modern Egypt," where this same Mahmud Sami, a poet and a highly educated gentleman, is

educated in the Azhar—a dignified old man, with beautiful white teeth. He had known Mahmud Sami as a boy, and wondered why the English Government had attacked him as a rebel.

"Mohammed Ikram-Ullah, Rais of Delhi, and Mohammed Ishak Khan, of Meerut, men of position, who invited us to let them know of our arrival in their towns.

"Amir Ali, who was very anxious to explain his true position as leader of Mohammedan thought at Calcutta; but his attitude with regard to the Ilbert compromise is not that of a leader. Mohammed Ikram-Ullah has just told me he supported the compromise at the meeting they held. He wants to please the Government. We then argued the question of his hat. He defended himself by explaining that it gave him more consideration in a crowd. On railway platforms and such places men in Indian dress were hustled and pushed about by the railway servants. This is no doubt true. He appealed to Bose, who had come in, to say whether it was so, and also whether he had not supported the Indian Association on the Ilbert and other questions. Young Mukerji, who had sat on in silence, listening, said to me as he went out: 'I am glad you told him about his hat. We all hate that.'

"These visits took us till three o'clock, and we had not even a moment to get breakfast. Then we went to the Zoological Gardens, where there are some astonishing tigers, and dined at home with Walter Pollen, thus ending the year 1883.

"I forgot to mention my conversation to-day with Bose. We discussed the probability of a revolution, and he said the danger was very great.

described as an "illiterate" man—a foolish judgement, typical of the writer's ignorance of Egyptian character.

People were losing their confidence in Lord Ripon, after having lost it in the Government at home. They still looked to English public opinion, but a spark might at any time fire the train. He asked what amount of influence men like those whose names were on the Indian Committee exercised, and I told him 'very little.' I was not at all sanguine of any great increase of sympathy with them from the British public, and I strongly advised the Indians to look to themselves, and themselves only, for help. We then talked over the details of an agitation. He is to organize meetings in every part of India, and telegraph constantly to me in London for publicity through the press. This is the only way, I maintain, of gaining them any real relief. They must frighten and coerce the English people into giving them their rights. I am writing strongly to Eddy Hamilton, pointing out the danger."

CHAPTER VI

A MOHAMMEDAN UNIVERSITY

"*1st January*, 1884.

"TO-DAY our visitors were:

"Mohammed Yusuf, a Member of Council, to whom I broached my idea of a university, but he is of the worldly school, and says he would rather have his sons educated at the Presidency College. He dresses, however, becomingly, in dark clothes, and with a gilt crown on his head.

"A Sheykh from Yemen came next, who brought a letter of introduction from Arabi, whom he had visited in Ceylon. He talked about the Mahdi, and told us that all the Arabs in Yemen and in Hejaz would join him if he crossed the Red Sea. They were weary of the Turks. The Mahdi had already a Wazir in Yemen, who was gathering adherents to the great terror of the Ottoman Mushir. The Turks had lately inveigled the Harb chiefs into Mecca, and imprisoned them, which was the cause of the confusion in the country. Midhat was still a prisoner at Taïf. The old man himself evidently believed in the Mahdi, and explained to us how all the signs and prophecies had been fulfilled about him. He was delighted when I said 'Allah yensoru'; and when he went away I observed that Mohammed Yusuf, in spite of his English education, reverently kissed his hand.

"Five friends of Jemal-ed-Din called to express their sympathy with 'The Future of Islam.' They are all young men, students and enthusiasts, hating England, I am afraid, with all their hearts. They are readers of 'Abu Nadara,' and they told me the address of the Ceylon Mohammedans had been printed in the last number. I showed them Sanua's last letter to me, which interested them greatly, especially the page in Arabic he had added for Sabunji, whom they also know in connection with the 'Bee.' What, however, pleased them still better was Arabi's letter, which some of them devoutly kissed. Only one could speak English, but they all had liberal ideas about religion, in fact Jemal-ed-Din's. These young students talk with the greatest boldness on all subjects, and I like them for it.

"Old Mukerji also came, with a great grand-daughter, a lovely little girl with a skin like stained ivory, and lips of coral, and eyes with the purest white and the brightest black. These Mukerjis are a family of the highest caste in Bengal.

"Dined at Dr. Hörnli's to meet some twenty Mohammedans. I am to speak my ideas on education in India, to-morrow, at the Anjuman i Islam meeting. It is certainly an experiment, but I know what I have to say, and, I think, also how to say it.

"*2nd Jan.*—Akbar Huseyn called to talk over his translation of 'The Future of Islam.' He is quite satisfied with the new preface, which I gave him yesterday, but will leave out some of the passages referring personally to Sultan Abd-el-Hamid. This, I hope, will satisfy all parties; and the book, to do good, must not be condemned as unorthodox. It has, however, he tells me, already done individual good, and he cited the instance of two of his friends who had been much affected by it, one of them to the extent of inducing him to abandon atheistic ideas and resume the practices of religion. This is most satisfactory; he says that he is sure it will be universally read in its Urdu form. I told him in return of my intention of visiting Constantinople, and trying to induce the Sultan to take up the idea of a Pan-Islamic Synod. We both agreed that, after the defeat in Egypt, Islam could not afford to wait for a more legitimate Caliph. What is especially gratifying in all this is that those who are bringing out the translation are members of the old school, not of the new. By the new school its ideas were sure to be accepted, but I hardly expected the other to go so far. We talked also of the Mahdi and his claims. They would all like to believe in him, but the opinion here is that 'the only real test of his mission is its success.'

"Ferid-ed-Din also came, introducing the Nawab Rajah Amir Hassan, the leading personage of Lucknow. He invited us to come and stay with him there; and I do not feel quite sure whether this is to be as representing Prince Suleyman Kadur or not. He did not talk very good English, however; so there is doubt.

"This constant talking and writing is beginning to affect my nerves, and we went out earlier than usual for a drive, calling on the Princes Jehan Kadur and Suleyman Kadur. The first lives with his uncle, the King of Oude, in Garden Reach, but he was out. The second has taken a house in the Circular Road. We took him, I expect, by surprise, for we found him in his shirt sleeves, in which state he entertained us. He seems an amiable, good man, but as he talks no English, and there was no interpreter, our conversation was in dumb show.

"Then we went to the Exhibition, where we met old Siva Prasad, and had a long conversation with him. Though he begins by the proposition that he entirely approves the administrative system of the British Government, in practice he complains of nearly everything which other people complain of.

He says they don't understand the people's wants, that they overtax them, and are perpetually raising the assessment. He holds land under them, and says it is impossible so much as to dig a well without the rent being raised. Reduced to its simplicity his argument is purely an historical one—namely, that India was worse off in the matter of peace and order before they came. 'For the sake of this,' he said, 'let them strip us to the skin. So long as body and soul hold together, and we have a rag to our loins, we will be thankful, only we would ask some permanence in their revenue demands—fifty per cent., eighty per cent., ninety per cent. if they will—but not always an increase for every improvement we make.' He then described the action of the assessment officers, just as others have done. Yet, for his English views and anti-National attitude, he has been burnt in effigy in his native town. This speaks volumes as to the 'loyalty' of the Hindus. He had written to the Maharajah, who will entertain us at Benares.

"The meeting of the Anjuman i Islam was a great success. All present, some two hundred, were in strictly native dress, with the single exception of Abd-el-Latif's son. The proceedings began with what seemed a very able lecture or sermon in Hindustani, delivered by Ferid-ed-Din, a man of the old stamp, but full of intellectual vigour. He explained, it would seem, his ideas of the wants and needs of Mohammedans in the matter of education, and described my views of reform as contained in the 'Future of Islam,' from which he made quotations, and mentioned the fact of Anne's knowledge of Arabic as an example for all Mohammedans to follow. (We were both there.) And he also mentioned the university scheme. All this was very well received.

Then Abd-el-Latif spoke, attacking Seyd Ahmed and his school, and then I, too, made my discourse, Abd-el-Latif translating it sentence by sentence, as I went on. It is rather difficult to be eloquent under such circumstances, but after the first I got on well. I told them how I had travelled up the country from the south, and how at Madura I had heard the Mohammedans complain that they had no one to teach them English, and no one to teach them their religion. I likened their position to that of the Catholics in England, and told them what efforts had been made by these in the way of founding colleges on a religious basis, and a university. I next described the ideas the Nationalists had entertained at Cairo of reforming and extending the university education of the Azhar, and I urged them, now that circumstances in Egypt had interrupted this great idea, to take it up in India. I believed a great opportunity was offered them thus of assuming the intellectual leadership of Islam. I then explained in detail my plan that a university on a religious basis should be founded in some city where living was cheap, and which should be sufficiently central to serve the wants of all India. I did not mention Hyderabad, as the idea ought to come from the Nizam himself. I urged on the Princes present (for there were representatives of every reigning Mohammedan house) to come forward and endow professorships, and poorer men scholarships. It would be an act of religion, not only an act of philanthropy, and so would gain them merit in this world and the next; and by connecting their names with the endowment they would perpetuate themselves in the memory of good men. I then stated my intention of myself founding such an endowment, a professorship of religious history, and lastly thanked them for the welcome they had given us. When I had landed in India I did not know whether the Mohammedans there would understand the sincerity of my sympathy, but the result had surpassed all my expectations. I begged them to believe that I would give my life, if need was, to help their cause, and begged them to remember me when I was gone, as I would remember them.

"The speech seemed much appreciated, and a vote of thanks was proposed to both of us for our services in the cause of religion. All the principal people of the old school were present, and I noticed some of our poor student friends, Jemal-ed-Din's disciples, one of them acting as shorthand writer of the proceedings. I shall repeat my argument in the towns of the north to whosoever will listen; and I fancy the idea will be taken up. But the rich men sitting in the front row looked a little uncomfortable, especially an old fellow with his feet tucked up on his chair, who is said to be the possessor of millions. I must now try and get Amir Ali's countenance also, for it is essential that we should unite all parties.

"*3rd Jan.*—Old Sheykh Abd-el-Rahman Ibn Hassan Ibn Abd-el-Mari, of Marawa, near Hodeida, looked in again, and gave me a deal of valuable information about the horses in Yemen. He says the best breed is called 'Beit el Khamaïs,' and belongs to the Sherifs of the Ahl Hsaidar, formerly kings of Yemen. They live in the town and district of Abu Arish, near the seaport of Ghizan, and near the Assir frontier. These horses are generally bays, with black points of medium height, and 'mutlakh el shimal.' 'They are better,' he said, 'than any of the horses of Nejd, even those of the Anazeh.' A year or two ago the Sherif, Ali Ibn Mohammed el Barad, had a son who was taken as a hostage by the Turks, and shut up in prison at Hodeida. His father sent men secretly to Hodeida, with five mares, and they got the boy out of prison by dressing him as a girl. They rode away without stopping to Abu-el-Rish, which is one hundred and fifty miles by the map, and the boy and one other arrived, on the fifth day, on two mares of the Khamaïs breed; the other three being of inferior blood, died on the road. These horses are not to be bought even for 1,000 or 2,000 dollars. But the Sheykh thinks Ali el Barad would give me one if I went to see him. The next best breed is in Jôf el Mareb, where Sidi Huseyn, a Sherif of Jôf, has *asil* horses of the breed 'el Zahir.' These are very tall, some bay, and some white. There are also Kehilans, and Abeyans, and Hamdanis, as in Nejd. The old man invited us to stay with him at Marawa, and then pulled a letter from his pocket, which proved to be a very ingenious begging letter, in verse, calling upon me as protector of the Moslems to help him, a poor Sherif, to build three houses for his three sons to settle them in life. I gave him one hundred rupees, whereupon he rose and politely departed.

"Two young Mohammedans next called, Mohammed Abd el Gaffar and another. The former wanted permission to translate the 'Wind and the Whirlwind' into Urdu verse, which I readily gave him. I shall put him into communication with Sidi Lebbe, at Kandy, as he seems good with his pen, and is correspondent of the 'Abu Nadara.'

"Kazi Raza Huseyn also came with a friend from Patna to invite us to stay with him while there. He is Kadi of Patna, and we shall thus enjoy Mohammedan hospitality, the first, I should fancy, that for many years has been offered to an Englishman in India. Our other visitors were Abd-el-Rahman Ibn Abd-el-Latif, Ferid-ed-Din, and Akbar Huseyn. Ferid-ed-Din will announce our arrival at Allahabad on the 10th, and will receive us at Cawnpore on the 14th.

"Rajah Nil Krishna, son of the Maharajah of Krishna, came to invite us to attend a meeting on Indian education at his father's house on Saturday. He talked strongly and bitterly of the disappointment of the Indians at receiving no practical help from Lord Ripon. 'Why did they teach us to read about liberty and justice and self-government,' he said, 'if after all we are to have none of these things?'

"We called in the afternoon on Mrs. Ilbert, but missed seeing her husband. Hunter, the statistician, was there, and I tackled him as to his figures on the land assessment. He maintained them to be correct, and said that, as to the Madras Presidency, he had taken them from official reports. But like everybody else he did not know Madras. He admitted, however, that the land assessment of the Deccan was a blot on our Indian administration. I said: 'A very large blot,' for the Deccan is half India. He then referred me to Mr. Quinton, who was sitting near, as the first authority on land assessment. But, on inquiry, I found he, too, knew nothing of Madras, and seemed to have his ideas confined to Bengal, the North-West Provinces, and the Zemindar system prevalent there. I told him that every native, without exception, put the land assessment at from forty to fifty, or even sixty per cent. on the *gross* produce. But he would have it that it must mean the net produce. In districts of the north, where the permanent settlement does not act, the assessment is calculated on the *rent* received by the Zemindar. They do not seem, either of them, to understand that in three parts out of four of India there are no Zemindars, and the Government is sole landlord. Also they talk as if the irrigated districts were the rule, not the exception. Hunter is, nevertheless, evidently a very able man, and anxious to hear the views of outsiders. He offered to show me the whole of the land question in Bengal in a single afternoon's visit to some villages near Calcutta.[1]

"At night there was a full dress party at Government House, all the native nobility and notability present. I made acquaintance with several new people, among others the Maharajah of Krishna, an intelligent and distinguished man, besides meeting most of our native acquaintance. I noticed that both Abd-el-Latif and Amir Ali were rather shy of being seen talking to me, the latter especially, but, as I had something to say, I took possession of him and made him sit down with me. I told him my university plans, and found him at first rather huffy about it. He said that no Mohammedan in India cared for a merely religious education, but was vexed when I hinted that there were some of them who cared only for success in life. He did not believe anybody would subscribe. He had tried to get subscriptions for educational schemes and had failed. While we were talking Lord Ripon came by, and Amir Ali jumped up and pretended not to belong to me. But when he saw that Lord Ripon stopped to talk to me he became more cordial. And, afterwards, I got him into good humour by telling him, as a great secret, of the Hyderabad scheme. He first objected that the Hyderabad State was going to ruin; but I told him that would be soon set right, and that the Nizam was interested in the university, and he said, if that was the case it would succeed, and promised to help it on in every way in his

[1] See Sir William Hunter's letter in Appendix.

power. I told him that my idea was that great latitude should be given to religious differences of opinion, and he might have a school of rationalism there if he chose.

"Lord Ripon was very amiable, and expressed a hope that he might see us at Hyderabad on the occasion of the installation; so I conclude the Nizam has told him we are expected. Salar Jung also told me he had spoken to the Nizam, and found him ready to support the university scheme. Keay made a successful speech this afternoon at the Town Hall, but I did not go, as he did not specially ask me to be there, and I had heard all his arguments already.

"*4th Jan.*—We had no visits to-day, but went to Government House at 11 o'clock to hear the Ilbert debate. It was a tame affair, but not altogether uninteresting. The Viceroy and Councillors sit round a large table, and the spectators, allowed in by ticket, sit also round, at a little distance, on chairs. Ilbert, who is a little, rather young looking man, related the history of the bill, slurring over the compromise as much as possible. Mrs. Ilbert was sitting next to us. Then Hunter spoke, quoting some words of Malabari's in the 'Indian Spectator' as an evidence that native opinion accepted the compromise. I asked him afterwards if he really thought this sentence represented either the general opinion, or even Malabari's own opinion, and he said he supposed so. Amir Ali next gave his opinion in a speech which, I think, was the best made, though it was wonderfully different from his private talk. He introduced, however, very cleverly a letter the Queen had written at the time of the Proclamation, which was very effective, and he reserved his attack on the compromise for the Select Committee. He told me afterwards that he had been promised to have his amendments paid attention to if he would only support the Bill. I think he would have done better to speak his mind. Kristodas Pal was as unsatisfactory. He dared not speak out and tell the Council how angry his people, the Hindus, were, and though he made some pertinent remarks on details, his speech was feeble. Hunter told me they had got hold of him with difficulty, but he would vote with them. All this is very disappointing, though I was not prepared for much, and I confess the commercial man representing the planters' interests stood out well in contrast, for he threatened the Council with new agitation if the letter of the compromise was not adherred to. We then adjourned to luncheon, and after luncheon somebody discovered that an important clause in the Bill might be read in two contradictory ways, and the debate was again adjourned to Monday. The Nizam and his court were present—very much interested, as it seemed, in all that was going on. I had talk with several members of the Council, and found them all with the idea that there was no real excitement among the natives on the question. They will never see anything until the fire breaks out.

"Later we went to a party at Belvidere, and again met the Hyderabad party. I had five minutes' talk at last, alone, with the Nizam, and asked him to put himself at the head of a movement for a university. He was the leader of the Mohammedans in India, and the people looked to him for their redemption. He promised most readily and emphatically that he would do so, and I suggested to him that he should speak to the Viceroy about it the day he was installed, and say that he wished to commemorate his accession by a great act in favour of education, and I cautioned him to say nothing about it to any one but Lord Ripon. This too he promised; and I am to send him, through Salar Jung, a draft scheme for approval, between this and our meeting him again at Hyderabad. Thus my plan in visiting India is working itself out in a surprising manner. *El hamdu l'Illah!* I had also talk on the same subject with Prince Ferukshah. He is a great friend and admirer of Amir Ali, whom he extols as a truly patriotic and disinterested Mohammedan, and I am glad to hear it. I spoke to him about the university. Like Amir Ali, he at first said it was impracticable; but when I explained it, and told him that I had already had promise of support from several eminent persons, he became more interested, and ended by wishing it all success. He is Europeanized, but wears a black cap instead of a hat, and is a most civilized and intelligent man. It is a pity they hate each other so that they cannot join in any common action. While I was speaking, Abd-el-Latif came up; and I noticed that Prince Ferukshah did not speak to him, but turned away. Fools!

"*5th Jan.*—Seyd Mohammed, Abd-el-Latif's son-in-law, called, a much cleverer young man than Abd-el-Latif's son. I like him much, as he is thoroughgoing and outspoken. We talked about Shiahs and Sunnis, and he told me that here, in Calcutta, there is no kind of ill-feeling between them, or any important difference of ideas. The Shiahs are not numerous, perhaps five per cent., but they have some men of high position, such as the King of Oude and his family and Prince Ferukshah. I asked him whether the Shiahs sided with Amir Ali, he being a Shiah; and he said on the contrary they were nearly all of the Conservative Party. Prince Jehan, I remember, was at the Literary meeting.

He then explained the course of education received by a Bengal Mohammedan. He begins at a vernacular school at seven years old, in which the language is Bengali only. Then he goes for three years to the Madrasa at Calcutta, where the education is in English for four hours, and Arabic or Persian or Urdu or Bengali, for one hour daily. At fifteen or sixteen, or later, he passes, by Entrance Examination, into the University. At none of these places is he taught religion. At the vernacular school the teacher is generally a Hindu. At the Madrasa, the Arabic and Persian teachers are Mulvis, but they are chosen by the Government from among the least religious and most loyal of the Ulema. Also the Government know nothing of their qualifications in Arabic or Persian, as they do not understand those languages. In the University the education is again almost wholly in English, so that those who have passed the whole course seldom know any other language, to read and write it with ease. They then become cut off from the mass of Mohammedans, regard them with contempt, and are so, by them, regarded. They consequently lose all influence with ninety-nine per cent. of the community.

"While we were talking, Mohammed Yusuf joined us and asked me where he should send his children to school in England, and I answered him with the story of the advice to those about to marry. This pleased Seyd Mohammed amazingly, and Mohammed Yusuf also promised to follow my advice. We agreed that there was no objection to young men visiting England when their ideas and their principles were formed, but to send a Mohammedan boy to an English school was simply to sacrifice his religion. I then explained to the new comer the university scheme, and I hope his boys may join it later. It was Seyd Mohammed who sent Abd-el-Gaffar to me yesterday about the 'Wind and the Whirlwind,' and no better proof could be given of the feeling of this section of Mohammedans towards the English Government. I told them of my intention to visit Constantinople and to try and induce the Sultan to head a reformation, and they warmly approved.

"Mulvi A. M. called to say good-bye. He was under the impression, not having been there, that my speech about the university had not been well received, and this is probably the view taken by Amir Ali's party, but I am certain the contrary is the case. A young university student, Seyd M., who came, also assured me all the Mohammedan students would take up the idea, especially if I could get Jemal-ed-Din as a professor. These students are an independent body between the two great parties, and they worship Jemal-ed-Din. It is, therefore, to them that the direction of religious thought will fall as they grow older. Thus has the persecution in Egypt spread the doctrine of reformation far and wide.

"While we were talking, Cordery was announced, and the others went away. Poor Cordery! I am sorry for him, as he is terribly down on his luck about all this business. I told him at once that I had seen Lord Ripon, and spoken to him about the state of things at Hyderabad, for I thought it unfair, as I had stayed in his house, to leave him ignorant of this. He said he was sure it was Laik Ali who had had the thing published in the 'Statesman'; but I assured him that to the best of my belief it was not so. I cannot conceive that Laik Ali should have done anything so foolish, especially when he knew from me that Lord Ripon was going to give him a full hearing, and was favourably inclined. But I fear it has done him harm, as some of the information, at least, must have come originally from him, though he probably never meant it to be published, at least not till the last extremity. There the matter, however, stands. I forgot to say that Mrs. Clerk told us yesterday, as a great secret, that the Nizam had asked for Laik Ali as Diwan from Lord Ripon, and that they considered the matter as settled. I have a fancy, from things I have noticed in Salar Jung's manner the last few days, and also in Vikar-el-Omra's, that they have been talked to, probably by Stewart Bailey, about me, as a dangerous acquaintance, and one in whose company the Government of India might not like them to show themselves. This struck me after going to the railway station this afternoon to wish the Nizam good-bye. Vikar-el-Omra was certainly odd in his manner. I missed seeing Salar Jung, or I should have spoken to him on the subject, and as it is I shall write to him before deciding to go back to Hyderabad. There were a couple of thousand poor Mohammedans come to see the Nizam off. One of them rushed after the carriage, and, in spite of outriders and aides-de-camp, climbed up and touched the Nizam's knee, the old Peishkar poking at him meanwhile with his stick. We had agreed to stay at the Clerks while at Hyderabad; but Cordery has asked us to go to the Residency if we do go, so I have made excuses to Mrs. Clerk. Hyderabad is such a nest of intrigue, that, unless I can do good to the university scheme by so doing, I shall not go back there. I attended a Debating Club meeting at Maharajah Krishna's at 4 o'clock, and heard Dr. Ghose lecture, and Bannerji speak. The latter is certainly a wonderful speaker. He took up each point of the lecture, and treated each in masterly fashion. Otherwise the proceedings were uninteresting.

"Dined at home with Walter Pollen.

"*6th Jan.*—Our last day at Calcutta. Abd-el-Latif came, and we had a long talk. He urged me strongly to go to Hyderabad to see the university scheme started. He assured me of the goodwill of all the Mohammedans of Calcutta towards me. His tone was cordial, even affectionate. He came to see us off at the railway station, and we arranged that I should send an account of my speech at the Anjuman meeting to the 'Times,' so as to show that my ideas were accepted by the Mohammedans of India.

"Later I called on Hunter and argued the land revenue question with him again, and he told me he had given great offence by bringing the matter of over-taxation forward. His book on India was considered so unfavourable to Government that it had cost him his post at the Statistical Office. Lord Ripon has sent for him on more than one occasion, and begged him to moderate his language in Council—this I was not to repeat. On the whole I like Hunter. He is more honest than most of them, but after all he is an official. Going to the station, we stopped at Amir Ali's to say good-bye, but heard he was ill with fever. I wonder whether this is to avoid voting on the Ilbert Bill. On the whole, I leave Calcutta much satisfied with all I have done, heard and seen, though not sorry to be once more on the move."

CHAPTER VII

PATNA, LUCKNOW

"*7th Jan.*

"ARRIVED at Patna at half-past 9 o'clock, and found about eighty of the leading Mohammedans at the City station awaiting us. Our host, Seyd Rasa Huseyn, drove us in a handsome barouche to his house, where we have been very comfortably lodged, and sumptuously entertained, and have made the acquaintance of, I believe, every Mohammedan of importance in Patna. Patna is one of the Mohammedan strongholds, as they number 50,000 out of a total population of 150,000; and they still have many rich families and noble families of the time of the Empire. The Province of Behar, they tell me, contains also a certain Mohammedan population of ryots, 30,000 or 40,000, who are descended from the Pathan invaders, and are a warlike race, retaining, however, nothing of their former rank but their name Malik, the mass of the ryots being Hindus or converted Hindus. The character of these is quite unwarlike. The Mohammedans, therefore, hold their heads higher here than in most places.

"We received visits all the morning, meeting our old friend Mohammed Ali Rogay from Bombay, Nur-el-Huda, Ferid-ed-Din, and others, also Mohammed Abbas Ibn Huseyn Bafiti, Sheykh es Saadat of Medina, a young Arab, who invited us cordially to come and stay with him in Medina, whither he returns in a few months. He says that if ever we write and tell him we are coming, he will prepare to receive us, and gave us his address and took ours. He repeated this invitation more than once, and I am sure it was sincerely given. The other acquaintance was that of Sirhadé Huseyn, who once wrote to me from Cirencester. After luncheon we were driven out to see something of the town and country. The town is old and picturesque, but we saw no specially fine buildings. We got out and inspected a village by the river side, but it was too near the river to be quite a fair specimen of Behar agriculture. One of the inhabitants, whom we questioned, told us it belonged to a rent-free Zemindar, and he was a tenant on a permanent rent, that is to say, fifteen rupees an acre, for three acres. We calculated the gross produce at thirty-six rupees, so he nets sixty-three rupees a year, or over five rupees a month, a fortune, but it is land of the best quality, and he grows maize and potatoes. It is not irrigated, so does not grow sugar cane. We asked whether he felt the salt tax, and he said 'No.' He was in debt twenty rupees this year, though he had never been in debt before. He and his family had held the land for generations.

"We sat down, sixteen or twenty, to dinner, and adjourned at 9 o'clock to the house of Nawab Villayet Ali Khan, the chief nobleman of Patna, where, in a large hall, about one hundred and fifty Mohammedans assembled to hear me give a lecture I had promised on their prospects. I shall not give my speech here, which was almost entirely extempore, because it is to be printed in one of the local papers. Suffice it to say that it included, with other matter, most of what I had said at the Anjuman i Islam, and was extremely well received.

"*8th Jan.*—We left Patna by the morning train, attended to the station by our host and Nawab Villayet Ali, with some thirty others, and a disagreeable incident occurred, as the train was starting, owing to the violence of a Scotch doctor, who threatened our friends, and especially the old Nawab, with his stick if they remained near his carriage window. I jumped at him, of course, and after calling him a blackguard for his conduct, gave him in charge at the next station, Dinapore. The railway authorities tried hard to screen him, and proposed to me to compromise the matter, but I insisted on having his name, and after about ten minutes he produced his card as Dr. K., Army and Navy Club (in pencil), Sealkote. So I have written a strong letter to Lord Ripon, warning him of the state of things, and of the bitterness of native feeling in consequence of their habitual ill treatment by the English."

This was a worse case than quite appears from this entry. The Nawab, with his party of friends, were on the platform wishing me good-bye, with all possible decorum, when the Scotchman, who turned out to be Chief Medical Office of the Punjab, put his head and shoulders out of the next compartment and struck with his stick at the Nawab and his friends, bidding them, with an insolent air of authority, to stand back from the neighbourhood of his carriage window. This happened just as the train moved on, and I had to wait till the train again stopped before I could take action. Fortunately, however, Patna has two stations, and in five minutes we came to the second. There I entered the Doctor's compartment, and insisted upon having his name, which he refused, and it was only by threatening the station-master with reporting the case to Lord Ripon that I got him to intervene. Several of my Patna friends had come on by the train, and supported me, or I doubt if I could have prevailed with him to do his duty. The matter being treated in this way madc a prodigious sensation, as it was the first time an Englishman had openly taken part with the natives against his fellow countrymen.

"We arrived at 4 o'clock at Benares, and are the Maharajah's guests in one of his empty houses, being attended to by one of his head servants. The river at Benares is striking, but less beautiful than I had expected.

"*9th Jan.*—In the morning I wrote a letter to Lord Ripon about the incident of yesterday, in a tone to compel his attention, and I enclosed it to Primrose with a hint that I should publish it if the matter was not promptly set right.

"We then went out to pay our respects to the Maharajah at Ahmednagar, crossing the river in a boat. The Palace at Ahmednagar is certainly one of the most striking buildings in the world. The Maharajah received us most kindly. He is a really 'grand old man,' blind with a cataract, but delighted to 'see' us. We had a rather long conversation with him, touching on religion and the disadvantage of a too-English education for men of the East. In which opinion we cordially agreed. He had his little Court of old servants round him, as he sat on the sofa, smoking his hookah, and his son, an amiable youth, sat in front on a chair, translating for him our conversation into Urdu. There was nothing of the new world in all this. He also talked about various Englishmen he had known, Sir John Strachey among others, whom he laughed at for his airs of grandeur. On one occasion he had come to pay a visit and had taken offence because the servants were not all at the door to receive him, and so had gone home. I told him he would laugh more if he could see Sir John Strachey in England, glad of anybody who would take the trouble to say 'how do you do' to him. This caused a chorus. Yet the officials fancy the 'natives' rate them at their own pretensions.

"After seeing the temple and the tank and the various sights of the Palace, we were rowed down the river in a barge, a really splendid sight, stopping once or twice to be shown the insides of houses. Bagdad must have been like this in its great days. But, what is strange at Benares, there is not a single house south of the river. Holkar's house, which has slipped bodily into the Ganges, shows how all that is solid on the river front will one day go, leaving, as at Bagdad, only the mud huts they now screen. The temples here are insignificant compared with those of the South. It has been a pleasant day of comparative rest after all the talking we have lately done.

"10*th Jan.*—Calling accidentally at the Post Office, we found important letters from England; and, amongst other good news, I find my Colombo letter is published in the 'Times'; also I am informed that orders were sent to Lord Ripon not to receive me at Government House.

"We were taken again on the river, which is a still more wonderful sight in the morning than it was in the evening, and, through the Maharajah, we had arranged to pay a visit, without which our Mohammedan tour would have been incomplete, namely, to the last representative of the Moguls, an elderly gentleman who lives in an old palace on the river, on a pension, he told us, of 649 rupees, 6 annas, and 3 pice a month, paid him in lieu of his Indian Empire by Her Majesty. He had had another 249 rupees with his wife, but she died last year, and now he wanted his case laid before the public. He was immensely pleased with our visit, for it seems no one ever thinks of paying him any attention, because he is poor; but we inundated him with compliments and courtesies, and he was moved to telling us of his descent from Arungzeb through the Emperor of Delhi, whose eldest son was his grandfather, and who, being disinherited by his father, left Delhi and settled at Benares. Sad old relic perched in a half ruinous house, like a sick eagle, looking down on the river and the crescent-shaped city, with his little group of tattered servants. We were pitying him from our hearts, melted at his pedigree, when he suddenly changed his tragic tone, and asked whether we would like to see a cock fight, and, when we assented, jumped briskly on his legs and led the way to the palace yard, where cocks had already been brought in crowing. The cock fight, as a cock fight, was a delusion. The birds were evidently too precious to be allowed to hurt each other, and their spurs were carefully swathed in bandages, so that no harm was done. This innocent amusement kindled him for a minute or two, and then he relapsed into his old listlessness. Wreaths were brought for us and perfumes, and we bade him farewell, and went on our way. I would not have missed this visit to the last of the Moguls for millions.

"We went on to Allahabad in the afternoon, and are staying with Lyall[1] at Government House. There were a large number of Mohammedans to meet us at the station; among them Ferid-ed-Din, quite hilarious with the recollection of the row at the Patna station. We were hurried off, however, to Government House, where there was a large dinner of uninteresting officials. How dull Anglo-Indian society is! But when everybody was gone, I unfolded to Lyall my ideas of Mohammedan reform, and the

[1] Sir Alfred Lyall, K.C.B., G.C.I.E., then Lord Governor of the North-West Provinces.

university scheme, which last, to my astonishment, he cordially approved, promising, if it was started in his province, to aid it with a public grant. He also suggested Jonpore or Rampore as suitable places.

"Ferid-ed-Din came to settle about the presentation of the address and the lecture, but, after consultation with Lyall, it has been agreed that the latter is to be abandoned. Ferid-ed-Din suggested asking him to it, but this Lyall declined to do. I don't quarrel with him for this. But it is painful to see what terror he inspires in the 'natives.' Ferid-ed-Din, in spite of his boldness, was struck speechless in his presence, and stood before him barefooted. I told Ferid-ed-Din to put his shoes on, but Lyall said he had better stay as he was. Yet Lyall is very far from being a narrow-minded man, and we have discussed the most burning questions without reserve. Talking of the Ilbert Bill, he said it was, as far as the Anglo-Indians were concerned, a local Bengal measure. It was quite true the Assam planters regarded it as an attempt to do away with their right of beating their own niggers. The jury system could not work there, as it would leave them free to do exactly what they chose. We discussed the chances of revolution. He would not agree that it would come in five years, but perhaps in twenty. But the people of India were a weak race, and would never be able to stand alone. They would be a prey to seafaring nations on their seaboard, and to the Russians and Chinese on their land frontier.

"We played lawn tennis, at which Lyall is good, in the afternoon; and after dinner we went to the Mayo Hall, a public place where about three hundred Mohammedans presented us with an address of an effusively loyal nature, to which I replied in a carefully moderate tone. Everything went off well, but the thing was tame compared with the Patna meeting, for the fact of our being at Government House has raised, in spite of us, a barrier between us and the people. They dare not come to see us there, and dare not talk openly anywhere. I feel suddenly shut out from all light, as when one goes through a tunnel on a railway journey.

"In England all seems going well. Churchill has made a grand speech at Edinburgh about Egypt, and I am glad to see advocates moral principles of government according to the programme I sketched for him. Gladstone's mantle of righteousness, which has slipped off his shoulders, may be picked up now by anybody. Also I have several letters about my Colombo letter in the 'Times.' It was published on the 13th, as Churchill's speech was made on the 16th. From Egypt, however, there comes news less good. Sherif has indeed resigned, but Nubar is in his place, and there is talk of increasing the staff of English employés, and prolonging the occupation for five years.

"*12th Jan.*—Akbar Huseyn and his brother came in the morning, and we wrote out an account of the meeting last night, and sent it to the 'Pioneer.' In the afternoon there was a garden party, and I talked to Sir Donald Stewart, the High Court Judge, about the Patna business. It surprised him, as it surprises every Englishman, and fails to surprise every native. He said the only similar case he had brought before him in his twelve years of judgeship, was one in which certain native pleaders had been insulted in their robing room in Court. This, however, does not affect the question of such things happening, because it shows only that no native ever dreams of complaining, or would have a chance of having his complaint inquired into if he did. On the other hand they have been settling a case this very day, in which a Hindu railway clerk beat an Englishman, and have sentenced the clerk to ten months imprisonment. Several of our Mohammedan friends were at the party, among them Ferid-ed-Din, but I noticed that they mixed with none of the English, talking only to each other or to certain Hindus.

"At dinner there were several intelligent people, especially a Mr. Patterson, who is on good terms with the natives, and spoke of them as I have not yet heard an Englishman speak. But he served with Garibaldi in Italy, and so has ideas of liberty the rest have not. The other was a young Strachey, son of Sir John, a true chip of the old block, with his father's way of sitting with his head on one side like a sick raven, and the same spectacles and soft voice, a clever youth. I had another long talk with Lyall about the prospects of a Mohammedan reformation, and he reminded me of our dinner at the Travellers in the summer of 1881, with Morley and Zohrab, and of how I was then looking for a prophet in Arabia to proclaim him Caliph. He thinks Egypt will certainly now be annexed.

"13*th Jan.*—I was nervous all day yesterday at getting no answer from Lord Ripon. But at dinner last night the post arrived, with a most gracious letter, which makes me feel ashamed of my own violent one. I shall now leave the matter entirely in his hands, and I am glad of it, for it might interfere with my larger plans to have to fight a newspaper battle on such a field.

"Since writing this, Lyall has spoken to me also about the Patna business, and tells me Lord Ripon has sent him a copy of my letter, and begged him to urge on me the excision of such portions of it as treat the general question, because, Lyall says, if it were brought forward in that form just now, there would be a terrible row all over India, and it would upset Lord Ripon altogether. He has had a terribly hard time lately, and another angry question would be too much for him. He said he could promise me on Lord Ripon's part, that if I would rewrite the letter in this sense, Lord Ripon would see justice done in the matter. He was not a man to do less than justice, and he, Lyall, would advise that Dr. K. be brought down to Patna to apologize to the Mohammedan gentleman, and that an order should be issued to the Railway Company for the better protection of natives. Of course I readily agreed to all this, and have now rewritten the public letter, and posted it, with a private one of thanks, to Lord Ripon. Nothing could have been better. But Lyall charges me I should tell no man—no Englishman that is—for I have already shown my first letter to several Mohammedans, and sent a copy of it to Villayet Ali. Rajah Amir Hassan called on his way to Lucknow, where we are to stay with him.

"In the afternoon we went with Mohammed Kazim, a friend of Ferid-ed-Din, to see some villages across the river, and saw also the Hindu pilgrims encamped in the river bed, at the junction of the waters. I feel in high spirits to-day at things having gone so exactly as I intended them to do in connection with the Patna incident. I could not really have published the first letter at a moment like this, and now Lord Ripon is under an obligation to me, and I shall have a right to speak about the university.

"Another long talk with Lyall. He told me that the Ceylon authorities had telegraphed about me to those of Bengal, and I fancy, though he did not say so, that he has been instructed to look pretty closely after me. It is also evident that Ferid-ed-Din has been warned not to go too far; and Lyall advised me to allow myself to be directed by Rajah Amir Hassan at Lucknow, as to whom to see and not to see, which means that he, too, has been warned to keep me out of dangerous company. I have been very frank with Lyall about my plans and ideas. Government opposition now would only strengthen me with the Mohammedans. They would do far better to help than to hinder me, for my ideas do not really run counter to any liberal interpretation of the continuance of British rule in India. Lyall, as a man, is everything that is charming and sympathetic; as an official he has graduated in a thoroughly bad school. It was he who, more than any one else, ruined Salar Jung's administration in Hyderabad, and he admitted nearly as much to me. Salar Jung, he said, presumed upon the fact of his good government to claim what he could not get, that is, independence of the Paramount Power. There were certain things which the Government of India would always insist upon advising about, and having its advice followed. But Salar Jung did not see this. He thought he could rely on his own cleverness, and extra-official sympathy in England. But this could not be allowed. On that point he agreed with Lytton that Salar Jung was a dangerous man. It was not part of the Imperial policy that the Berar provinces should ever be restored.

"14*th Jan.*—The 'Pioneer,' instead of publishing the account of the meeting at the Mayo Hall, has printed a vicious little paragraph, saying that the natives of Patna regard me as a paid spy of the English Government. This is too much, and I expostulated with Lyall about it on the ground that the 'Pioneer' is a semi-official journal, a fact which, with certain qualifications, he admitted, and sent at once for N., the sub-Editor—Allen, the Editor, being away. After a sermon from Lyall, N. was shown in to me, a lackadaisical youth in a check suit, apparently still in his teens, and so frightened he could hardly speak or find his way to a chair. I was sorry for the boy, and dealt with him mildly when he stammered an excuse that the paragraph had been inserted as a joke, and he promised repentance, and to print the address verbatim as well as my speech, and also to print, when it should arrive, any letter from the Patna Mohammedans. Lyall tells me he is a youth who spends his time playing lawn tennis, and picks up his information in such places. They make use of him, however, to insert communiqués (one of them was Cordery's explanation a few days ago), and Colvin is thick with Allen, the Editor, lodging, I understand, in the same house with him at Calcutta. Colvin, he says, has always worked the press. He himself has made the rule only to work anonymously to the extent of writing articles he was prepared, if challenged, to avow. But he is of opinion it is best to keep out of it altogether. It is Colvin, no doubt, who has prompted the spiteful tone of the 'Pioneer' towards myself. But how ridiculously these newspapers rule the world.

"*7th to 15th Jan.*—We went to Lucknow, the party here breaking up at the same time, Lyall going on a tour of the province, his wife and daughter to a ball at Lucknow. Mulvi Wahaj-ed-din and about twenty others came to see us off at the station, but we have seen nothing of them, for they won't come to Government House to be treated like servants. Nothing happened on the journey except that at Cawnpore about one hundred Mohammedans had assembled to see us while the train stopped. One of them recited some verses in Arabic, and an address was promised, but they had had no time, they said, to write one. There are not many Mohammedans at Cawnpore, and only one can speak a little English, so our interview was limited to compliments, bowings, and hand shakings.

"At Lucknow we were received by all the great people, two of the Oude princes, and our host, Rajah Amir Hassan, who drove us to his house in a state carriage and four. He made many apologies to us for the poorness of his abode, which was, in fact, a small palace, and explained that his own palaces had been burned down at the time of the Mutiny, and this house was given him in exchange by the English Government. It was late, and we had no more time than to dine and go to bed, the Rajah dining with us, the first time in his life, he told us, he had ever dined with Europeans, nor had he ever entertained an Englishman in his house.

"*16th Jan.*—We have had a great deal of conversation with our host, who is a man of much intelligence, though a rather bigoted Shiah. He explained to me the dogmatic differences they had with the Sunnis, the principal of which, he said, was that the Shiahs asserted God's justice, and that the prophets had been without sin and infallible. He also went through the old discussion about Ali's succession to the Caliphate with warmth; and told me a number of other curious things connected with his sect. Lucknow is its stronghold in India, as the Court was Shiah during the last eighty years of its existence. We then talked of Hyderabad. Sir Salar Jung had been a great friend of his, and he had recommended Seyd Huseyn to him.

"In the afternoon he drove us round the town and

showed us the Imambara, where he said a prayer on the tomb, touching it with his right hand. Also to the Residency ruins, while he told us the history of the Mutiny from his own point of view. His father had sided with the mutineers and been the chief leader of the Shiah faction among them, till the massacres occurred, when he left them in disgust and went to his own fort, at Mahmudabad, where he took ill and died. Twelve of Amir Hassan's brothers and cousins were shot, blown up, or hanged by the English, and he alone was left, a boy of ten, to be educated by them. All the family property in Lucknow was confiscated and destroyed, for the English destroyed one third of the city, and so he comes in for an inheritance of woe. Looking, however, at the ruins, which are very beautiful, he said: 'We have agreed to forget our history, and the days of our glory. But the English refuse to forget it. They leave their ruins standing to perpetuate the memory of bloodshed. If I could do it, I would persuade the Lieutenant-Governor to have them razed or rebuilt.'

"The Rajah is only thirty-six years old, but his hair is very gray, and he looks fifty. He complains of his liver, and I have strongly advised him, for the good of his soul and body, to make the land pilgrimage from Kerbela to Mecca, and he says he will certainly do so. He does not go into English society, because he dislikes being disrespectfully treated. The officials are very tyrannical. Of General Barrow he spoke very highly, as of one who had saved them from destruction after the Mutiny, and he showed us a statue of him the Talukdars of Oude are going to set up. He is President of the Talukdars' Association, and takes considerable part in public affairs, besides having started some indigo factories. Altogether he is a superior man.

"17th *Jan.*—We went to the 10th Hussar ball last night, in the Chotar Menzil, a beautiful room robbed by the Government from the princes of Oude. Wood, the Colonel, is an old friend of mine, and we met Brabazon and Lady Lyall and the Franklins.

"There is a furious article against me in the 'Pioneer,' written evidently by Colvin, or inspired by him, to the effect that I am stirring up sedition in Patna and other Mohammedan centres. The text, however, of it is the 'Wind and the Whirlwind,' and its tone is exactly what I could most have wished. Good hearty abuse as a revolutionist can do me nothing but good. In the same sheet they publish the text of my Allahabad address.

"I am to give a lecture here and receive an address to-morrow, and have been busy preparing. In the middle of the day we went to a horse sale of the 10th Hussars, and had luncheon with them; and then we drove through the city with the Rajah, he lamenting over the ruins. A great road has been run through the city by pulling down the houses of poor men. Hardly any got compensation, and the ruins make a causeway raised about twenty feet above the general level. This is called Victoria Street.

"We had several visits: First, Mohammed Ibrahim, chief Mujtahed of the Shiahs, a dignified old man who talked good Arabic. He did not fancy a university at Hyderabad, because the Government was Sunni. He lamented the decay of religious institutions here in Lucknow. Secondly, Prince Mirza Mohammed Madhi Ali Khan, a polite and amiable personage who talked no English, but had sent us last night an enormous tray of fruits and sweetmeats. Thirdly, Ihtimam ed Dowlah Nawab Haidar

Huseyn Khan, an elderly nobleman of Lucknow. Fourthly, Rajah Tasadak Rasul Khan, a nobleman related to the princes, in very fine clothes. I find, however, that no Sunni has been to see us, nor any of the small people of the town, who are the most interesting. Perhaps our host is carrying out Lyall's instructions; perhaps he discourages Sunnis. It is tiresome, but cannot be helped.

"We were taken to-day to see the Shiah Madrasa, a poor little place, where seventy pupils, men and boys, are taught religion, logic, and arithmetic up to the rule of three. I was begged to examine them, and asked who was the Mogul leader who had sacked Bagdad, but was told that no one knew history. Then I put the problem of the herring and a half costing three half-pence, and six boys, on slates, worked out the problem, two correctly.

"*18th Jan.*—We went out in the morning to see the Hoseynabad Imambara, which is certainly the most beautiful thing in Lucknow, though less imposing than the great Imambara. Here we took off our shoes, which pleased the Rajah greatly, and at his suggestion we refused the wreaths offered us by the guardian, this on the ground that, it being a charitable endowment, the money spent on these wreaths given to English visitors was misspent. The way in which this endowment is misappropriated is astonishing. The guardian is a Hindu, appointed by the English trustees with a salary of four hundred rupees a month, and quite recently they have spent £10,000 on building a ridiculous clock tower as a memorial to Sir George Couper, the man most hated by the Mohammedans of Lucknow. These are the things that bring the English name into contempt.

"Prince Mahdi Ali called again and one or two

others, but there seem to be few Mohammedans here who know English, except among the younger men, and these did not come to the house. In the afternoon, however, they came to the meeting. We talked with the Rajah about the land assessment, and he gave us the following as the proportion between the ryot, the Talukdar, and the Government. Of a field producing one hundred maunds, the ryot would keep sixty (that is three-fifths, of which fifteen or twenty would represent the seed corn, and forty or forty-five for his profit and labour). Of the remaining forty maunds the Government takes twenty or twenty-five, leaving fifteen or twenty to the Talukdar. He said this would be an average reckoning.

"The meeting in the Kaisar Bagh Hall was the most successful we have yet had. All the religious chiefs, Sunnis and Shiahs, and many of the noblemen of Lucknow, and altogether about one thousand persons were present, as well as about a dozen Englishmen. Three addresses were presented, and I made a long speech of an hour and a half, which, as it is to be printed, I will not give here.

"Lyall has written to apologize for the article in the 'Pioneer,' which he says he knows comes from Calcutta, and he will give orders that I am to be well received everywhere in his province. This is good of him, though nobody can do me much good or harm now. My only anxiety is Hyderabad, and I think I shall write to Lord Ripon and ask him whether he wishes me to come or not. Unless he gives me his countenance, my going back there will do more harm than good. We came away by the night train to Aligarh.

"19*th Jan.*—Mulvi Sami Ullah, Seyd Ahmed, and a number more of the Aligarh Mohammedans, met us at the station, and we are staying in Sami Ullah's house, a bungalow furnished in extra English taste, and having a certain chill simplicity which savours of the convent. One expects a crucifix and a holy water stoup in every room. The Mulvi's dress is almost a cassock, and he has something of the manner of a Don. I can understand why the Aligarh men are not liked. I myself feel rather constrained with them, for one does not know whether to treat them as pious Mohammedans, or latter-day disciples of Jowett. Not that they are not extremely amiable, but there is a tone of apology in their talk to me, as much as to say 'we are not such infidels as you suppose.'

"I am rather disappointed in Seyd Ahmed. He is certainly a *beau vieillard*, but does not inspire me with entire confidence. His features are coarse, his hands coarse, and I should not be surprised if he turned out to be a *faux bonhomme*. But this is a first impression, and he speaks very little English. I have not had a real opportunity of judging him even superficially. We went over the College, which is certainly a wonderful work. It is on a large scale, but without pretence, and no money has been wasted on ornament. The boys were out playing cricket, which they did as well as an average lot of English schoolboys, and seemed to take full interest in the game. Among them was the new English Principal of the College, Mr. Beck, a pretty little young man with pink cheeks and blue eyes, certainly not an average Englishmen; and an average Englishman certainly could not succeed here. So Beck may succeed. He is probably clever.[1]

[1] Mr. Beck certainly succeeded and acquired a notable influence with the young generation of Mohammedans. His death, some years ago, caused universal regret.

"The Collector, Mr. Ward, and the Judge have called, by Lyall's orders, and I had some talk with the former about the ill feeling between Englishmen and natives, which he seemed to think could not be helped. I don't suppose it can. The Judge seems a better sort, but when we went to take tea with his wife, she at once asked Sami Ullah to 'take a peg,' and then apologized for her thoughtlessness. A good sort all the same.

"We sat down, a dozen, to dinner, but as no one could speak English well, it was a dull party. There were two Rais in the company who belong to the old-fashioned party, and with them I had a little talk. On the whole Aligarh bores me.

"I forgot to say that Mr. Ward mentioned it, as an instance of rough behaviour on the part of the natives, that a day or two ago an Englishman having accidentally shot a Hindu boy, the native police had arrested the man, made him walk some miles, and detained him two days at the police station, and then brought a charge against him. He said the wound was little more than a skin wound, and that the bullet had glanced from the ground while the Englishman was shooting blue deer.

"*20th Jan.*—Letters have come from England, and a great number from Patna, strengthening the general case of the insults offered to natives. I shall now write to Lord Ripon again. We paid a visit to the dispensary, where we happened to see the boy wounded in the neck by the bullet, half an inch deep the English doctor said, and within very little of the jugular artery. Also to the Mosque, where we were received with great honour by the chief preacher here. The Mosque has just been restored with excellent taste. I noticed that Sami Ullah did not take off his shoes to go inside. The repairs have cost

£10,000, partly paid out of a *wakf*, partly by subscription. They have made me promise to make a speech to-morrow, but it will be difficult not to give offence, for party feeling runs high.

"We drove to a village and ascertained a few useful facts. The proportion of seed corn to harvest is one to six, and they give their cattle salt twice a week. We dined at Seyd Ahmed's, a mixed party of Mohammedans and Englishmen. Seyd Ahmed told me he quite agreed with my fifth chapter of the 'Future of Islam.'

"*21st Jan.*—The meeting was a failure compared with the others. Most of the old Mulvis would not come, I suppose because it was convened by Seyd Ahmed. But they sent me a very nice address in Arabic, and some of them were there, including one who is a dwarf. I did not know quite what to say between the two parties, and I doubt whether Seyd Ahmed altogether liked my discourse. It was certainly not a success. Still I think it may do good. It will put them on their religious mettle.

"Since writing this, I hear that my speech was immensely appreciated by the greater number of those present, only they did not like to express their feelings strongly in Seyd Ahmed's presence. I have talked, too, with Seyd Ahmed, and hope no offence has been taken by him. I fancy he has considerable experience of people differing from him, and he tells me he shall lay to heart the suggestions I made. I like him better than I did at first, and have no doubt he is a good and sincere man. But my taking part, in a way, with his enemies cannot of course be agreeable to him, especially as he is just starting on a trip to the Punjaub to collect funds for his college. Ikhram Ullah of Delhi is here, and goes with him, being Seyd Ahmed's nephew and disciple. It was on him we counted for introductions at Delhi; but he has promised to go back and start us there. I feel a little doubt as to how we shall get on. The 'Pioneer,' I hear, has rather frightened peoplc, and Ikhram Ullah tells me we are watched by spies. However, the thing is almost done now, and our reception at Delhi is not of vital importance. I have written to Lord Ripon to ask his leave to be at Hyderabad for the installation. It is evident to me now that the Calcutta Foreign Office has warned Salar Jung and Vikar-el-Omra against intimacy with us, perhaps also the Nizam. With Lord Ripon's countenance, however, we need not mind that.

"At night there was a dinner at the Aligarh Institute in my honour, at which Seyd Ahmed presided, and the Collector and other English officials were present. I sat between Seyd Ahmed and Mr. Ward. The latter talked about the future of India, and said he wished to see a parliament in India. Anything was better than being governed by the English Parliament. He complained that the English in India were disfranchised. They had no vote in England, and no representation here. Seyd Ahmed read a speech in which he proposed Her Majesty's health, which was drunk in tea, and then my health and a great many expressions of loyalty, and Sami Ullah also spoke, and then Seyd Ahmed sang, with much spirit, a few Arabic verses in my honour. After which I replied briefly, explaining that I was not come to India to stir up strife, but to help the cause of peace and goodwill. That I should like to see the Indians and English living in harmony together, but the condition of social intercourse was social equality. There were none at this dinner but men of Seyd Ahmed's school, but about fifty others came in in the evening. Anne came also, but did not dine.

"*22nd Jan.*—We left for Delhi by the morning train, Mulvi Mohammed Abbas Huseyn, the chief of the Shiahs, presenting me with a separate address before starting. He is one of the old-fashioned ones, and I like him especially. He wears the white turban, and dresses like an Egyptian Alem. At the station everybody was present, Seyd Ikbal Ali had come all the way from Faizabad to see us, Seyd Ahmed and all of them, who started a 'hip hurray' as the train moved off, but Mohammedans are not good at cheering. I promised Seyd Ahmed to send him a subscription, and wished him, very heartily, success."

CHAPTER VIII

DELHI, RAJPUTANA

"*22nd Jan.* (*continued*).

"AT Delhi we were met by Ikhram Ullah with three of the chief noblemen of the town, Nawab Ala-ed-din, Ahmed Khan, chief of Loharo, a prince Mirza Suliman Jah, of the Mogul family, and Ala-ed-din's son, Emir-ed-din Feruk Mirza. The Nawab accompanied us to the hotel, where he had taken rooms for us, and, as he speaks English, we had a long conversation, principally about Egypt. But I found him very ignorant as to the state of affairs there. He asked very particularly about the Sultan, and I answered, as I always do, that I believed him to be a good man in private character, and with the wish to improve his Empire, but quite ignorant of the world, and surrounded by a set of avaricious Pashas. I cannot discover any enthusiasm in India about the Turkish Empire, and very little about the Sultan.

"In the afternoon I went out alone to return the visits of the Nawab and princes. The Nawab explained to me that he was a pure Turk (Turcoman) by descent, his family having come only three generations back from Samarcand, and having always married with women of their own blood. He was, till last year, a semi-independent sovereign, and he abdicated in favour of his son, and is now living on a small income at Delhi. He also told me that his uncle, an illegitimate son of his grandfather, had been hanged here in Delhi for the murder of Mr. William Fraser, he says, unjustly, though he evidently thinks it served him right for having usurped the greater part of the family property. He says that he got the property by bribing this Mr. Fraser, and that he was accused of the murder by the Government in order to confiscate the estates, which were very large. He showed me a picture of this uncle as a young man riding out with his attendants, and another of the Mogul Court, in which his father and this very Mr. Fraser figure. The old gentleman is a curious old-world type, with a fair knowledge of English, and the reputation of being a good Arabic and Persian scholar, as well as a sportsman and good rider. He has only one wife, 'thank God.'

"With the Prince we talked Arabic, which he speaks better than most of the Indians, and he was helped in it by an Alem, his cousin by marriage, who spoke it colloquially. We discussed the Mahdi, whom they were delighted to hear me speak well of, and Arabi, for whom they expressed great respect, and Tewfik's character, and the Sultan's. All these things interest them extremely. The Prince is a cousin of our friend at Benares, and enjoys a pension of five hundred rupees a month. He lives in a little old house in the old town, and keeps a little old Court of old servants like his cousin. But he is a much more intelligent man, younger and better educated. He was immensely pleased with my visit, and has promised to take us to see the Kottub on Thursday, which is eleven miles off.

"This hotel stands on the ramparts, and is a really nice place, its proprietor a negro of Algerian extraction, but born in France and a Christian. He knows a few words of Arabic and no more, dresses in ultra English dress, has served as naval engineer on board Her Majesty's fleet, and is more of a John Bull than anybody I know except Zohrab. His helmet is monumental.

"I may here note that I heard from Akbar Huseyn of a case in which liberties had been taken by an English official with a Hindu woman, whose husband's relations, finding her 'no longer of any use to them,' killed her and laid her outside his tent. The case was taken up, and though there was no kind of doubt as to the facts, those who brought it forward were proceeded against by the Government as having brought a malicious charge, and were sentenced to a fine of one thousand rupees each, and three months imprisonment. My informant added: 'They will never allow a charge to be substantiated against an official for fear of injuring the British character.'

"*23rd Jan.*—Ikhram Ullah brought us four Mohammedan gentlemen, with whom we conversed about the political position to be taken up by Mohammedans in India, and their opinion seemed to be that there should be more common action with the Hindus. But one of them was of opinion that the Hindus were impracticable, because they would not permit the killing of cows. He and Kadi Huseyn, a Shiah, talked English, but the Sunnis talked none.

"Later we went with Robinson, our black host, to see the fort and the great mosque, among the few wonders of the world. The mosque is far and away the finest mosque, the palace far and away the finest palace; and, except Madura, they stand together first in the universe. The palace is full of intense interest, for it was here that the great events of the last three hundred years happened, and in modern times that the last Emperor of Delhi, after the retaking of the city by the English, was tried ignominiously for murder. A dentist whom we met today tells us he happened to go into the hall of audience during the trial, and saw this last of the Mogul kings crouched before the Military Commission, dressed in a piece of sacking and a coarse turban 'like a coolie.' Here, too, the English soldiers slew and destroyed some thousands of innocent men in revenge for the death of about one hundred. The old Loharo chief assures us 26,000 persons were killed by the soldiers or hanged or shot or 'blown up' during the eight months following the capture of the city. The city was deserted, and whole quarters and suburbs razed to the ground. Such are the resources of civilization. The dentist says he saw nineteen men hanging together in one spot, and put the number executed at several thousands. I suppose no Englishman will ever dare write the real history of that year.

"We dined with the Nawab, his son, Prince Suliman Jah, and Ikhram Ullah, and had some instructive conversation. The son, Emir-ed-din Feruk Mirza, who is now reigning chief of Loharo, gave me an amusing account of how young princes were brought up by the British Government when it happened to become their guardian. They are taught to ride and play lawn tennis, and the Resident writes that they are enlightened and loyal princes. Then they are placed on the throne, but find it dull, and go to Calcutta where they spend their money. Then they come back and grind their subjects with taxation, and the Resident writes that they are barbarous and unfit to govern. Lastly, the Government intervenes and administers the country for them. He is a very intelligent young man himself, and his father complains of him because he is too old-fashioned. But I expect he knows better than the old man the ins and outs of our modern diplomacy. The old man is a curious type. During the Mutiny, he tells me, he remained in the city because he could not leave it. But he kept up communication with the English, and for this reason he was not hanged, as most people were, or his property entirely confiscated. It is quite evident to me, however, that, while expressing loudly his loyalty, all his sympathies are with the old *régime*. What he did not like about the mutineers was that most of them were Hindus. But Heaven forgive me if he loves the English. Things, too, have changed mostly since then, and it is my firm conviction that in the case of a new mutiny every man, woman, and child, Mohammedan and Hindu, will join it. The Nawab is a bit of a humbug, but I like him all the same. He belongs to a school which is rapidly passing away, the school which allied itself with the English Government from motives of interest, or sometimes out of a sincere admiration for some individual Englishman. All this is gone. The old men's loyalty has become lip service, and the young men hardly conceal their thoughts. Nothing is more striking in India than the absolute want, at the present day, of native enthusiasm for any particular man. Lord Ripon had this till lately, but he is the last who will have had it.

"*24th Jan.*—We were to have gone on an expedition with Prince Suliman to the tombs of his ancestors, and the Kottub; but it has been put off, luckily as it turns out, for Colonel Moore came in to-day to see us from Meerut. I would not have missed him for much, as he is the only Englishman I have met who quite understands the natives, and sympathizes with our ideas. He is acting as bear-leader to the Duke of Connaught, where he lives in an uncongenial atmosphere, for he describes the Duke and Duchess as being of high Tory ideas about English rule in India, quite unsympathetic with the people. Even if they wished to see anything of them it would be impossible, for there is great jealousy on the part of the Indian Government.

"We talked over the whole situation in India, and agreed that it was impossible so absolutely unsympathetic a Government should not come into collision, some day, with the people. The Indians were the gentlest people in the world, and the easiest to govern, or we could not maintain our rule for an hour. As it was, they had only to combine against us passively to make the whole machine stop working. About Egypt, where he acted as Chief Interpreter, he gave us some valuable information. He knew the whole of the Palmer history, and had read the report whose existence the Government denied. In it Palmer stated that he had spent £25,000 on his first journey between Gaza and Suez on bribing the Bedouins. This money was secret service money, immense sums of which had been expended. He had seen and talked to Sultan Pasha, and described him as a 'miserable fellow.' On the day of the Khedive's entry he had been in the streets and heard the mob cursing the Khedive and all his family, and cursing the English. He had refused to stay in Egypt, as, knowing Arabic, he did not like being perpetually insulted. On the other hand he was no Arabist. He had not seen Arabi, and did not believe in his patriotism.

"Colonel Moore took us round the city, along the ridge which the English held during the siege, and explained the strategical position clearly; and he showed the spot in the Chunda Chowk where the bodies of the King's two sons were thrown by Hodson after he had shot them. He had taken them prisoners at Humayum's tomb, and had promised them their lives, but explained that a crowd had gathered round on his way back to the city with them, and so he had taken a rifle from the troopers, and shot them both where they sat in their carriage. The King he had spared, and he had been sent to die a prisoner at Rangoon. It is a hideous story one side and the other; but what is certain is, that for every hundred English killed, the English exacted a thousand native lives, mostly of innocent men. So, too, the Bedouins seized by Warren in revenge of the Palmer murder were not those who did the deed. This admission from Moore, who, better than any man, knew the details of this business, is of importance. He said the official lies told about Egypt passed all bounds of belief.

"While we were sitting talking after our drive, a letter came, about which Primrose had telegraphed me some days ago. It was from Baring, delivering to me officially a message from Sherif Pasha to the effect that I should not be permitted to land in Egypt. Moore was much amused to learn how matters stood. I expect Baring is personally annoyed at all I told him having come true. On the other hand, Primrose telegraphs that Lord Ripon says I am at full liberty to accept Cordery's invitation to the Residency at Hyderabad, a much more important matter to me just now than visiting Egypt. I look upon the university scheme as certain of success.

"*25th Jan.*—I have written out a 'draft scheme of the Deccan University,'[1] and posted it to Salar Jung with a letter for the Nizam. I am satisfied with it. Also I have written a letter to Gordon about his mission to the Soudan, which was announced in the telegrams two days ago. I consider that he will certainly come to grief if he holds to

[1] See Appendix.

the opinion he expressed to me last year about the necessity for Egypt of retaining Khartoum. I have a letter of Eddy Hamilton's in my possession now, saying that he, Gordon, was considered in Downing Street to be out of his mind. But time works strange revenges. All this, with about a dozen other letters, I wrote yesterday.

"My letter to Gordon is as follows:

"Delhi, *24th January*, 1884.

"My Dear General,

"I feel obliged to write to you about your mission to the Soudan. I see it announced to-day by telegraph, without explanation of its object, but I cannot wait till more definite news arrives, and I desire to warn you. It may be you are going there to make peace between the Mahdi and our troops in Egypt, to acknowledge his sovereignty in the Soudan, and arrange terms for the evacuation of Khartoum. If so, I can only wish you God speed. It is a good work, and you will accomplish it. But if, as I fear it may be, from the tradition of some of those in power, the object of your mission is to divide the tribes with a view to retaining any part of the country for the Khedive, to raise men for him, and scatter money, it is bad work, and you will fail. It must be so. Neither your courage nor your honest purpose, nor the inspiration which has hitherto guided you, will bring you success. I know enough to be able to assure you that every honest Mohammedan in Egypt and North Africa and Arabia sympathizes with the Mahdi's cause, not necessarily believing him to have a divine mission, but as representing ideas of liberty and justice and religious government, which they acknowledge to be divine.

For this reason you will only have the men of Belial on your side, and these will betray you.

"I beg you be cautious. Do not trust to the old sympathy which united Englishmen with the Arabs. I fear it is a thing of the past, and that even your great name will not protect you with them. Also consider what your death will mean: the certainty of a cry for vengeance in England, and an excuse with those who ask no better than a war of conquest. I wish I could be sure that all those who are sending you on your mission do not forsee this end. Forgive me if I am wrong in my fears; and believe me yours, very gratefully, in memory of last year,

"WILFRID SCAWEN BLUNT."

"To-day we spent in visiting the great monuments south of Delhi, in company with the Loharos and Prince Suliman Jah, who organized the expedition. We breakfasted at Humayum's tomb, over whom our friends the Loharos said prayers, he being their ancestor, not Prince Suliman's. It was touching to see this, and to notice a little offering of withered flowers on the tomb of a man so long dead. We went to the top of the monument. Prince Suliman, who is well read, or rather well learned, in history, gave us the story of Humayum and his dynasty, and pointed out to us on the Hindu fort the tower from which his great ancestor fell while looking at the stars. They brought him here and buried him, and his widow raised this pile, under which the rest of the members of his family lie. Thirty-five emperors and kings of Delhi lie buried, he told us, within sight of where we stood. Parrots were building in the chinks of stone; but there are guardians still of the tomb. It was here that later the last King of Delhi fled, and was taken by Hodson, with his two sons, while they were praying, and on the way back from here that he shot the young princes, our friends' uncles. We asked him whether they had been brought back here to be buried, and he smiled sarcastically. They were thrown like the corpses of dogs into the street in Delhi, and none knows where they now lie. The King himself lies buried in Rangoon. From this we went across to the beautiful mosque and more beautiful tombs of other ancestors, and of a dead Persian poet, which we found decked with fresh flowers. Our friends talked all the while of these dead heroes as still living, and, when the young Loharo exclaimed 'This country is full of poets and kings and learned men,' I, for a moment, thought he meant at the present day. But it was of those under ground he was talking. The living people of the place are only poor guardians of the tombs who live on alms.

"With the Kottub I was less interested—though we climbed to the top—and mourned with our friends the decay around us. It is here that the bloodiest of all the battles between Hindus and Moslems was fought, 200,000 being slain. We talked of Tamerlane, and I denied he was a Moslem, but my friends warmly supported his character in this respect, and said he was a friend of the Seyyids, though they knew of his cruelty and savage conquests and his pyramids of skulls. But he, too, was their ancestor. With the Prince we talked in Arabic. He is a Shahzadeh through his mother, the daughter of the King of Delhi, and he is great grandson of the Emperor Akbar.

"Coming home, while we were changing horses, I talked to them of the university, about which they enthusiastically promised to busy themselves. It appears that Ikhram Ullah, being Seyd Ahmed's nephew, had told them nothing of this scheme. They spoke strongly against Seyd Ahmed as a 'nature worshipper,' not a Moslem, and the young Loharo will get up the Committee here at Delhi. This visit took the whole day, and we only got back to our hotel at sunset.

"*26th Jan.*—We left Delhi for Ulwar. In the gray of the morning the old man, the elder brother of the Prince but by another mother, called with messages of farewell and a little box containing the Prince's photograph, and some small ornaments, a present from his wife, which being of no value we gladly accepted.

"At Ulwar we were met at the station by the Diwan and the Mohammedans in the Maharajah's employ, and were driven to the house of His Highness's doctor, Dr. Mullen, an Irishman, and an excellent fellow, with a real knowledge of the country, and much sympathy with the people. According to him, Ulwar and Rajputana, generally, are very lightly taxed. The assessment made by Colonel Paulett is only one-sixth of the net produce, and the Maharajah constantly remits arrears. Of him he spoke very highly as a young man who did his duty well as a ruler, and as being an excellent judge of character. He also praised the Diwan. We discussed most of the political and social problems of India, and he takes rather an optimistic view of things from his experience being almost entirely of Rajputana. But he admitted that in other parts there was a very dangerous ill-feeling between the English and the natives, though he said they would never rebel again after the lesson of the Mutiny. I disagree with him here. On the whole an honest good fellow who does his duty and seems to be liked by all.

"In the evening we called on the Maharajah in

his country palace, and found him with his Court, looking on at lawn tennis. He is very fond of horses and of sport, but it is difficult to have conversation of an intimate nature with a man in his position. Mullen tells me he, the Maharajah, was not highly struck with Laik Ali when they met at Calcutta, but that the Diwan thought well of his abilities.

"The Mohammedans of Ulwar are much in decay. Sheykh Wajidah told me that most of them are hardly Mohammedan except in name, dress like Hindus, and have no education. He himself is from Lucknow, and his friend Enait Ullah, the Commissioner-in-Chief, is also from the North-West. The Maharajah is very liberal to Mohammedans, but the community is not flourishing. They said they had heard of me as a friend of Islam, and were delighted at the university idea. They did not like Seyd Ahmed.

"*27th Jan.*—Visited the city palace, which is one of the most beautiful in the world. We were shown the library, where there was a splendid Koran, and portraits of the Emperors Baber, Humayum, and Akbar. The first two pure Mongols in face, with little slant eyes, the other a regular Brahmin in appearance, as he was in character. Also the armoury.

"In the afternoon we came on to Jeypore.

"*28th Jan.*—Jeypore is a less interesting place than Ulwar, and we saw it in a less interesting manner. The only Mohammedan I met was the hotel guide, an Agra man, who had been educated in the Agra College. He told me there were a good many rich Mohammedans at Jeypore, both Zemindars and in the Army, besides shop-keepers, forming one-third of the population. The chief Mulvi's name is Sadr-ed-Din.

"We called at the Residency, dull people; and waited at home for a couple of hours before the train started, expecting the visit of Mir Kurban Ali, a member of Council, to whom I had written announcing our arrival. But he did not come, which shows how difficult it would be to establish relations, except through introductions.

"We went on through the night towards Bombay.

"*29th Jan.*—All day travelling through an interesting country not unlike Nejd, only far better wooded. The only incident, an English lawyer at the buffet asking me whether I knew that 'Mr. Blunt of Egyptian memories' was in the train. He told us a good deal about Hyderabad, where he has practised; was there when Salar Jung died, and had had an appointment to see him on business that very morning; was of opinion he had not died a natural death, though the Residency doctors had certified it was cholera, but no post mortem was made. Some had put it down to tinned oysters, and several persons present at the picnic had been unwell but recovered. Salar Jung's collapse was sudden and so complete he hardly spoke, and left no orders or directions about anything. There was a great deal of talk at Hyderabad about the probability of faction fights, but he himself did not think it would come exactly to that.

"*30th Jan.*—Arrived at Bombay for breakfast. A pile of letters and newspapers. Gordon already half way to Khartoum, taking with him the ex-King of Darfour. He is sure to come to grief, and I hope my letter will catch him in time.

"Called on Malabari, who, I think, is a little ashamed now of the line he took about the Ilbert compromise. He seems to think they will never get anything now without something like a revolution, which is wholly my own opinion. Also called on Mr. Mandlik, the Hindu Government pleader, who holds the highest position of any native's at the Bombay bar. I told him the Patna story. He told me he had often been insulted himself; on one occasion turned out of a railway carriage neck and crop between Benares and Allahabad. Every native in Bombay had been subjected to such incidents, and he mentioned the instance of the Chief Translator to the Government, promising to furnish me with proofs.

"*1st Feb.*—Finished letters, and then started by midday train for Hyderabad. At dinner, in the refreshment room, saw, for the first time, a native in his own dress. He looked rather shy and nervous, like a *femme honnête* at Mabille, and I asked him if he did not expect to be rudely treated. He said 'Oh, they look at me, but I am not afraid.' He was a Mohammedan tradesman, and before going he gave me his card. When I told him my name, he said he had heard of me through the newspapers.

"*2nd Feb.*—All day in the train, which was several hours behind time owing to the crowds of people flocking to the installation—everything at the refreshment room at Wady eaten up by the Viceroy, who is just ahead of us—flags, greens, and flowers at all the stations—finally arriving at 9 p.m., to find that Cordery and all his guests are at Bolarum, so that we have had an eleven mile drive on the top of the railway journey. Solomon and the luggage only turned up this morning, 3rd February, having slept out somewhere on the road."

CHAPTER IX

THE NIZAM'S INSTALLATION

"*3rd Feb.*

"WE are established in tents at a camp just outside the Residency, where Kurshid Jah does the honours to all strangers in the Nizam's name. It consists of a large *shamiana* and fifteen principal tents arranged in a street, with flowers, in pots, down the whole row—very pretty certainly, but it wants the natural attraction of camp life, the individual choice of site one always finds in Arabia, and there are no beasts of burden near it, so that it has an unlocomotive look, 'like a swan on a turnpike road.' However, here we are. The tents seem to be occupied principally by members of the various suites, for the Commissioner-in-Chief is here, as well as the Viceroy, and the only *bona fide* traveller besides ourselves is Gorst. He tells me Churchill has written to me urging me to come home at once, as a great campaign is beginning in Parliament. We talked over Churchill's speeches. He said he would have to modify the one on the franchise, but approved of the Irish one, as I do, although I don't agree with a word of it, wishing to see Ireland independent. He asked me what I thought of the Egyptian speech, and I said '*C'est magnifique, mais ce n'est pas la guerre.*' It has probably had something to do with the upset of Sherif's ministry, but it has spoiled Arabi's chance, at least for the present.

"This has been a day of profit. We breakfasted at the Residency with the Viceroy, who received us very cordially, and then drove down to Hyderabad, where we called on the Clerks and Keays to get news. Clerk is evidently very much down on his luck, as he tells us Salar Jung is. They consider that Cordery and Kurshid Jah are carrying all before them. The idea of cholera in Hyderabad is all a 'plant' to get the Viceroy away from sources of intelligence. There has been no cholera, but Kurshid Jah cunningly chose, when his choice was given, to superintend the arrangements outside the town, leaving the internal arrangements to Salar Jung. His idea was that the Viceroy would decide the dispute about the Diwanship, and that the Viceroy would take Cordery's advice or Durand's; but I think he has outwitted himself, for Lord Ripon will leave the choice to the Nizam, and so in all probability it will fall to Salar Jung. Bushir-ed-Dowlah is in a great rage because the question of his precedence over Kurshid Jah has been decided against him. At first he threatened to leave the country and never return, but when he heard the news of the Nizam's installation being fixed for this year he was pacified, as he believes the Nizam can reverse the decision. His secretary, Colonel C., told me this, and that when the news arrived he laughed 'from the top of his head to the soles of his feet.' And he, Bushir-ed-Dowlah, is also delighted at the birth of the Nizam's son and heir, because it cuts Kurshid Jah's son out of the succession. And so he has given up his idea of exile. Keay is full of a new letter he has written to Lord Ripon about the railway scheme, which certainly seems a famous swindle. I sent a letter by him to Salar Jung, begging him to see me to-morrow, and to send Seyd Huseyn and Rasul Yar Khan. The nuisance of being out here at Bolarum is beyond conception; and Lord Ripon has told Anne that he is much disgusted at it. Walter

Pollen, who has to do aide-de-camp's duty to-morrow, will have to drive seventy-two miles backwards and forwards in the day.

"We dined at the Residency, Anne sitting between Lord Ripon and Mr. Grant Duff, I next to Primrose, an arrangement made on purpose; and he and I talked the whole time. We began about Baring's letter and my relations with Downing Street and the Foreign Office, about which I spoke with absolute frankness, as well as about my relations with Churchill. He said the letter had surprised him; and it is evident Eddy has written to him lately, for he said he believed I was for Halim's return to Egypt. He talked with the same apparent frankness, and we discussed the advantage of telling the truth in politics. He assured me neither Lord Ripon nor he ever lied about public matters; the most he himself ever did was in the case of impertinent questions being asked him, when he thought a lie was sometimes necessary. I told him Lyall's views on the subject, and we discussed Lytton's character, and Dufferin's. He asked me my opinion of Dufferin, and I told him I did not consider him at all a serious man; but I thought he would make, in some ways, a successful Viceroy, because he would take the Indians in with his good manners and sympathy and pretty speeches, but he would do nothing for them in the way of giving them liberty. He told me he had been in correspondence with Malabari; and that it had been touch and go work when the Ilbert Bill was compromised. Malabari had written to him very frankly on the subject, and he had shown the letter to one of the civilians, whose only remark had been, 'What cheek of a native to write like that.' I warned him not to try such tricks as the compromise twice; and he seemed quite to admit that it was a shady business, and that nothing but Lord Ripon's immense popularity pulled him through. 'Lord Ripon,' he said, 'was very near going down to posterity in India as a traitor instead of a benefactor.'

"We then talked about the Patna business, and he said inquiries had been made; but I told him it was useless making them through the civilians, and that Lord Ripon should send down one of his own aides-de-camp—and I suggested Walter Pollen—to hear their complaints. He promised as soon as they got back to Calcutta to have the inquiry properly made. But I must insist further on this. I got him also to take down Ragunath Rao's name for Lord Ripon to see him as he went back through Madras, and Mandlik's at Bombay. The latter, however, he already knew. I saw Trevor watching us. He was sitting opposite, but could not hear what we were talking about. Cordery, too, looks very uneasy. I don't think Lord Ripon has talked to him at all yet.

"After dinner Lord Ripon came to me and took me aside into an inner room, and asked me my opinion as to whether the Nizam would speak frankly to him about his wishes, as he considered that these wishes ought to be the first consideration in appointing to the Diwanship. I told him that it entirely depended on his own manner towards the Nizam, and that if he took the Nizam by the arm, and spoke kindly to him and reassured him, and told him that no ill consequences would follow, and he would not be dethroned or deported or otherwise punished, he no doubt would speak exactly what he thought. I felt sure he had been intimidated by people here (meaning Cordery), and would require encouragement. Here at Hyderabad he was quite a different being from what Lord Ripon had seen him at Calcutta. I had seen him looking frightened here, as if afraid to speak. Lord Ripon then spoke about the difficulty there was in finding any one to advise the new Diwan for his good. All the English about him wanted money and things for themselves. I said that it required somebody who really wished well to the Hyderabad state, that I felt sure there would be no difficulty in making things go well if the will was there. I could do it myself, I was confident, if I only had time to devote to it. But who in the world was there? I then told Lord Ripon about the university scheme, and seeing him interested, said that I had hopes the Nizam would make himself its patron—indeed, I believed he had the intention of speaking to Lord Ripon about it—and hoped he would give it his approval. Lord Ripon said he quite approved of it, and thought it would do great good, and agreed with me that a religious basis was essential to all education, and he should certainly encourage the Nizam to proceed with it. He answered me, laughing, that he acquitted me of all idea of preaching sedition. This is very satisfactory.

"*4th Feb.*—It struck me, during the night, that Moore would be the man to make things go here, and I shall certainly propose it to Lord Ripon, that he should be appointed special adviser to the Diwan. At breakfast sat next to Primrose and Father Kerr, and afterwards talked to Primrose about Lord Ripon's coming interview with the Nizam, and impressed upon him strongly the necessity of reassuring the Nizam, for I was certain intimidation was exercised on him by Cordery. I also explained my view of the action of the Foreign Office with regard to Hyderabad, how they had feared Lord Ripon might give back the Berar province, and so had connived at misgovernment in order to make this impossible. The retention of Berar was a cardinal point of policy with the Foreign Office, and they did not scruple about the means. We were then interrupted by Primrose being sent for by Lord Ripon, and while I was waiting till this was over, the guard of honour and band arrived for the Nizam's visit, and we went back to our tent to be out of the way.

"Primrose told me to-day that he was in correspondence with Godley, but very little with Hamilton, that he had been quite as averse to the Egyptian War as Godley was: and I warned him that they must not think of sending Indian troops against the Mahdi, as the Mohammedans would be very indignant. (He said there was no chance of that, and that it had been a great question in 1882 how the Mohammedans would take the sending of troops.) But they had a great respect for the Sultan as long as he appeared as their champion; they would not listen to him if he went against them; they did not care much for his spiritual claims, witness that they were publishing my book in Urdu at Calcutta.

"The Nizam's visit was announced by a salute of twenty-one guns, and I hear from Walter Pollen that after the ceremony His Highness had a long talk of over half an hour with the Viceroy, and came out looking much excited; so I fancy he has told all his thoughts. At luncheon were Bushir-ed-Dowlah and Salar Jung, and I sat next the latter, and improved the occasion, and had a talk with him also afterwards on the verandah. I told him of my conversation last night with Lord Ripon, and assured him that the choice of a Diwan would be left to the Nizam. This, he said, he had been told by Mr. Durand on his way back from Calcutta. But he asked me several times, and earnestly, 'Are you sure Lord Ripon means well to us, to the Hyderabad State?' I told him I was sure of it, but not of the Foreign

Office. The Foreign Office and the Viceroy were two very different things. 'Oh yes,' he said, 'we know that. But are you sure of Lord Ripon?' I said: 'Very sure, and I intend to propose to him to appoint some Englishman, whose duty it will be to counsel the Diwan, not in English, but in Hyderabad interests.'

"I then talked to him about the university, and he said the Nizam would certainly take it up, but not till after the ceremonies. He would not have time to think of it. But I urged on him very strongly not to let the Nizam miss the opportunity of announcing at least his intention to the Viceroy. He seemed surprised to hear that Lord Ripon should have approved the scheme, but said, if that was the case, the Nizam should certainly speak to him. I then gave him some good advice. I said: 'You are likely now to be made Diwan, and so you will have, after the Nizam, the highest position of any Mohammedan in India. If you aspire to lead the Mohammedan world you must be careful not to offend their prejudices. You should hold a middle course. The general of an army does not go forward reconnoitring. He stays with the main body. This you must do. Be careful not to be too European in your dress or thoughts, or at any rate language, for this will give offence.' He said: 'It is hard for one brought up as I have been.' 'But,' I said, 'you must sacrifice something if you are to play a great political part. Don't at any rate throw yourself too entirely into the Aligarh set.' He said: 'Oh, I don't care about Seyd Ahmed. My father always used to say he was a humbug. He cared only for display.' I said: 'I don't want you to go so far as that, but be moderate and be careful.'

"I trust that Laik Ali may become Diwan, for,

under good guidance at starting, he may make a very good minister. I am sure he means well, but he is a bit childish, and his manner is not quite so good as one would wish. He has an abrupt way of talking, which strangers might take for rudeness; some have, as I know. I noticed that Cordery's manner to him and Bushir-ed-Dowlah was not *empressé*. Bushir-ed-Dowlah was in high spirits. Salar Jung has not told Rasul Yar Khan of my arrival, giving as his reason that yesterday he, Rasul Yar Khan, being Sadr es Sadur, was occupied all day with the Nizam, praying with him on the occasion of his birthday. I feel pretty sure, however, that there was some other reason, and hold to my belief that he and the Nizam and Vikar-el-Omra were warned against me in Calcutta, probably by Stewart Bailey. His manner to-day was very cordial as in old times, but I noticed he seemed a little uneasy, as if watching to see who might be watching us.

"Father Kerr sat at my other hand at lunch. He is sad, having just received a telegram announcing his mother Lady Henry Kerr's death, whom I used to know so well years ago at Huntlyburn.

"We stayed quiet all the afternoon, and dined at the camp, as there is a large official dinner at the Residency. I sat next to Mr. Lambert, the head of the secret police, who said he had heard from Primrose about the Patna affair, and was making investigations. I gave him an exact narration of the thing, which he did not seem to have had correctly; and he expressed unbounded astonishment at it, as an incident the like of which had not occurred in his twenty-one years' experience. He would not hear of its being a common thing for natives to be insulted on the railways, and seemed even a little to doubt my accuracy. But I think I convinced him, at any rate, about the particular incident. As an instance of the contrary, he told me how Villayet Ali had written to him and asked for a special compartment for himself and friends to go to the Exhibition a little while before, and how he had willingly written to the station master about it. But the tale seems to me to prove, if anything, the danger natives run—or why should a special compartment be needed?

"At half-past 9 o'clock we went to the Viceroy's *levée*, and Lord Ripon, as soon as he saw me, came to me rubbing his hands, and said, 'Well, I have had my talk with him [the Nizam], and I flatter myself, at last, that he has told me everything.' Lord Ripon did not say precisely what this everything was, but I gathered from him in our subsequent conversation, which lasted about a quarter of an hour, that there had been some 'eye-openers.' 'There is no doubt either,' he said, 'about his wishes. He spoke them strongly and decidedly; and my opinion clearly is that they ought to be followed.' I did not press to know whom it was the Nizam wished for as Diwan, for I shall learn that later, but I feel no doubt it is Salar Jung. I asked Lord Ripon, however, whether on the whole he had been favourably impressed by the young Prince, and he said: 'Oh, very much so. He has ideas and opinions of his own. But I told him things which I fancy he is not likely to hear again, and which will be good for him.' So I suppose he has given him a thorough good talking to about his morals. Lord Ripon was anxious to know, and asked me to find out if possible, what the Nizam's own impression of the interview had been, and I shall probably be able to do so to-morrow.

"I then suggested to him my idea about an official adviser being appointed to the Diwan, whoever he might be, with written instructions to work in Hyderabad interests, not those merely of the Indian Government; and I expressed my opinion strongly about the Foreign Office policy in respect of the Berars. Lord Ripon would not admit that I was correct in my view of the case, but his protest was feebly made. The essential in any settlement of the Hyderabad problem is to remember that the Resident cannot be trusted to advise for good. What Lord Ripon said was: 'Would not this be introducing new Englishmen into Hyderabad? It seems to me that there are too many already. I should like to make a clean sweep of them all.' I said: 'By all means make a clean sweep.' I suggested, however, that Moore might be intrusted with the new duty, as a man who really understood and sympathized with the native races, and really wished them well.

"We were talking a quarter of an hour in this way, very much in evidence, and I noticed poor Cordery watching, and Clerk once even came up and interrupted our conversation. I don't know what they can all think of my position here as the Viceroy's adviser, in spite of the 'Wind and the Whirlwind,' and everything else. Indeed, it is a singular one, and it shows how strangely politics are managed here, and at home, too, for that matter, for I am going about with a decree of exile from Egypt in my pocket, no more nor less than if I was a proclaimed rebel.

"5*th Feb.*—A day to be marked with white. We went quite early into Hyderabad to the Clerks, where we had tea, and then went on to the Chou Mahaila Palace, which is the old palace where installations have always taken place, and where Mahbub Ali was this morning installed. The city was a magnificent sight, crowded with people and decked with flags, the people most of them sitting on the ground, and even some of the soldiers on duty so seated, as they used to be at Haïl. Everything was most orderly, with the single exception of one man, probably an Arab, who seemed to have been making a disturbance, for he had a sword drawn in his left hand, and was being led away by four or five others. We arrived at the same time as Cordery, and walked through the palace garden to the open hall where the Durbars are held. Here the nobles were assembling, and those officers of the English cantonments who had received invitations, perhaps one hundred and fifty of each, the natives occupying the right, the English the left of the thrones. We had reserved seats, Anne's close to the thrones, mine a little way down, and I sat next to Lambert and close to Gorst. We had an hour to wait, but we occupied it talking to Rasul Yar Khan, Seyd Huseyn Bilgrami, and others of our friends, who were in fine feather, for our balloon has gone up at last, and at 2 o'clock last night Salar Jung was named Munir el Mulk and Diwan. The news began to be whispered round, though it seemed too good to be true, for, till the last moment, it had been believed that Cordery and the Foreign Office would carry the day. But it was soon proved by the arrival of the Peishkar, who came to take his seat next the thrones but was bundled out of it, to his confusion, and made to take his chair several places down. Poor old man, he seemed quite dazed, for it was the first he had heard of his disgrace.

"There was a good deal of confusion, too, among the nobles, and C. whispered to me that his Nawab, Bushir-ed-Dowlah, had fainted just as he stepped into his carriage, the news being brought to him that his chair had been put below Kurshid Jah's, and so had gone home to bed. But the triumph of the Salar Jung party was crowned when he and Saadut Ali arrived with the Nizam, all three wearing yellow turbans in sign of their alliance. Salar Jung, I must say, showed considerable dignity and absence of visible elation; but the *coup de théâtre* to us who knew what lay behind the scenes was all the more striking. The Nizam and Viceroy arrived together, and sat down together on two chairs in front of the two equal thrones, and, after some announcement made by Mr. Henderson, who did the duty of herald, Lord Ripon made an excellent speech full of good advice and piety, though I was a little disappointed that he did not allude to the Nizam's position as head of the Mohammedans of India, but perhaps this was thought indiscreet. Lord Ripon alluded, however, to old Salar Jung's services to the State, and declared the policy of the Indian Government to be that of peace and goodwill towards the Nizam's, and the encouragement of good government and progress.

"The speech affected me almost to tears, and it seemed to affect the Nizam, whose answer, drawn up for him by Sèyd Huseyn, was almost inaudible. He behaved, however, with considerable dignity during the rather trying quarter of an hour when, seated on his throne by Lord Ripon's side and girt by that nobleman with a new diamond-hilted sword, put on on the wrong side, he waited to be photographed, for such was the banal termination. Swords also were given to Salar Jung, Peishkar, and Kurshid Jah, the latter's with an ivory hilt, reminding one of a large paper cutter, perhaps lest he should go home and commit suicide with it, for he must have been very angry. I hear the poor Peishkar was so utterly confounded that he walked home immediately after the ceremony without waiting for his carriage, and was picked up somewhere in the street by his servants, having lost his way. But this may be an exaggeration. Lord Ripon has a pleasant voice speaking, but his style is that of a sermon, which, however, suited the occasion, and all the Hyderabadis, except the disgraced nobles, seemed delighted with him. I believe this appointment of Salar Jung to be generally popular. But Rasul Yar Khan told me there were some who were not best pleased.

"Then we drove back to Mrs. Clerk's, where the Commissioner-in-Chief and Sir Frederick Roberts were also invited to luncheon. Sir Donald Stewart is a dear old fogey, but with wits enough to appreciate Colonel Moore, and Sir Frederick is a gallant officer of the unostentatious, strictly professional type. I like them both. We stayed there the afternoon, and went in the evening to a great banquet at the Palace, in the new part of it, which is extremely handsome and built in excellent taste only about twenty years ago by an Italian architect. The illuminations, both in the Palace and in the city, and for miles round, surpass anything I ever saw attempted in Europe, even at Paris in the palmy days of the Empire. There were at least two hundred guests at this dinner, which was held in a very long hall. Anne was taken in by the Viceroy, but I had to shift for myself, and was fortunate enough to get hold of Seyd Ahmed, the Persian attaché and translator of the Foreign Office, an Afghan with whom I had a most instructive conversation. He had been educated by some missionaries at Peshawar, and is to a certain extent denationalized, but is a good Sunni, and seems still fond of his own people. He was employed in that mission to Shere Ali which was refused admittance to Ali Musjid. I asked him his candid opinion about the Afghan War, and he said he could not approve it either at the time or now, though Shere Ali had brought it on himself by intriguing with the Russians. He said, moreover, that any Mohammedans who might have pretended to me that they approved the war were hypocrites, for all were strongly against it. The Mohammedans of India were, nevertheless, loyal as a body, though not all. They were so from interest. He lamented the quarrels which divided them, and was sure I was doing a good work in bringing them together. If they only were united, and knew their strength, the Government would be obliged to do something for them. But they were far from united. He did not approve of Seyd Ahmed of Aligarh, though far from a bigot. He had been brought up an utter bigot till he went to school at Peshawar, but now his ideas were changed. He also told me he had travelled with Major Napier in Persia, and corroborated much of what Malkum Khan had told me of the Persians. He was of opinion that they were doomed to fall to Russia, they were so much diminished in numbers, only three to five millions in a territory as large as India. Afghanistan was far more prosperous. He would not hear of his countrymen being treacherous, except to Englishmen, who they thought were spies, or in cases of blood feuds among themselves. He thought I might travel safely among them, and the best way to go would be through Persia. He had heard Malkum Khan's history, much as I had heard it from Malkum Khan himself. I met Vikar-el-Omra after dinner, who seemed in his old friendly mood. I asked him how he liked the new political arrangement, and he said he thought he did, but Salar Jung was very young to be Diwan. I believe his idea had been a council of seven, with himself as one of them. So he is naturally a little disappointed. I told him I thought the success or non-success of Salar Jung would depend mainly on the kind of advicc given him by the Resident. We slept at Bolarum.

"*6th Feb.*—A telegram from Ferid-ed-Din begging me to congratulate the Nizam in the name of the Mohammedans of Allahabad and the North-West Provinces, and also a letter signed by some hundred of the chief Mohammedans of Patna expressing their confidence in me. I have written to Salar Jung with the first message to beg him to remind the Nizam of his promise to speak to the Viceroy about the university, for it appears that Lord Ripon told Anne he had expected the Nizam to broach the subject. But they seem lukewarm about it, and, if they don't take it up more seriously than they seem now inclined to do, I shall wash my hands of them, and look to Lucknow as a better place. It would ruin the scheme to establish it here without thorough and determined support.

"We went to a review with Sir Frederick Roberts, and had a good deal of talk about Egypt and the Mahdi. There is a telegram to-day announcing a new victory and Baker's flight from Tokat. It seems, too, certain that some at least of the Khedive's troops went over to the Mahdi. This will seal the fate of Khartoum, I hope, before Gordon arrives there. But the military here all count on a campaign with Indian troops. I warned them, however, that such an adventure would be most unpopular with the Mohammedans of India, and with all classes of natives.

"We lunched with the Viceroy, but everybody was busy with the mail which goes this evening, and my only conversation was with Cordery about architecture. I feel that he is very angry with me, and no wonder. I hope Lord Ripon won't leave him here. It is not in human nature that, having been foiled in his plans and forced to recognize Salar Jung as Minister, he should cordially support him, and less than cordial support will not do.

"There was another great banquet this evening, at the Bolarum mess rooms, given by Cordery to the Viceroy and the Nizam, and before it Lord Ripon again took me aside, and asked if I was satisfied with the arrangements he had made, and if I had found out what the Nizam really thought of the lecture he had given him. I said I was sure it had had the best effect, and later I made certain of it by asking the Nizam himself, whom I found exceedingly nice about this, and about the university, which he seems really interested in. He did not however, as I had expected him to do, speak to Lord Ripon about it at the dinner; but he will to-morrow, at a Council which they are to have at the Residency, and he has told Anne that he wants to have the university here near the town, perhaps at Serinagar. He seemed also immensely pleased at the interest taken in him by the Mohammedans of India, and if he is encouraged he is sure to go on well. I told Lord Ripon all this again after dinner, and again proposed appointing an official adviser to the Diwan, independent of the Resident, and Lord Ripon said there was certainly something in the idea, and I am to have a private talk with him to-morrow.

"Everything, therefore, is going on wheels. Seyd Huseyn Bilgrami, however, with whom I had a long talk, says the Government of India will never consent to such a plan, and asked me besides whom they could possibly trust to advise them for their good. I mentioned Moore, and he said he knew him and had a high opinion of him, but the Government would never consent. I told him Lord Ripon was capable of doing many things the Government of India did not like, and I have some hope the idea may be taken up. Otherwise we must get rid of Cordery. It seems Lord Ripon is likely now to stay out his time in India, which is a good thing, as it will give things a start. I told Seyd Huseyn I was sure, if they were going badly, the Nizam might write to Lord Ripon, or perhaps it would be better, on smaller matters, Seyd Huseyn should write to Primrose. I was glad to see Seyd Huseyn at this banquet of Cordery's, as it shows his position is re-established. It is just two months since Cordery announced his intention of exiling Seyd Huseyn, and, in fact, gave him notice to quit. Of course Cordery is angry.

"Colonel Dobbs, whom I sat next to at the dinner table, declares the Foreign Office will not allow any official proceedings to be taken against the 'Statesman' for its libels, but that Abd-el-Hak will probably bring a private action. He also talked about the railway scheme, which he defended, but not, as I thought, very successfully. He said he thought there would be no greater loss than at present over the old railway, and it might be found to pay. He is a director of the old line, and attributed its non-payment to the action of the Indian Government, which for political purposes had insisted, in opposition to Sir Salar Jung, on having the line run through an unremunerative country. All these admissions are of value from a man avowedly hostile to Salar Jung. Geary, editor of the 'Bombay Gazette,' sat at my other hand, and we had a deal of conversation.

"In talking to Lord Ripon I mentioned my disappointment at his having made no allusion to the fact of the Nizam's being the head of the Mohammedans in India, but he said 'We didn't dare do that. We had to remember that though a Mohammedan prince, he has many more Hindu than Mohammedan subjects.' I did not press it further.

"*7th Feb.*—We spent the morning at the Residency, looking over some colts which Ali Abdallah had brought for Sir Frederick Roberts's inspection, and after luncheon I had a long talk with the General about Egypt, especially as to our military position there. I asked him whether it was not a mistake to occupy a country against the will of its inhabitants, instead of seeking their friendship. And he said certainly it was elementary in military matters to hold as little disaffected territory as possible. This was the mistake which had been made in Afghanistan. It had been his idea there to leave the Afghans to choose their own ruler, which would have been the best way of gaining their friendship. But the authorities had decided on having a man of their own choosing, and they had put up Abd-el-Rahman, and were now obliged to subsidize him heavily to keep him on his throne. I told him no amount of subsidies would keep Tewfik on his. He then asked me why Arabi had not defended the Canal, and I told him that it was from the idea he had that England would come to terms with him, and he did not want to offend all Europe. He said they would have come to terms if Arabi had won the battle of Kassassin instead of losing it. He then observed that he considered Egypt a very difficult country for us to hold, that it could be easily invaded from Syria. But to this I would not altogether agree, as there was only one road by which troops could possibly march, and that was not an easy one. I told him, however, I considered that the Power which wished to hold the Suez Canal should certainly look to its position in Syria, and we then discussed the best line of defence against Russia. I told him I thought the line from Scanderum to the Euphrates the shortest, and therefore the best, and I drew him a sketch map of the hills and rivers. He said he had been consulted about the possibility of holding Diarbekr against the Russians, but had come to the conclusion that it would be almost impossible now that Kars was gone. To this I quite agreed. Another advantage, too, of the line between Scanderum and Aleppo is that it fairly marks the division of the Arabic and Turkish speaking populations. I fancy, however, another line of defence could be found further south if this one would not do. I like Sir Frederick. He is a man without pretence, and I have no doubt a real good soldier.

"In the afternoon we drove to the Mir Alum Tank in procession behind the Viceroy, much, as we believe, to Cordery's disgust, for he raised difficulties about the carriage, and certainly discouraged our going. But Anne had been particularly invited by the Nizam himself, and the Viceroy supports us openly. So we went. The Nizam was very amiable to us, and Salar Jung asked me to stay on a day or two and come to breakfast with him, and talk things over. We steamed round and round the lake for an hour, and then had our photographs taken in a group, where I figure between Salar Jung and Cordery—I have no doubt to his still greater disgust—just behind the Viceregal chair—Anne, and Mr. and Mrs. Grant Duff seated with the Nizam and Lord Ripon;—Vikar-el-Omra, Saadut Ali, Mohammed Ali Bey, and a certain grouping of aides-de-camp behind, one of whom was Walter, make up the party. This will be historical.

"We dined at the Residency, but went to bed instead of to the ball given at the Bolarum mess, for we are really at the end of our tether.

"*8th Feb.*—This morning, after breakfast, Lord Ripon sent for me, and we talked over the Patna business. I read over to him the strongest passages of the letters I had received about it, and suggested that it would be far more soothing to their outraged feelings if he sent one of his own aides-de-camp (*e.g.*, Walter Pollen), than if he had the enquiry conducted through the regular channels. He promised to consider this, and, I think, will act in accordance. Next, I asked him to see Ragunath Rao when at Madras, and he promised to do so, and he took his address, and I warned him he was not in favour with the officials. Then I spoke to him about Gordon, who is reported in this morning's telegram to have been captured by the Mahdi's people; and I told him if it should be found necessary, I believed I could go to the Mahdi without much danger, and I told him, under secrecy, of the Sheykh I had met who was in communication with the Mahdi, and who, I believed, would go with me. But he said he feared the Government at home looked upon me with too much disfavour to think of making use of me, though for his part he should not mind recommending it, if asked his opinion.

"Lastly, Lord Ripon talked to me, though I did not begin it, about the position here. He asked me to speak to Salar Jung, first, about the finances of the country, and urge him to declare the whole deficit, or floating debt, at once. He had reason to believe it was a large one. Next, to recommend him not to quarrel with Abd-el-Hak, who, he told me, was strongly supported by the India Office, and was too clever a man not to be dangerous if neglected. It would be better—though I was not to deliver this as a message—to provide him with a place. It would be only prudent to shut Abd-el-Hak's mouth. The railway scheme was powerfully supported at home, and he believed there was some exaggeration in the charge it would be on the Nizam's Government. He thought it might pay. At least it was not certain to be a loss. I did not, however, understand from Lord Ripon that the scheme was approved beyond the possibility of disavowal, though Seyd Huseyn, whom I saw later in the afternoon, seemed to think it was so. Lastly, I was to assure Salar Jung that as long as he, Lord Ripon, remained in India, he would see that he was properly supported. What might happen after his term of office was over he could not say, but they would have a year, or thereabouts, to establish things on a firm basis, and ought then to be able to take care of themselves. I asked whether, supposing things were again going badly between Salar Jung and the Residency, he might write to Lord Ripon. But Lord Ripon said, 'You had better not give them any such message. They are pretty sure to write without your suggesting it, and I shall keep my eye on the Hyderabad State, and shall be sure to hear if anything is going on wrong. I am glad I have been here, because now I know something of the people and the place, and I shall always take a deep interest in its welfare.' I asked him if the Nizam had spoken about the university, and he said he had. He had expressed his intention in general terms, and apparently without understanding it much, of founding a university, and he, Lord Ripon, had approved, remarking only that he must count the cost, and not embark in any scheme which should burden the finances. I told him we wanted his patronage more than his money, and I promised to see that he was not unfairly pressed to contribute. Then I thanked Lord Ripon for his kindness to me, and took my leave.

"The party at the Residency broke up to-day, the Viceroy and Grant Duff going back to Madras, and we to the Clerks at Chanderghat. The Commissioner-in-Chief went yesterday, and Sir F. Roberts goes to Bombay. Cordery stays a day or two at Bolarum, and goes away, he told us, in April or May, to England for three months leave. This means that he will not return, and there is talk of Henderson as his successor. I don't fancy him. *C'est un grand sec*—the ideal of the office man—not at all what is wanted. We lunched with Seyd Huseyn Bilgrami, who is now practically Minister, and had a long talk about the situation. He said he would certainly draw up a financial statement showing all the deficit, and that he intended to make it his rule to be quite straightforward in all his dealings, on the principle that honesty was the best policy. I told him, of course, that I approved, and that he must remember that the Hyderabad State existed on sufferance, supported only by public opinion at home. The policy of the Indian Foreign Office was one of encroachment, and, but for English opinion, they would annex every independent State; nor would public opinion protect them, except they showed themselves worthy of protection, I said: 'In all your dealings show yourselves honester than the Indian Government. It is not saying much or asking you to do much, but this will be your best protection.' About the railway he seemed to think there was no help for it; but he did not fancy the idea of having dealings with Abd-el-Hak. Abd-el-Hak was a desperate intriguer, and should be suppressed; he was not so clever as people thought; the letters he wrote were not his own; he was incapable of writing anything worth reading. They must make the best they could of a bad job with the railway; it had been imposed upon them with a view to ruining the State; it could not possibly pay more than its working expenses, and there would be a charge for twenty years on the State of £200,000, a tenth of the revenue. It certainly is an outrageous business. About the university he seemed to think there would be much practical difficulty, though he decidedly wished to have it here when I said that we did not absolutely depend upon the Nizam's help. He promised, however, to read over the draft, and talk about it again on Sunday, when I am to have a conference with Salar Jung. Unless they take the thing up more warmly than this, I am inclined to think we had better look elsewhere.

"We had a discussion at luncheon with his brother and Cheragh Ali about the Mahdi, one or two being opposed to him on the ground that he was adverse to the Ottoman Empire, and on the more general one that 'If he is not the Mahdi, he is an impostor; if he is, we ought all to join him'—a thing nobody seemed willing to do. The majority, with Seyd Huseyn, however, agreed that he was a Mohammedan representing Mohammedan interests, and so ought to be supported, and this is very strongly my own view. Dined at the Clerks', and went to bed early.

"*9th Feb.*—Rasul Yar Khan came and spent the morning with us, talking over the university scheme, which he warmly approves, but warns me that it runs great risk of failing in the working out, and would have me keep the management in my own hands. But this I cannot do. He says it must anyhow be independent of the Government here. He will do all he can for it in any case. Also a poet, who calls himself the Bulbul of the Deccan, called with a complimentary ode in the Nizam's honour in English and Persian. He says he can write poetry in seven languages, but his English verse is funny. He travelled, as a boy, with Sir something Binney in Persia, and is now Court poet here.

"Later we went to the races, and I had a few words with Salar Jung about the university. I told him, unless he was prepared to take it up energetically we should look elsewhere than to Hyderabad. The people of the north were determined to have a university, and if not here, would have it at Lucknow or Delhi. He spoke, however, strongly about it, promising to give it all his support, and quite admitted that the advantage received by the Hyderabad State would be as great as any it could give. I told him we did not need the Nizam's money, but his patronage, on account of his great name. He talked of Kalbarga or Aurungabad as suitable places, but Rasul Yar Khan is for Golconda, as being nearer to Hyderabad and containing plenty of buildings. We are, however, to dine to-morrow with Salar Jung, and discuss the whole matter, and the day after at a farewell dinner with the Nizam. If I can bring this to a good end I shall have done enough for one winter. I doubt if ever a university was imagined, planned, preached, and accepted before in six weeks from its first conception. This, however, is only gathering in a harvest I have ploughed and sowed for, and watered with my tears, for almost as many years.

"I have spoken to Clerk about it, and he is strongly in favour of Aurungabad, where he says there are heaps of old buildings, and he introduced me to Mir Abdu es Salaam (Ferdunji, the Parsi Talukdar is the next most important man at Aurungabad), chief Subar there, who happens to be at Hyderabad, and who invited us to stay with him at Aurungabad. Dined with Seyd Huseyn. He showed me, before dinner, a long telegram dictated by Cordery, which has been sent to the 'Times of India,' and of which Seyd Huseyn has obtained this secret copy. It explains the nature of the new council here, which Cordery seems to have invented as a fresh dodge for pulling the strings. It also says the railway scheme is to be pushed on, and explains the reasons which induce him and Trevor to take leave this summer.

"10*th Feb.*—Another visit from the Bulbul, who has brought a copy of Arabic verses composed in our honour, and requests that we will forward to Lord Ripon a rhymed address in seven languages. I have corrected his English version, purged it, that is, of its most absurd blunders, but it still remains a highly amusing composition. He brought his son with him, a bright boy of fourteen.

"Seyd Huseyn came next, and we talked the university scheme over fully. He foresaw great difficulties of administration, which I have no doubt he does not exaggerate. But I think his real doubt was as to the reality of the support I am counting on in the north. This I was able to remove by showing him the addresses I had received, especially from his own town, Lucknow, which bear the signatures of all the great Mulvis. I put it, however, plainly to him whether he was prepared to support the scheme thoroughly, as otherwise I should not risk establishing it at Hyderabad, and he promised to do his very best, especially when I had explained to him the political bearing it would have, and the influence it would bring to the Hyderabad State. We agreed, therefore, to act together in this matter, and it is only now a question of details. He does not fancy Golconda, saying it is unhealthy, and that the buildings there could not be given. He thinks Serinagar far better, but all would have to be built there from the ground. I fancy he would like to have the thing under his own eye and management, as he was formerly professor at the Lucknow College. I do not, however, want the university to be too entirely under Government control here, as one never knows who may succeed to power. A Mohammedan university, unless guaranteed by charter, would run a poor chance in the Peishkar's Hindu hands. Mohammed Kamil then looked in and spoke of the enthusiasm there was among the Mohammedans here for Lord Ripon, because he had saved the State from destruction.

" Lastly came Mademoiselle Gaignaud, the Salar Jung's French governess, who told us a number of extraordinary things connected with Hyderabad life and politics. The late Sir Salar was the best and noblest of men, never said an unkind word or did a dishonest action in his life. All, even his enemies, respected him; and the old Emir el Kebir, the bitterest of them all, sent for him on his death-bed, and recommended his sons to his care. I asked her about Sir Salar's own death, and she told me she had no doubt in the world that he was poisoned. He had not complained of anything till 9 o'clock on the Wednesday evening, the evening of the water party at the Mir Alum tank, and he died at a quarter past seven on the Thursday. On the Tuesday he had dined at the Residency. The symptoms were not those of cholera. There was no vomiting, except such as he himself caused by putting his fingers down his throat. He complained only of a burning in his throat and chest, and great thirst. After death his colour remained unchanged. Of the two English doctors, one said it was not, the other, Beaumont, said it was cholera, but no post mortem examination was made. She drew a fearful scene of the confusion in the Zenana on the occasion, and of the old minister being plied with potions mixed by two holy men, who wrote words in Arabic and Persian and Sanskrit on leaves, and made an infusion of them, the English doctors being only called in after 3 o'clock in the afternoon, when there was no more hope, and his pulse was gone. A crowd of women friends and relations, eight hundred of them, had collected in the house, and when they heard of the Minister's death, for he died in the outer part of the house, they shrieked, and cursed, and screamed, and rolled upon the floor, tearing their clothes, breaking their bracelets, and behaving like mad creatures, nobody fully recovering her senses for a week.

"We dined to-night with Salar Jung. It was a merry party, no English but ourselves and young Hugh Gough who was brought up at school with them. Rasul Yar Khan was there, and Seyd Ali Shustari the poet, who made great fun of his rival, the Bulbul, and the son of a late minister of Oude, and Mohammed Ali Bey, and half a dozen intimates. At dinner there was a deal of fun made about the recent political crisis, the poor old Peishkar's trouble at finding his chair changed, and his wandering in the streets afterwards, and Kurshid Jah's disappointment, and Trevor's discomfiture. Trevor knew nothing till the moment of the installation, nor was anything absolutely settled till 7 o'clock that morning, when the chairs were changed. Salar Jung told us he had had the management of everything in the city himself, down to the *menu* of the banquet, and had planned all the illuminations with his own hand, and the whole had cost no more than 22,000 rupees, while Kurshid Jah had spent, I think he said, four lakhs on what was done outside the city.

"After dinner I had a long private talk with Salar Jung, first of all giving him Lord Ripon's messages and recommendations about the finances, about Abd-el-Hak, and about the promise he made him of support. All these he promised to respond to, and the more readily as Lord Ripon had already spoken to him about them, having taken an opportunity in the train after I saw him. Salar Jung spoke in the warmest terms of Lord Ripon, and I have explained to him the situation as regards English politics thoroughly, and he promises to let me know if new troubles arise, as also to give me copies of certain documents which it may be advisable to make public. He promised to follow the advice about Abd-el-Hak, and to place on record a temperate protest against the railway scheme, leaving the whole responsibility for the injury done to the Hyderabad State on English Government shoulders. We then discussed the character of the principal English statesmen; and he told me that Lytton had been especially kind to him when in England, and he thought very likely he might now regret the harm he had plotted to his father. I told him, however, to trust none of them; and I don't think he will be easily taken in, either by Goschen or Dufferin, should either come as Viceroy to India.

"About the university he is now, I can see, in earnest; he promised to subscribe personally, and also on the part of the State. But I cautioned him to be moderate about the latter. He also considers

Kalbarga as decidedly the best place, as there is a fine old mosque there, recently restored by his father, and plenty of old buildings which we can have. He promises that the Nizam shall write me, without delay, such an answer to my letter to him as we can publish, so as to start the thing; and to push it on with all his might during the next year, while Lord Ripon is still in India. He will write to Kalbarga announcing our arrival on Tuesday. This is by far the most satisfactory talk I have had yet with Salar Jung.

"I see in the papers that it is a false report about Gordon, so I hope he may yet get my letter in time, and take my advice. Things, however, are looking very like a new war.

"11*th Feb.*—We had several visitors to-day, the Bulbul and his son, who brought a poem in our honour, and Seyd Ali Shustari, who brought another poem, and laughed at the Bulbul's. We had a long discussion with him about the Mahdi, who, he said, could not be the real Mahdi because there had not been seven years of famine immediately before his appearance; besides, he was to come suddenly out of the sand in Hejaz, and to be an Arab. This last, however, I assured him he was, and he agreed that at least he was Hami el Muslemin, if not Mahdi, and chuckled greatly over the successive victories against Hicks, Moncrieff, and Baker.

"Mohammed Kamil came to make arrangements for me to make a speech to the Mohammedans, but there is not time to do the thing properly, and besides Cordery might interfere, so we did not agree to it. But they are all to write me a letter which I will answer. Then Rasul Yar Khan, whom I urged to get up an address of thanks to Lord Ripon for having saved the State of Hyderabad from ruin, and several English people.

"I had a long talk with Clerk about the university, and he promised to do all he can to help it on. He thinks Kalbarga will do very well as its site, though he likes Aurungabad better. Salar Jung has written a note promising the Nizam's answer for to-morrow, and he has telegraphed to the officials at Kalbarga to order all attention to be paid us to-morrow when we stop. Sabapathy, from Bellari, came, too, with Seyd Ali Bilgrami and others, and Mirza Agha Khan, the Nizam's Persian tutor, whose employment seems over, as he talks of going to England for three years. He certainly belonged to the Kurshid Jah faction.

"We dined at the Palace, the Purani, where the Nizam has now installed himself with his mother and grandmother and one wife, the mother of his son and two daughters. There were several Englishmen and women of his suite at table, and for the first time in history, wine was served. Of course the Nizam drank none, but it was an innovation of his own devising, and not, as I think, a happy one. The presence of the English prevented any lively conversation, and I think the Nizam was rather sleepy, as he had been up and at work since sunrise. Salar Jung seems to have put his shoulder to the wheel in earnest, and if they only go on as they have begun, all will go well. We bade good-bye to them all, and the Nizam promised to send us his photographs, and Salar Jung, what is more important, the letter, and then we went home.

"*12th Feb.*—It is five months to-day since we left Crabbet, and now we have our faces turned homewards. We went by train to Kalbarga, Rasul Yar Khan accompanying us as before as far as the second station. Henderson, the secret policeman, was in the train, and we had some conversation with him about Hyderabad affairs, and especially about the railway scheme, which he thinks will pay, at least in a few years time. I asked him what it was that had made our Government at home press on the scheme as it had done, and he said he 'supposed it was the Baring interest.' This reminds me that in recording my conversation with Salar Jung on Sunday, I have not given the whole of his views about this railway scheme, and his father's connection with it. It would seem that when Lord Ripon restored amicable relations with the minister at Simla, he gave him a definite promise that, if all went well, he would restore the Berar provinces to the Nizam as soon as the Prince should come of age. This became known to the Foreign Office, and it is without doubt the cause of all the trouble that has since happened.

"Young Salar Jung is strongly of opinion that the railway scheme was pushed on with the distinct object of disordering the Hyderabad finances, and his father seems to have been well aware of its dangerous nature, though he played with it probably in order to propitiate the Indian Foreign Office, for he said to Clerk the day after agreeing to the first negotiations, 'I have put my foot I know into the serpent's mouth; but I shall always be able to withdraw it.' It is, however, distinctly denied by all who knew him that he ever really approved the scheme, or intended to carry it through. The history of how it has been pushed forward by Cordery since his death is so scandalous that it is impossible to believe he should have been acting without orders. He has told me enough himself to prove that this was the case, and, although the Foreign Office missed their object of fully ruining the Hyderabad State, they have succeeded partially. It is beyond a question that had Cordery been able to persuade Lord

Ripon to put off the Nizam's coming of age for two years, and so prolonged the Regency, the finances would have been ruined past redemption. As it is, they have succeeded in this, that Lord Ripon with all his goodwill has not been able to keep his promise about the Berars, which will still remain as the perquisite of the Indian Civil Service. Cordery will leave Hyderabad, but his zeal will be rewarded elsewhere, and Lord Ripon dares not disgrace him. I could not have believed these things if they had not happened under my own eyes, and if Cordery had not himself shown me so much of his hand.

"At Kalbarga we were met by Kader Bey, the chief Talukdar, and Rustemji and Enait Ali, his subordinates, anglicized Indians all, and well informed, though uninteresting. With them we visited, in the dusk of the evening, the fort and mosque of Kalbarga, a splendid place which we at once decided would do in every respect for the university.

"*13th Feb.*—Went out at sunrise to visit villages, and put our usual questions. They are distinctly more flourishing than nearly any we have visited, and Rustemji, who is by no means a small believer in English systems, declares they are not exceptionally so. In one village we, for the first time, received the answer that 'Nobody was in debt for they had enough to live upon.' Neither do they complain much of the salt tax, though salt is dearer here than in Bellari, only saying that it used to be cheaper, that is, twelve seers instead of nine to the Halli Sicca rupee. The Hyderabad Government charged five per cent. over and above the English Government price. The assessment is about thirty per cent. on the gross produce, at which figure, too, Rustemji puts the Bombay assessment. The seed corn he calculates at from fifteen to twenty per cent., but a villager we asked put it at one in twelve. I strongly advised these revenue men to advocate a reduction of the assessment, which they agreed would bring ryots in from British territory, and pay in the end. They thought fifty years assessments would pay, too, on these lines.

"Spent the day in the bungalow as it was very hot, and at half past 4 o'clock went on to Bombay, after having instructed two of the Mulvis of Kalbarga in my ideas, and gained their support for the university."

N.B.—The following is the account given me by an Indian gentleman in whom I have confidence, of the final act of the long official intrigue here described at Hyderabad, which had for its object the permanent retention of the Berar provinces by the Government of India: Twenty years after Lord Ripon's visit, another viceregal visit was paid to Hyderabad, and the Nizam was pressed by Lord Curzon at the close of an entertainment at the palace to accord him a perpetual lease of the Provinces for the Indian Government, and the Nizam, in deference to his guest, verbally consented. In the morning, however, he would have recalled his promise, and it was only on compulsion, and on threat of deposition, that he signed the treaty laid before him as a binding document by the Resident. The form of a lease was chosen to evade Lord Ripon's honest assurances at the time of the installation, and there are many precedents for the subterfuge. The Nizam, my informant added, refused for four days to take food after this occurrence.

CHAPTER X

BOMBAY

"*14th Feb.*

"ARRIVED at Bombay at 11 o'clock. I see the 'Bombay Gazette' has published the Patna letter, and there is important news from Egypt. Sinkat has fallen to the Mahdi, and Mr. Gladstone has ordered 4,000 English troops to the Red Sea. Next we shall hear that Khartoum has fallen and Gordon has been killed, and then there will be a regular Soudan expedition on the scale of the Abyssinian one. I shall protest against the employment of Indian troops."

We spent the next few days mostly in the Arab stables with Abd-el-Rahman, Eid el Temini, and other dealers from Nejd, arranging for the taking of horses to England for the intended Arab race at Newmarket. It resulted in our taking back four with us to England.

"*18th Feb.*—No letter has come from the Nizam, so I am writing again to get one. They are really the most aggravating people to deal with. A vote of censure is expected in England, and if the Ministry go out of office Lord Ripon will follow, and there will be an end of the university and everything else. Gordon has arrived at Khartoum, and has issued a proclamation announcing the slave trade to be henceforth free. This is in accordance with a conversation I had with him last year, for I remember well his admitting that, in spite of all, he had done more harm than good by his crusade against the traffic. The only point indeed we differed on was as to the necessity of retaining Khartoum for Egypt. I have always been for limiting Egypt to its old frontier at Assouan, and abolishing slavery in Lower Egypt, and encouraging its abolition elsewhere. But the Anti-Slave Trade Association does not want slavery abolished any more than a huntsman wants to abolish foxes. Their livelihood depends too entirely on it.

"We spent the afternoon at the stables with Abd-el-Rahman Minni and Eid el Temini, and arranged with the latter that he should go with us next winter to Nejd, starting from Jerusalem and travelling by Kheybar to Aneyzeh. He is himself of the Harb Tribe, but he knows them all, and we could go to the Ateybeh, who are now in high feather, having beaten Ibn Rashid and the Shammar several times. The son of Saoud has joined, and is living with them, declaring that he will not go back to Riad until Ibn Rashid is destroyed. He is on good terms now with his uncle Abdallah, but remains with the Bedouins. Abd-el-Rahman will give us letters to them all, and he says there would be no danger or difficulty in going to Riad. They would all be delighted to see us. So, therefore, let it be. We need to see the desert again, and we need to visit Medina.

"19*th Feb.*—Had luncheon at Parel with the Governor, Sir James Fergusson, whom I remember in old days. He is a good fellow of the old Tory type, believing that all is for the best in the best of possible worlds, and firmly convinced that the Anglo-Indian administration is worked perfectly by high-minded and disinterested men, having the welfare of the natives at heart. He himself undoubtedly has, but I cannot think he knows all that happens under his Government. Talking of the Mahdi, he quoted his own head *chuprassi* as having told him that the man in Africa could not be he. He admitted, however, that the forest conservancy had been a great evil, and was making the hillmen very angry. The ryots on all other points were highly delighted at our rule. He would not hear of any danger of a revolution, because seven years ago a Mahratta Brahmin had been discovered trying to excite rebellion, and in his diary had been found complaints of the people being as dull as stones to his preaching. The assessment everywhere in Bombay was low, the people everywhere but in the hills and at Poonah were well affected, and he thought a war with the Mahdi would be popular. This is possibly true to some extent in the city of Bombay, because war would bring wealth in the shape of contracts and employment. I told him frankly my views, and he was at pains to convince me that they were wrong. He has asked us to stay with him a few days in Government House before we go. To the races later, where we found Mohammed Ali Rogay and Ali Bey the Turkish Consul. They will dine with us to-morrow. Mr. Gladstone states in Parliament that he disbelieves Gordon's having proclaimed free slave trade.

"*20th Feb.*—Wrote letters all the morning and then went to call on Prince Agha Khan, where I met a Persian Mulvi of repute, and had a long talk about the Mahdi. This reverend gentleman would not hear of his being the real Mahdi, who, of course, ought to be a Shiah, but they seemed to think him better than English rule in Egypt. I could not get the Prince to give a decided opinion one way or the other. His father was head of a sect in Persia, and was driven out with some thousands of his followers, and they settled at Bombay, where he was considered to the day of his death a saintly personage. His son inherits something of his position, and is visited by many devotees from Persia, but he is inclined to worldly interests, and thinks a great deal about horse racing. He showed me his stud, and I am glad to say has agreed to send his best horse Kuchkolla to Newmarket for the Arab race.

"Mohammed Ali Rogay and Ali Bey came to dine with us. We discussed the condition of Turkey, the Sultan, and the prospect in Egypt. Ali Bey is of opinion that the fortune of Islam is bound up with the maintenance of the Ottoman Empire, but he would see a new system introduced into the administration, for the Mohammedan population was dying out. 'There are no young men in the villages,' he said, 'none but old ones left.' I could not, however, get anything more definite out of him than a suggestion that the personal power of the Sultan should be curtailed, and the Government intrusted to a Council, that the official language should be Arabic instead of Turkish, and that the revenue collected in the provinces should be spent in the provinces.

"*22nd Feb.*—Gordon's proclamation in favour of the slave trade has been fully confirmed, and Gladstone's later denial seems only to have been a dodge in view of the Vote of Censure, which has been thrown out by a majority of eighty-one. On the whole I am glad of it, as, though the poetical justice would have been admirable, we should lose our game altogether just now with the Tories, as they would certainly annex Egypt and invade the Soudan.

"I went to call on Malabari, and afterwards to the stables, where I had a long conversation with Abd-el-Rahman, partly about the condition of the inhabitants of Bombay, but principally about horses. We talked of Rogay, who, Abd-el-Rahman says, makes two mistakes. He is a disciple of Seyd Ahmed (he told me so himself the other day), and he mixes himself up with politics. This, Abd-el-

Rahman deplores. But they are friends, and he says he is a good-hearted man. Abd-el-Rahman is a vice-chairman or something of the Anjuman i Islam, and will attend the meeting which is now put off till Friday. His heart, however, is in horses, as becomes an Arab and a horse dealer, and we soon got back to them. Abd-el-Rahman tells me the Nejd horses take longer to get into condition when they come over poor than the Anazeh horses. He says three quarters of the racing Arabs are bay, which is certainly the case at present, as The Doctor is the only first-class gray horse now running. Among the ponies this is not so much so.

"*23rd Feb.*—Yesterday evening I received the letter promised me by Salar Jung, which has been wandering about, having been first sent to Kalbarga. It is most satisfactory. The Nizam signifies in it his readiness to see the university founded at Hyderabad, he records the Viceroy's approval, and he invites me to return to Hyderabad to complete the work.[1] This 'crowns the edifice.' I am now only anxious to get home.

"Ghulam Mohammed Munshi called. He has spent twenty years, he tells me, trying to get up a Mohammedan school at Bombay, and has at last succeeded. He seems a good old man, though apparently a follower of Seyd Ahmed. He was the first organizer, too, of the Anjuman i Islam here, and was sent to see me by Abd-el-Latif, who had telegraphed to him. He gave me some particulars about the Bombay Mohammedans. Agha Khan has 30,000 followers who count as Shiahs, but they are hardly Mohammedans, as they neither pray nor read the Koran nor fast. They are called Khojas, and the sect began not in Persia, but in Kutch, being

[1] See Appendix.

originally poor; they are now rich and prosperous traders and shopkeepers. The late Agha Khan kept them very strictly, forbidding them to attend the public schools. The rest of the community are Sunnis. The original Mohammedans of Bombay are called Kokhnis. They are Shafites, as they were converted by the Arabs, and are shopkeepers. The rest are descended from northern immigrants, and are mostly Hanafites. He tells me the Mulvis are very much averse to education, but they are all coming to the Anjuman meeting on Friday, when there will be about five hundred persons present.

"Dined at Mr. Gonne's, where I had some talk with Sir William Wedderburn, a very superior man indeed. We discussed the agricultural question, and agreed, I think, on every point, except that he seems to hope for more good from Lord Ripon's local self-government scheme than I do. He said: 'The village is the unit. What we want is to have one village, only one village, really examined, and the fact ascertained that it does not pay the cost of its cultivation.' Agriculture in India does not suffice to keep the people alive. In old days it was an accessory only; now it is their sole resource. Formerly they were weavers, mechanics, carriers, as well as farmers, and now these trades are stopped, and they cannot live on the land. He agreed with me about the necessity of a permanent settlement everywhere. He said: 'The assessment is not merely a land tax, nor merely a rent. It is more than both of these. It is a poll tax, and a tax on labour, for it takes more than the whole agricultural profit, the excess being levied on wages received for other than agricultural work done.' This is a good description of the facts. I told him what Gordon had said to me about the hopelessness of expecting anything being done for the Indian people until they had made a revolution; perhaps if the Government went bankrupt it would do as well. But he said it was incredible how long governments could go on after they were practically insolvent. We are to have another talk to-morrow.

"*24th Feb., Sunday.*—A visit from Sir Jamsetji Jijibhoy who called to invite us to see the Towers of Silence with him. He is a young man of great simplicity and apparent honesty, who seems to do his duty in public matters, but rather to avoid politics. There is, however, nothing more absurd than to suppose that the Parsis are not on the native side of the quarrel with the Anglo-Indians. Their position was well explained later by the editor of the 'Rast,' Kaikhosna Norrosji Kabraji, with whom I had a very long conversation. He said that the Parsis came originally from Persia, twelve centuries and more ago, having been driven out by the Moslems. The Hindus had received them, but on certain conditions. They were to abstain from cow's flesh especially, and to use certain Hindu forms in their marriage ceremonies. They were persecuted constantly, and repressed, and were in danger of dying out when the English came to Bombay. For this reason they have always supported the English raj, and would support any Imperial Government which should succeed the English. They had become very prosperous and wealthy, and education had brought them a wish to take part in public affairs. They were now with the Hindus in the struggle going on for Home Rule, though they had no wish to weaken the connection with England, which was all to their advantage. I asked him about their priests, and he told me they were very ignorant, that their ritual was in Zend, which few of them understood. It was a language closely allied to Sanskrit, a good Sanskrit scholar being able to read Zend, but few knew either. The richer Parsis, however, had taken full advantage of public education, though they complained, like the Mohammedans, of a lack of religious instruction. He did not think education in England a good thing for Parsis, though he had sent his son there to read for the Civil Service Examination. He only knew one Parsi who had returned improved from England. That was one of the Wadia family. Most were spoilt by it. One had ended by marrying his aunt. Others had stayed in England altogether. He had been instrumental in getting up the 'God save the Queen' movement with Canon Harford, having translated it into Gujerati. I explained to him the Egyptian and Soudan situations, and he has already begun to write in his journal against sending Indian troops. I also explained the political situation in England, and promised to see his son and give him good advice.

"Ali Hamid Bey also called, and we are to dine with him on Friday, before the Anjuman meeting. I like the young man.

"At 4 o'clock Sir William Wedderburn called, and we had a long talk. He considers that the chief reforms to be looked to are: 1. To have a fixed sum allotted for the Civil List, so as to make the multiplication of offices impossible. At present, sons and nephews and cousins of Members of Council are stuck into the uncovenanted Civil Service *ad libitum*. They get posts of two or three hundred rupees a month, and cannot live on it, and so do their work badly. It is just two and three hundred rupee places that would form the prizes of the native Civil Service. Sir William thinks the English civilians should be few and well paid. They are now multiplied needlessly. 2. To do away with the Indian

Council in London. They are now made a Court of Appeal, but they are all members of the old covenanted clique, and so are incapable of unprejudiced decision. 3. He is in favour of a permanent settlement everywhere at one-sixteenth of the net produce. 4. He would have an option of paying in kind or in money. 5. He would have agricultural banks.

"He described the state of things at the end of Lytton's reign as bordering on revolution. Armed bands were beginning to go about, having the sympathy of the people. They were put down with great difficulty. In the Bombay Presidency, Sir Richard Temple contributed much to this state of things. Lytton's policy of show corrupted them all, and Temple exaggerated it. Temple was a man without principles, good or bad, and his idea of getting on was to head every cry popular with the Anglo-Indians. Thus, during the famine, when the cry was 'Save life at any cost,' he had immense heaps of grain collected conspicuously in every station, much of which rotted and was lost, and he issued a minute to the effect that two pounds of grain should be the daily ration. Then came a reaction. It was found that the country was being ruined by this wholesale distribution, and he issued another minute that one pound was a quite sufficient ration, the truth being that one and a half was about the reasonable portion. He was answerable, too, for the severity of the forest laws. Because it was a popular cry that timber should be preserved, he issued a minute confiscating whole districts to this purpose.

"Dined at Sir Frank Souter's. Abd-el-Rahman and Kamr ed Din Tyabji and a couple of Parsis were there, Sir Frank having what is considered here great sympathy with the natives. But it seemed to me that without intending it, he was insulting them in nearly every word he said, although he is evidently a most kind-hearted man. These mixed native and Anglo-Indian parties are colourless things, and the conversation is all unreal, neither side speaking its real thoughts. I suppose, if the truth had been told, it would have been something of this sort. *Souter:* 'You are welcome to my house and honoured guests, because I am an English gentleman, and I think it right that natives should be civilly treated. But I know that you are still half savages, and hope you will take no liberties.' *The native guests:* 'We come to dine with you because it is a good thing to stand well with those in power. But you grow rather brutal after your sixth glass of champagne.' It is astonishing the amount of liquor consumed here in India.

"25*th Feb.*—Malabari called, and I had a long talk with him about my plans and ideas, and he has promised to help them on all he can. He is going to get up a small meeting of Hindus and Parsis, but I told him I would sooner not make a speech for fear of saying too much. We lunched with Mr. L., a typical Anglo-Indian, at the Yacht Club,—a tall, dry man, Judge of the High Court, who has carried on through life the recollection that he was a sixth form boy at Eton, and in the cricket eleven. He would like to see Afghanistan annexed, and himself sent to administer justice there. With him General H., who, just as Sir James Fergusson quoted his chuprassi, quoted his native troopers as authorities for the contempt with which the Mahdi was regarded by Mohammedans in India.

"To the stables, where we spent a pleasant hour talking and making arrangements with Eid el Temini about visiting Nejd next winter. We decided it would be best to start from Bussora and Koweit, and we agreed to meet him there about the 1st of December. Dined at Dr. Blane's, and sat between Lady S. and Miss T. The former complained of the shabby way the Anglo-Indian officials were treated by Government, and thought it hard India should not be governed entirely for their benefit. They all hated India so much that they ought to be handsomely treated for being obliged to live there. What would India do without them, and what would England do without India? How could England ever have conquered Afghanistan without Indian troops? How could she have conquered Egypt? This is a sincere woman. Miss T. is a serious person. She would see the agricultural condition of the Indian ryot raised by inducing him to plant fruit trees and keep market gardens. She has been four months in India, but has not yet gone beyond Bombay.

"*26th Feb.*—The Diwan of Kolapur, a Mahratta Brahmin, called. He confirmed Sir William Wedderburn's estimate of Sir Richard Temple, but added that he was the best informed of any Governor they had had. It was not from ignorance that he erred, but because he only looked to his own advancement. I asked him about the land revenue of Kolapur, and he said it was about twenty per cent. of the gross produce, the same as in Bombay, but the districts varied. The Bombay Deccan was very poor land, not so good as Kolapur, and there might be some districts as highly assessed as one-third. I asked him if he thought Indian finance in a satisfactory state. He said the agricultural revenue will diminish, because the land is becoming impoverished, but they may make up in other ways by opium and salt taxes. The salt tax was much complained of, both on the sea coast, where it interfered with the fishing industry, and inland, where the cattle were suffering from want of it. He could not explain why, in Northern India, they should not give salt to their cattle, but supposed they were able to give them better food. He was on the Famine Commission and spoke very highly of Sir James Caird, though he said that from want of time he had not been able to understand certain questions, and so had made mistakes. He seemed to think that Wedderburn was too kind to the ryots, and doubted the success of his bank scheme, at any rate financially. He had, of course, a very high opinion of him, both as an honest man, and as one who knew. He likes Fergusson, but says he knows nothing that is going on. Wrote multitudinous letters, among others to Amir Ali and Abd-el-Latif, exhorting them each to unite with the other over this university scheme. But I hardly expect they will.

"The photographs have come representing us with Lord Ripon and the Nizam and Grant Duff, me standing next to Cordery, behind the Viceroy's chair. There is humour in this; and I shall send copies to my various friends in token of the university scheme having succeeded. It will give them courage. After all, Ragunath Rao could never get to see Lord Ripon, and he writes rather comically about it. We are staying with Fergusson at Parel.

"*27th Feb.*—There is an article in the 'Bombay Gazette' this morning about the university, well and courteously written, and which I am told is probably by a Mr. West of the High School. It is, of course, against it, but will attract attention, which is what we most want, and cannot by any possibility do harm. At breakfast I told Sir James Fergusson that I was going to a meeting of Hindus and Parsis, and asked him for a carriage to go in. He told me very frankly he did not like my going from his house, though when I explained that it was not a public meeting, and that it would be held at the house of Kashinath Telang, an honourable member of his own council, he agreed to send me. But he spoke to me very strongly and very earnestly about the danger of my exciting the native mind by appearing to sympathize with their grievances. He could not understand how, as an Englishman, I could reconcile it with my conscience to do this. The Government of India was a despotism of a paternal and beneficent character, which was day and night working for the people's good, and any agitation would only impede its efforts. There were, of course, ambitious natives who had their own ends to serve by making out a case against the Government, but he could assure me their tales were lies. He knew, of his personal experience, that the Government officials were entirely anxious to do what was right, that the people looked up to them as their protectors from injustice, and that he believed there was no better Government in the world, or one more respected. He asked me what subjects I proposed to discuss with them, and hoped I should eschew politics, and he spoke so earnestly and well that I had not the heart to say how precisely his good faith proved all the native argument. No one can doubt Sir James's loyalty. But who are his eyes and hands and ears? His chuprassi, who tells him that the Mohammedans despise the Mahdi; Sir Frank Souter, who tells him, on his experience as a police officer and a friend of the natives, to trust no native's word; Mr. L., who would like to extend his High Court jurisdiction to Afghanistan, and the old Commander-in-Chief. I said, however, that I could not promise not to talk about politics, but I would say nothing inflammatory, and I felt quite certain that no sympathy

I could show them or suggestions that I could offer, would make them more dissatisfied, or make them any clearer-headed about a remedy than they were already. He asked me what they complained of, and I instanced the absence of any real Court of Appeal for grievances. At this he broke out and protested that nothing could be less true, that every day appeals were made to him, and the decisions of lower officials reversed by their superiors or himself. All were anxious to do justice to the poor, sometimes only too anxious. Only the other day he had had to censure an officer for making too strong a complaint as to the oppression of the people. He had written that the people were being ruined by the Government. There was no want of sympathy for them anywhere. I said: 'Yet you censured him.' He said: 'Yes, because he spoke too strongly.' I like Sir James, because he is quite honest and plainspoken. But were not the Austrian officials in Lombardy equally sure that their Government was the best in the world, and did not Lombardy rise and cast them out? Ignorance is a greater danger than ill-will.

"To the meeting. I confined my questions almost entirely to agriculture and finance. The general opinion of the meeting about local finance was that its condition was not satisfactory, that the assessments were far too high, and that the resettlement every thirty years was a bar to capital being invested in the land. 'In the old days,' one speaker said, 'we used to look on the land as our best investment; now we avoid it. If a permanent settlement were introduced we should again invest in land, just as they do now in Bengal.' (This in answer to the question, what would be the result of a permanent settlement?) 'The land would thus fall into the hands of capitalists, but the whole policy of the Government had been to discourage middlemen, because it looked on them as drones who kept a portion of the honey from coming to the proper hands, its own. This was a natural law of economy which legislation could not interfere with without harm.' The meeting was unanimously in favour of a permanent settlement as the only solution of the agricultural difficulty, and as, by itself, a sufficient remedy. I asked about the assessment, and it was agreed, after some argument, that about one-third of the gross produce was a fair calculation for Bombay. One half of the net produce was the pretension of the Government officers. Gujerat was the most fertile district, but the assessment was high. Wells were taxed, and so the sinking of new ones discouraged. A landowner of Gujerat, Yavinhal, told me his assessment had been raised on account of the possibility of making a well. I mentioned Sir James Fergusson's assurance that there was no wrong in India without a remedy, and asked if it was so. This caused general laughter; and Rao Shankar, the Oriental translator to the Government and a man in whom Sir James Fergusson has the greatest confidence, went so far as to say that he had never known the instance of an appeal from assessment having been favourably met. They were all against the salt tax, and one man mentioned the condition of the population of the Koucan, south of Bombay, as suffering most from leprosy. They could no longer cure their fish against the monsoon when fishing was impossible. The district between the Ghauts and the sea was very poor, so poor that the villagers only existed by coming in for mill labour, part of the year, to Bombay. The cultivation there did not pay its expenses.

"I asked them, since taxes must be raised, how they would raise them. They said: 'By import duties. We should all like these, as they would affect only the rich.' I asked them about the income tax, and here there was a difference of opinion, Telang being in favour of it, but others said it was only a little better than the license tax, and Mr. Ferdunji, C.I.E., a leader among the Parsis, denounced them both alike. It is evident that this tax is unpopular in India, but the license tax seems to combine its disadvantages as an inquisitorial tax, without raising sufficient money. The highest rate paid by any man, however wealthy, in Bombay, is only two hundred rupees, so it is a tax on the middle classes only, not on the rich. Those who have an income of five hundred rupees are exempted. They were all very much amused at Sir James's fear of my influencing their minds, and it is plain they have no great idea of his intelligence, though they hold him honest. Yet these are the pick of the native community, Members of Council, of the Corporation, and officials of all sorts. Who then are the people Sir James gets his ideas from? Who are the satisfied natives? I have not met a single one since I came to India. We did not touch directly on any political subject.

"At dinner, at Mohammed Ali Rogay's, we had a great discussion about the Mahdi, to whom all wish success. There were several men of the old school with whom I talked Arabic, and we talked also about the Turkish Empire and the new university.

"*28th Feb.*—A long talk with Sir James after breakfast. He admitted more than in our previous conversation. Thus he acknowledged the evil of the salt tax, and all the evil of the forest tax, though he said the latter was being remedied. The way the evil had been done was this. In 1878 a law had been passed in Calcutta ordering the enclosure of lands, and that they should be marked out within the year. With the 'usual dilatoriness' of the administration, this was put off till the last month, when arbitrary lines were drawn, with an explanation that these would be rectified later. Execution, however, was begun, and hundreds of families were turned out of their holdings without consideration, but things were now being remedied (after six years!). I asked what became of the people, and Sir James said 'Some emigrated, some disappeared.' Compensation, he said, was given 'wherever titles existed,' but these were people who had been encouraged to cultivate bits of the hill. The wrong was nearly redressed now.

"Sat at dinner next to Mr. West. He is a clever man, much wrapped up in his own conceit, and very intolerant. He is Vice-Chanceller of the university here, and attacked my ideas about founding a Mohammedan university. The Mohammedans were incapable of reform, being fatalists and fanatics; they had burnt the library of Alexandria; their creed could not adapt itself to circumstances. What would a Mohammedan community do at Rome under a Papal Government? How could they get on without mosques? At Kalbarga they would only encourage each other in ignorance and fanaticism, and the end of it would be that they would bring the Nizam's Government to grief.

"*29th Feb.*—Rode with Fergusson on a Turcoman horse, which had belonged to Shere Ali. He is very frank and amiable now he has spoken his conservative mind, and on many points we agree, for instance, on the necessity of import duties, and the reduction of the salt tax, and I think he is not altogether averse to a permanent settlement, though he will not hear of there being now any over assessment, or of officers having any interest in raising assessments. Only the other day the supreme Government had lowered some newly-made assessments twenty per cent. But this cuts both ways, as it seems to show that they were too high. We also agreed that it would be well to get the native states to disarm. I thought they would consent, but he was sure they would not, and was surprised to hear me say that in Hyderabad they would not much mind it. He is a good fellow, and, I am sure, does his best as a kindly despot and liberal landlord. But he is in the hands of his officials.

"I wrote a quantity of letters, while Anne went out looking after things. Then we called on Mrs. Malabari and arranged with Malabari that I should correspond with him, and he would help on the university scheme all he could in his paper. Then to dinner at Hamid Bey's,—Rogay, Bedr-ed-Din Tyabji, and others, also guests—and after it to a meeting of the Anjuman i Islam, about five hundred persons present. They presented me with an address, and I made a long speech expounding my ideas. We did not touch on politics. There was a beautiful sight in the heavens to-night, the crescent moon with the evening star exactly over it and quite close, like the Mohammedan device. This should mean a victory for the Mahdi either at Suakin, where they talk of an imminent battle, or perhaps the fall of Khartoum. I never saw a moon and star like this before.

"1*st March*.—We left India to-day, being exactly the anniversary of our leaving Egypt two years ago, and we are going home with something of the same vague hopes and fears. We have only taken our tickets to Suez, but I do not mean to land there, as it would only give them a triumph to have me arrested, and I can strike them a severer blow by moderation.

"As we were leaving Government House, Professor Monier Williams and his wife arrived. I had some talk with him about the things that interest me, and he invited me to come and stay with him at Oxford, and give a lecture on Mohammedan education. This I promised to do.

"And so we leave India, well satisfied with what we have done, but not a little glad now it is over."

CHAPTER XI

AN APOLOGY FOR FAILURE

SUCH was my Indian tour of 1883-1884. It will be rightly asked by those who have read thus far how it came about that I wasted so great an opportunity for good as then seemed open to me, and did not return the following year, or indeed in any subsequent year, to carry out the mission which appeared marked out for me. I often ask myself the same question. Looking back at the position I held for a moment with Hindus, Mohammedans, and Parsis alike, I am filled with regret that in the sequel I should have put it to so little purpose. If I had had the perseverance to pursue the course I had begun, and had followed it out unflinchingly to its full results, I believe that I might have brought about great permanent good for the people whose interests I had espoused, and perhaps with the Mohammedans encouraged them to a real reformation, social and intellectual, if not political. To do this, however, it would have been necessary for me to devote the whole of my life to this special work, and to give up every other interest which I had at heart and all my private affairs at home. It would have required something more than sympathy to bring me to the point; and I suppose my mind lacked the impetus of a full faith, without which complete devotion to a cause more than half religious could not be.

Nevertheless I left Bombay with an entire intention of returning the following winter, and of making a new tour for the collection of the funds necessary for the proposed Mohammedan University. I had already received promises of over £20,000, the greater part being the intended gift of my friend the Rajah Amir Hassan, of Lucknow; and, with the patronage of the Nizam and Lord Ripon's approval, the accomplishment of at least this part of my plans seemed already within my reach. If it was frustrated, the fault, though partly mine, was not wholly so. A series of misfortunes happened in the course of the year which combined to defeat it, and which nothing but very persistent determination on my part could have sufficed to overcome.

In the first place Lord Ripon, though he had established a state of things at Hyderabad favourable to reform as far as the native elements of the government were concerned, had not been able to impose his will altogether on the Calcutta Foreign Office. Trevor, indeed, left soon after, but the *personnel* of the Residency at Hyderabad, in spite of all that had passed, was not thoroughly changed. Cordery was allowed to remain on in power, and, as we had foreseen, the old intrigues were quietly renewed. The young minister, Laik Ali, was left without advice of any profitable kind by the Resident, and through his youth and inexperience made mistakes by which his enemies were not slow to profit. The confidence and friendship which had from the outset existed between him and the Nizam were undermined, and both were frustrated in their better intentions, and, in accordance with the time-honoured plan in dealing with native states, were encouraged to neglect their public duties and indulge in a life of pleasure destructive of their more serious energies. Thus the year was not out before it became clear to me, from the reports I received, that the Nizam's patronage of the university scheme was not one which could be prudently relied on.

Another misfortune was Lord Ripon's resignation of the Viceroyalty before his term of office was fully over. Frustrated in his larger design of endowing India with something like free institutions, and finding himself without real support from the Government at home, he recognized that it was useless for him to prolong his stay, and, amid the lamentations of native India, he returned to England a defeated, if not a disappointed man.

Under his successor, Lord Dufferin, things lapsed into their old groove, and all hope vanished of serious political reform. The Mohammedans were, indeed, favoured by the new Viceroy as far as their employment in the administration went, but anything like vigorous action among them was once more discouraged. Thus, snowed upon officially, the idea of an independent university, existing on its own resources and subject to no influence of official fear or favour, necessarily languished, and was abandoned by the timorous souls of those whom for a moment I had persuaded to take it up courageously. It is rare in India to find persistent energy in any undertaking not patronized by Government. The death blow to the scheme followed a little later when Rajah Amir Hassan, who had persevered in it so far as to commence founding a college for his Shiah co-religionists at Lucknow, was attacked by an illness which ended in insanity. Even if I had returned to India, it is doubtful whether I could have done anything to neutralize these misfortunes. As it was, I allowed myself to be discouraged by them into a gradual abandonment of my Indian plan, and turned my energies into other channels, which seemed to me at the time more practical.

My first enthusiasm was already cooled by a visit I paid to Constantinople in the autumn of 1884. It had seemed to me that the best chance of infusing general life into the university scheme was to obtain for it the Sultan's patronage. In spite of all I knew of Abdul Hamid's character, I thought it just possible that if I could get speech with him I might persuade him to use the enormous influence his name and Caliphal title gave him in Moslem lands in the direction I desired. But my visit was a failure; I found the Sultan personally inaccessible, except through such channels as I was unwilling to employ, and at an endless expense of time and money. At Constantinople the reign of corruption was supreme, nor was any approach to the head of the Moslem faith possible except by intrigue with the Court officials. It will be seen, when I publish the sequel to these memoirs, how entirely the atmosphere of the palace was opposed to serious ideas, and I left Constantinople convinced that it was useless any longer to fight against circumstances or attempt the impossible. Other interests at the same time allured me away, the urgency of the crisis in Egypt, the tragedy of Gordon at Khartoum, the general election of 1885, the Irish Home Rule movement, and the attempt I then made to enter Parliament as its supporter. Thus, while I still continued to interest myself in the fortunes and misfortunes of India, I never again aspired to take a leading part in its affairs.

All the same, I think I may lay claim to have contributed something towards the cause I had made specially my own, that of the Indian Mohammedans. On my return to England in the spring of 1884, I found Lord Randolph Churchill more than half disposed to go with me in my plans for them, and to make himself in Parliament a champion of Islam. It was partly through my persuasion and example that he started on his tour in India the following winter, and the letters I gave him for my Indian friends contributed not a little to his success in that direction, though in the sequel his political interests were too diverse to hold him permanently to any one line of action. His visit, nevertheless, taken in connection with his appointment in 1885 to the India Office under Lord Salisbury, marks a turning-point in the official policy towards the Indian Mohammedans which has ever since been followed. As a community they were encouraged, not, indeed, as I had intended, but as a counterpoise to the Congress movement of the Hindus; and gradually the idea expounded by me in "The Future of Islam" has come to be adopted as the Government's own and used to its own purposes.

Nor was I forgetful of the promise I had made to my Hindu friends of expounding to my fellow countrymen at home the griefs of which I had been witness in India; the infinite poverty of its people; the economic ruin they had suffered at our hands; the oppressive character of the land assessment constantly enhanced, aggravated as these things were by new forest laws and a salt tax levied on the very poor;—and, no less, the arrogance of their official rulers; the growing ill-will between class and class, and the causes of what was rapidly becoming race-hatred between Englishman and Indian. In the course of the summer of 1884 I embodied these in a series of papers contributed to the "Fortnightly Review," and republished by me at the end of the year under the title "Ideas about India," a little work, which being now long out of print, I propose here, as a natural sequel to the diary, to add in the form of final Chapters.

There will be found among them a scheme of constitutional reform not very different from that which we now see, after the lapse of a whole generation, timidly and half-heartedly propounded at the India Office, when all the grace of a spontaneous act of justice has been lost with a lost opportunity. Such as they are I give them unaltered, omitting only such portions of them as are merely redundant of the diary, and adding here and there an explanatory note recording changes which in the last quarter of a century have come about. Alas, such changes have been seldom for the better, and in its main features the condition of India is to-day economically the same as what it was in Lord Ripon's time, with only the accumulated burden of poverty which famine years and years of pestilence have brought about.

India's famines have been severer and more frequent, its agricultural poverty has deepened, its rural population has become more hopelessly in debt, their despair more desperate. The system of constantly enhancing the land revenue has not been altered. The salt tax, though slightly lowered, still robs the very poor. Hunger, and those pestilences which are the result of hunger, are spread over an increasing, not a diminishing, area. The Deccan ryot is still perhaps the poorest peasant in the world. Nothing of the system of finance is changed, nothing in the economy which favours English trade and English speculation at the expense of India's native industries. What was bad twenty-five years ago is, according to all native evidence, worse now. At any rate there is the same drain of India's food to alien mouths. Endemic famine and endemic plague, with British India's universal bondage to the village usurer, are facts no official statistics of prosperity can explain away.

Nor has the chasm of race antipathy been at all narrowed. All the causes of ill-will noted by me in

1884 are still existent in an aggravated form, and find stronger ground of action now; and there is one besides, unnoticed then, which may perhaps be added. There can be no question that the twenty-five years which have elapsed since 1884 have seen a change in the attitude of the white races of mankind towards their fellow men of other hue and lineage, and in their avowed conduct towards them. The old religious teaching, Christianity's best claim to the world's regard, was that all men were brothers at least in the sight of God, but this has given place to a pseudo-scientific doctrine of the fundamental inequalities of the human kind which, true as a statement of fact, has been exaggerated and made political use of to excuse white selfishness and white exclusiveness, and to reinforce the white man's pretension of rightful dominion over the non-white world at large. I call this "pseudo-science," because nothing really of the sort exists under the world's natural law. Darwin's rule of the "Struggle of Nature" and the "Survival of the fittest" included no assertion of superiority in one race rather than another, giving it dominion over the rest, nor has any species in the world's natural history prevailed in this way. Its survival has been, not by its greater strength or even by its greater cunning, but by its better adaptability to its local surroundings. Yet it is common to hear Darwin quoted as an authority favourable to imperial domination and race intolerance in lands unsuited to European survival, and it is precisely under conditions such as we find in India that these arguments find most favour with Englishmen. As a rule the English in the East, missionaries apart, are not much of Christians, and their tendency is to become less and less so in the progress of modern ideas.

On the other hand the Indian races, many of them quite as intellectual as the European, have been far from standing still. Quite apart from such education as they have been receiving in Government schools and colleges, the knowledge of the facts of the Western World and its ways has been spread far and wide among them by their ever-increasing intercourse with European travellers, and the facilities they have themselves acquired of travel. If every Government school in India were closed to-morrow, and every native newspaper suppressed, I doubt if the spread of such information would be greatly checked, this class of facts being conveyed from mouth to mouth rather than by writing; and it is at any rate certain that, at least in the towns of India, Englishmen are appraised pretty generally at their real value, and their moral weaknesses and intellectual limitations are known to every one, even the poorest.

I confess I do not see how this unfortunate tendency of things is to be mended by any rules or regulations issued to the Anglo-Indian Civil Service. I am the more in despair about it, because I have noticed precisely the same evil growth, though in a less dangerous form, in Egypt. When I first knew Egypt, seven years before the British occupation, the best possible relations existed between Englishmen and native Egyptians. There was much familiar intercourse and respect on either side, and English travellers, rare in those days, were proud to be invited to the houses of rich Cairo Moslems, while among the poor in the villages they were always welcome. But the false position assumed by our people since the occupation of 1882, that of rulers and ruled, the rulers being aliens and affecting airs of race superiority over the natives, has destroyed all this. Pleasant social relations can only continue where those concerned meet on an equal human footing, and of all inequalities the inequality of race is the most unsocial. In India things have gone so far that I doubt if any measure, short of placing the administration of the country wholly into native hands, by abolishing the covenanted Civil Service as a privileged body and reducing the Europeans employed to the position of well paid servants not masters, would induce Englishmen to forgo their pretension of exclusiveness, and bring them down to the level of their merits, whatever these might be, as useful paid employés.

As to the concluding Chapter, that on "The Future of Self-Government," I leave it without comment as it was written twenty-five years ago, though I should have liked to have drawn from it a moral and to have applied it to the state of things we see in India to-day. That, however, is forbidden me in deference to the present difficulties of government, and also as being alien to the historical character of the present volume. The suppression, nevertheless, of free thought and speech in India, by the new press laws, and the revival of arbitrary arrest and imprisonment without trial, is a subject which I cannot let pass without a protest, lest I should seem to approve. Such methods of government are not only repugnant to me, but are, I am sure, as futile as they are reactionary. If persisted in, they can only mean that the Government relying on them has no serious intention of true progressive reform.

CHAPTER XII

THE AGRICULTURAL DANGER

I BELIEVE it to be an axiom in politics that all social convulsions have been preceded by a period of growing misery for the agricultural poor, combined with the growing intelligence of the urban populations. Certainly this was the case in Europe at the time of the Reformation, and again, following the lead of France, in the last century; and, most certainly and immediately under our own observation, it has been the case in Ireland and in Egypt at the present day. Where there is complete ignorance, misery may be accumulated almost without limit by a despotic power. Where the mass of the population is prosperous, no growth of knowledge need be feared. But it is at the point where education and starvation meet that the flame breaks forth. This is a truism. Yet there are few who recognize how absolutely true it is of India.

No one accustomed to Eastern travel can fail to see how poor the Indian peasant is. Travelling by either of the great lines of railway which bisect the Continent, one need hardly leave one's carriage to be aware of this. From Madras to Bombay, and from Bombay again to the Ganges valley, distances by rail of seven hundred and eight hundred miles, one passes not half a dozen towns, nor a single village which has a prosperous look. The fields, considering the general lightness of the soil, are not ill-cultivated; but there is much waste land; and in the scattered villages there is an entire absence of well-built houses, enclosed gardens, or large groves of fruit trees, the signs of individual wealth which may be found in nearly every other Oriental country. The houses are poorer than in Asia Minor or Syria, or even Egypt, and are uniform in their poverty. There are no residences of any wealthier class than the poorest, and the little congregations of mud huts are without redeeming feature in the shape of stone-built mansion or whitewashed dwelling at all superior to the rest. Such exceptions one finds in every province of the Ottoman Empire, except perhaps in Irak, and one finds them in Persia. But throughout the great central plateau of the Indian peninsula, they are wholly absent.

Nor is the aspect of poverty less startling if one looks closer. Entering a Deccan[1] village one is confronted with peasants nearly naked, and if one asks for the head man, one finds him no better clothed than the rest. The huts are bare of furniture; the copper pots are rare; the women are without ornaments. These are the common signs of indigence in the East; and here they are universal. Questioning the peasants, one ascertains not only that they do not eat meat, for this is often against their religious custom, but also that they eat rice itself only on holidays. Their ordinary food is millet mixed with salt and water, and flavoured with red peppers; and of this they partake only sufficient to support life. Of luxuries other than the red peppers they seem entirely destitute.

In every village which I visited of the British Deccan I heard complaints of poverty resembling most closely those to which I was accustomed in Syria and Egypt—complaints of over-taxation of the country, of increase and inequalities of assess-

[1] I include in the term "Deccan" the whole geographical area of the central and southern plateau of India; not merely the Nizam's territory.

ment, of the tyranny of local overseers (not necessarily Englishmen) charged with levying the rates, complaints of the forest laws, of the decrease of the stock of working cattle, of their deterioration through the price of salt, of universal debt to the usurers. The only complaints conspicuous from their absence were those relating to insecurity of life and to conscription, the two great evils of Western Asia. And I will say at once before I go further that immunity on these heads goes far in my opinion towards counterbalancing the miseries which our rule would otherwise seem to have aggravated in the condition of the Indian ryot.

The special evils which we have imposed upon him are, however, only too apparent. In former days, though his land assessment or rent was very likely as high as now, it was mitigated for him by custom and by certain privileges which our system of administration has deprived him of. In bad seasons when his crop was poor he enjoyed remissions which are very seldom granted now. The lord of the land to whom he paid his rent lived within reach of him, and in days of distress might be cajoled into pity or possibly frightened into moderation. But the landlord now is a formless thing—the Government—which no tears can reach, no menace turn away. It is represented only by a succession of changing agents, strangers to the country, ignorant of the people and their wants, and whose names the ryots rarely learn to know. This is a constant complaint in their mouths, and the condition of British India under the modern system is a striking instance of the evils of absentee ownership. For the last hundred years it has been the constant aim of the Madras Government to destroy all ownership in land but its own, and it has so far succeeded that it stands now alone throughout the greater portion of the Presidency face to face with the peasantry. If these were happy the result might be good. But in their actual circumstances of chronic starvation it seems to me a very dangerous one.

With regard to the actual amount of the assessment, I made what inquiries I was able, endeavouring, so far as possible, to ascertain what proportion it bore to the gross value of the crop, and, although I state it with all due diffidence, I think I am not wrong in putting it at 35 to 40 per cent. for the Deccan district. It may well be considerably more, but I think it can hardly be less. In any case, I feel quite certain that Dr. Hunter's figures in his book (which, be it remembered, is the accepted handbook about India) are enormously wrong, where, quoting the Famine Commission, he states that "the land tax throughout British India is from 3 per cent. to 7 per cent. on the gross out-turn." Seven per cent. would of course be a very light rent in any country, but 40 per cent. would be inordinately high, and I am quite sure that impartial inquiry would prove that, in the Deccan at least, my own figures are far more nearly correct. In Bengal, I know there are lands assessed as low as 1 per cent.; but Bengal is a prosperous country, nearly the only one in British India, and is precisely the exception which best proves the general rule by exemplifying the causes of agricultural poverty.

It is, however, not merely the amount of the assessment which weighs upon these Deccan ryots, nor merely the inelasticity of its collection. If the natives themselves are to be believed, there are other causes of poverty directly due to the British connection which have had a far more disastrous effect upon the prosperity of the country than any taxation has produced. The reason, these say, why the ryot of the present day is poorer than his predecessor of fifty years ago is this. Under the ancient system of native rule, and during the early days of the Company, the agricultural population was not wholly dependent on agriculture. It had certain home industries which employed its leisure during those seasons of the year when labour in the fields was useless. There was the carrying trade which could be engaged in with the bullocks used at other times for ploughing. There was peddling of ghee and other home-made wares; and above all there was the weaving industry, which employed the women, and the men too during their idle time, and helped them to pay their rent. But modern improvements and modern legislation have altered all this. The railroads have very much destroyed the carrying trade; native industries have been supplanted by foreign ones, and the introduction of machinery and of foreign cottons has broken up every hand-loom in the country. The ryot, therefore, is reduced to the simple labour of his fields, and this does not suffice him any longer to live and to pay his assessment—therefore he starves. This account of the matter has been very ably set before the English public by Sir William Wedderburn, and I do not propose to argue it out here. But I can testify that it is the account also given by the natives themselves, and that I have no doubt that it is strictly true.

The official account is different. According to apologists of the Strachey school, over-population caused by the security of our rule is the sufficient reason of all distress, and it is possible that this may be correct of Bengal and other districts enjoying more prosperous conditions than those of which I am now speaking. But as applied to the Deccan it is manifestly untrue. For nothing like the whole area of cultivable land is taken up, and the population is scanty rather than excessive. The causes of distress and famine must be looked for rather in the growing impoverishment of the existing population, than in its numerical excess—in its enforced idleness during part of the year, and in the disappearance of the whole class of large proprietors who in former times used to lay up stores of grain to keep their peasantry alive in the droughts. It is my opinion, in common with that of the most intelligent native economists, that a permanent settlement of the revenue, such as there is in Bengal, would do more by the creation of a wealthy class of landowners in the Deccan, towards mitigating the periodical famines there, than any other form of legislation could, or the covering of the country with a whole network of railroads.

Other modern grievances of the peasant are, first, the new Forest Laws. These were introduced some years ago in consequence of the growing famines which, it was argued, were caused by the irregularity of the monsoon rains, which in their turn were caused by the denudation of the forests. Admitting as true all that can be said of the necessity of strong measures to prevent destruction in these, and to increase the area of vegetation, the *modus operandi* seems to have been needlessly violent, and most injurious to the people. One would have supposed that so wide an object as the regulation of the rainfall would have been provided for out of Imperial funds. But this was only done in part. The bulk of the loss fell on individual peasants. Wherever I went in the Madras and Bombay presidencies I heard of common lands enclosed and rights of pasture withdrawn, and this without any compensation at all being given to the possessors. The plea seems to have been that, in the days of the Mohammedan Empire, the Mogul was lord of all uncultivated lands, and that therefore, although time and custom had intervened for generations, the land might be resumed. The effect in any case has been disastrous. The leaves of trees are largely used in India for manure, and the supply is now cut off. The pasture has been reduced and cattle are dying of hunger. Where wood had been free from time immemorial, so much a load now has to be paid. In the Ghauts of Bombay matters seem to have gone farther still, and after the great famine or 1877-78 Sir Richard Temple had whole districts enclosed, evicting the ryots and destroying their villages. The ryots in turn set fire to the forests, and but for his timely resignation of office it is said the whole country would have been morally and physically in a blaze. I know that the ill-feeling caused by his high-handed action—which reminds one of that attributed to William Rufus when he enclosed the New Forest—has left behind it memories bitter as those in Ireland to this day. Bad or good, necessary or unnecessary, the Forest Act has much to answer for in the present state of discontent among the peasantry.

Allied to this, and even more general in its pressure on the poor, stands, secondly, the Salt tax. Its oppressive character has been much disputed; but in the Madras Deccan and the poorer districts of Bombay there should be no doubt whatever upon the matter. It is the one great theme of complaint, the one that touches the people most nearly and is most injurious in proportion to the poverty of the sufferer by it. The comparatively well-to-do ryot of Bengal and North-Western India does not feel it and does not complain of it. But wherever there is real pinching in the necessities of life, there the salt monopoly raises a clamorous cry. It is only the very poor who are obliged to stint themselves in salt; but the very poor are, unfortunately, the rule in Southern India. In the Deccan, moreover, its pressure is more galling, because natural salt lies on the ground, and the people are therefore starved of it as it were in sight of plenty. In several villages which I passed the ryots told me that they had been reduced to driving their cattle by night to the places where salt is found, that they may lick it by stealth; but the guards impound them if thus caught infringing the law; and latterly orders have been given that the police should collect in heaps and destroy all salt whatever found in its natural state above ground. In other parts I heard of a kind of leprosy attacking persons deprived of this necessary article of diet; and especially on the sea-coast south of Bombay the disease was spoken of as prevalent. The fact of there being no complaint with regard to the salt tax at Calcutta or in Northern India, has caused the Indian Government to be callous in this matter, and I fear the fact that it brings six millions sterling to the revenue is an additional reason why it is likely still to be overlooked. But it is one that is nevertheless very urgent in the poorer districts, where it is causing real and increasing suffering, and where it is regarded with well-founded anger. The price of salt sold to the people by the Government is reckoned at from 1200 to 2000 per cent. on its cost value.

Lastly, and this is the case all over British India, the peasantry is deeply, hopelessly in debt. It is curious to find this prime cause of the Egyptian Revolution faithfully reproduced in India under our own paternal and enlightened rule, and through the same causes. Agricultural debt came into being in either case with European methods of finance; and, although the subject has been thoroughly threshed out by previous writers, I shall perhaps be pardoned if I once more briefly explain the process. In old times, as I understand the case, in Oriental lands money was practically unknown to the peasantry. Their dealings were in kind, and especially the land tax paid to the Government was paid not in coin but in corn. The whole of the peasants' security, therefore, if they wanted to borrow, was their crop—and, if at sowing-time they needed seed, it was recoverable only at the harvest; at which time also the Government took its share—a tenth according to strict Mohammedan law, or it might be a fifth, or in times of grievous tyranny the half. Nothing more, however, than the crop of the year was forthcoming. No lender, therefore, would advance the impecunious cultivator more than his seed corn or the loan of a yoke of oxen, and there was no possibility on the Government's part of anticipating the taxes. The economic law of ancient Asia was to do things parsimoniously, to spend according to the means in hand, and at most to store up wealth for rainy, or rather rainless, days.

But with European administration came other doctrines. Wealth, our economists affirmed, must not be idle; production must be increased; resources must be developed; capital must be thrown into the land. The revenue, above all things, must be made regular and secure. In order to effect this, payment in money was substituted for payment in kind, a regular tax for an irregular portion of the crop;—and, while the rate was nominally lowered, no loss from accidental circumstances was to be allowed to fall upon the Government. So much coin must be forthcoming every year as the tax on so many acres. In countries like England where the system is understood, where markets are at hand, and money plentiful, this is undoubtedly the best and most convenient form of levying the revenue. But in the East its introduction has always produced disorder. In the country districts of India, as in Egypt, corn could not be sold in the public market at its full market price, and, when the day came for payment of the Government dues, the peasant had the choice either of selling at a grievous loss or of borrowing the money. He generally borrowed. I believe it may be stated absolutely that the whole of peasant indebtedness in either country originally came from the necessity thus imposed of finding coin to pay the land tax.

The change, however, put immediate wealth into the hands of Government, by lessening the cost of collecting the revenue, and so was approved as a beneficial one; and by an inevitable process of financial reasoning borrowing was encouraged. It was argued that capital, if thrown into the land, would increase the wealth of the agriculturist along with the wealth of the revenue. But how induce the investment of that capital except by increasing its security? In order to enable the agriculturist to borrow, he must be able to give his debtor something of more value than the crop in his field. Then why not the field itself? The laws of mortgage and recovery of debt by safe and easy process were consequently introduced, and courts appointed for the protection of creditors. This completed the peasant's ruin. Finding money suddenly at his disposal, he borrowed without scruple, not only to pay taxes and to improve his land, but also for his amusements. Whether I am right or wrong in the details of this history, it is an indisputable fact that at the present moment there is hardly a village in British India which is not deeply, hopelessly in debt. In the course of my inquiries I do not remember to have met with a single instance of a village clear of debt even in Bengal.

This is the last worst evil which English administration has brought upon the Indian peasantry, and when one considers all their poverty and the depth of their increasing liabilities one finds it difficult to have patience with the optimist views of men like Sir John Strachey, who see all that they have created in India and find it very good. That we have done much that is of advantage to agricultural India no one will deny, but have we not done it still more harm? We have given the ryot security from death by violence, but we have probably increased his danger of death by starvation. This is a doubt which is beginning to assert itself vividly in the minds of thoughtful Indians, and it is one that Englishmen too will do well, before it is too late, to entertain.

Admitting, then, the general fact of India's growing agricultural poverty, what should be our remedy? I confess to being a little sceptical of the legislative nostrums partially applied and proposed to be applied by the Imperial Government to a patient manifestly in want of a complete change of treatment and a long period of financial rest. Nor do I see my way to accepting such alleviations as the Bengal Rent Bill, or the founding of agricultural banks, or even local self-government, though all these things may be good, as a sufficient check to the evils fast accumulating. At best they may succeed in shifting the burdens of the people a little on this side or on that. They will not lighten them really by a single pennyweight, nor restore the confidence of the people in the humane intentions of the Government, nor put off even for a year the trouble which on the present lines of policy must certainly ensue. I do not believe in legislative remedies for the starvation of the ryot or in the possibility of relieving his position except at the sacrifice of interests too strongly represented both at Calcutta and in London to be assailed with any chance of success. Finance, not legislature, is the cause of all the evil; and until that is put upon a sound footing, the rest is of no real value.

When I was at Calcutta, I constantly discussed this matter with the leading native economists, and I know, too, their ideas in other cities; and at Bombay it formed the chief subject of attention at the meeting specially convened to instruct me with regard to the wants of the Presidency. I know, therefore, what Indians think about Indian finance, and I believe their reasoning is sound. According to these, the vice of the Calcutta budgets lies in the fact that, whereas in every other country the finance Minister looks solely to the interests of the country he serves, in India he looks principally to the interests, not of India, but of England. Two English interests have to be served first, before any attention can be paid to the necessities of those who supply the revenue. First, the Anglo-Indian Administration must be maintained in full employment, in pay, allowances, and according to native ideas in luxuries; and secondly, every kind of advantage must be given to English trade. It is unnecessary for me to argue out the question of the excessive costliness of the civil and military establishments of India. These are notorious in the world as surpassing those of all other countries to which they can be fairly compared in the present time or the past. And, although they may also lay claim to be the most efficient, it does not prevent them from being a vast financial failure.

It is a perpetual astonishment to travellers to note the scale of living of every Englishman employed in India, in however mean a capacity. The enormous palaces of governors and lieutenant-governors, their country houses, their residences in the hills, their banquets and entertainments, their retinues of servants, their carriages and horses, their special trains on their journeyings, their tents, their armies of retainers and camp followers—these are only samples of the universal profusion; an equally noble hospitality reigns in every bungalow on the plains; and endless dinners of imported delicacies, with libations of imported wines, tempt night after night the inhabitants of the most solitary stations to forget the dismal fact that they are in Asia and far from their own land. No Collector's wife will wear an article of Indian manufacture to save her soul from perdition, and all her furniture, even to her carpets, must be of English make.

I remember early in my travels having the good fortune to enjoy the hospitality of a country station-master on the Indian Peninsular Railway, and being astonished to find him living in better style, and in a house larger than most English rectories, while we were driven out after luncheon by his lady in a charming phaeton drawn by a pair of stepping ponies. There was no reason, however, for astonishment. He lived as all Englishmen in India do, that is to say, about five times as well as in his rank of life he possibly could do at home, and he was worthy of his good fortune. Only it must not be supposed that the natives starving outside are at all proportionately the better for the brave living of their rulers. I, an English traveller, profited as a guest, and I am half ashamed to say how sumptuously I fared. But the poor ryot was, in fact, my host—not the other—for it was he whose labour fed me, though he did not share the meal.

I say, a traveller cannot fail to be impressed, and, if he have any powers of reflection, disagreeably so, with this profusion. There is surely no country in the world where in the midst of such starvation there is so much waste; certainly none where the expense of it all is borne so wholly and directly by the poor. I wonder whether any one has calculated the number of miles of macadamized road in the various Anglo-Indian cantonments, not a yard of which has ever served any purpose beyond that of enabling the officers' wives to pay each other visits in their carriages? I wonder whether any one has calculated the numbers of absolutely useless clock towers and Gothic memorials erected by Sir Richard Temples to Sir Bartle Freres, and Sir Bartle Freres to Sir Richard Temples in the various Presidencies? I wonder whether any one has calculated how many hogsheads of champagne the water-drinking ryot has paid for in the last half-century as an unaccounted item of his yearly budget? These things strike the imagination of the traveller. They do not strike the resident in India. They are not arguments, but impressions; and yet they mean something.

If, however, the ryot must maintain the luxury of his English administrators before his own wants can be supplied, so, too, must he maintain the English trader to the ruin of his own trade. I am repeating native arguments when I complain that the necessity of considering the advantage of Manchester capitalists stands seriously in the way of an honest framer of the Indian Budget, and that, whereas the Finance Minister of every English colony is at liberty to raise money by import duties and generally does so, the Indian Minister is precluded from that source of revenue. I have argued the matter of Free Trade out with the native economists, and they seem to me perfectly to understand it. They know that as applied to England, a manufacturing country which imports its food, Free Trade is considered a necessity of financial life. But they deny that the doctrine applies with equal cogency to India. India, they say, is a produce-exporting country like the United States or the Australian colonies. It imports no single article of prime necessity, iron and coal perhaps excepted, and the cotton and other manufactured goods consumed there are luxuries only used by the rich, and especially by the Europeans. It is certain that no ryot in all India wears any cotton clothing of foreign make, or has his means of existence made one wit cheaper for him by Free Trade. Import duties, then, would tax the rich only, and the rich in India are hardly taxed at all. Yet, because Free Trade is of advantage to England, India must forgo her own advantage. This, the natives say, may be a political necessity, but it is not ruling India financially for India's good. I confess I do not see where the flaw in their argument lies.

They say, moreover, that Free Trade in manufactured goods has destroyed the native industries and given nothing in their stead. When the handlooms a hundred years ago were ruined in the English counties, the rural population migrated to the towns and found work in the great factories. But in India this has hardly at all happened. The ryot who used to weave is left without labour of any sort during his spare time, for distances are great and there is little demand for labour in the towns, and he remains of necessity idle, so that it is difficult to avoid the conclusion that a present of his labour has been made by Anglo-Indian finance to his English rival. The doctrine of advantage from buying in the cheapest market does not help him, for he buys nothing cheaper; and if the English manufacturer shares the advantage with any one in India, it is with the town consumer, not with the ryot. Every native economist, therefore, whom I have spoken with on the subject, would impose import duties on manufactured articles except machinery. Thus, they say, a tax would be levied upon the rich; and if it acted as a protection and stimulus to home manufactures, why, so much the better. With protection, factories could be established in the Indian country towns in which the surplus labour of the ryot would find employment, and so the injury done him be in part redressed. If this doctrine is unsound, I shall be glad to hear in what manner; for at present it seems to me to have not a little reason.[1]

I was surprised to find, in an assemblage mainly of rich men, that most of those who composed the Bombay meeting already alluded to were in favour of some form of income tax. Not that they altogether denied its general unpopularity, but from the necessity they recognized of taxing wealth. They said that in one shape or other incomes had always till recently been taxed in India, and that, though there were great difficulties in the way of collecting any

[1] Since this was written factories especially for cotton goods have been established by native enterprise in Bombay, but have been met in the interests of Lancashire by measures designed to limit their competition with imported goods. Lord Cromer with the same object imposed "countervailing excise duties" in Egypt.

sort of income tax fairly, it had always been accepted. The present licence tax, they assured me, was much more hateful and far less profitable than any true tax on income, and seemed framed on purpose to distribute its pressure most unfairly. It seemed hardly credible, but according to present regulations the keeper of a small shop in the native quarter was taxed as highly for his trade as the richest English banker on 'Change; all the charge upon the latter's income, though he might deal in millions, being twenty pounds per annum in the form of a trade licence. The present system was, in fact, only another advantage given by the framers of Indian budgets to English trade; and they assured me that the people who really prevented a proper income tax from being imposed in India were not the native tradesmen, but the English officials whose salaries would be directly touched by it. If it were possible to levy import duties and a tax on incomes, the agricultural poor might be relieved, but hardly in any other way. I offer these suggestions for what they may be considered worth.

The prime measure, however, of agricultural reform, on which all native India seems agreed, is the granting of a permanent revenue settlement to every province, such as was ninety years ago granted to Bengal, and limiting thereby the preposterous claim of the Government to all ownership in land. This right of State ownership has worked everywhere, or nearly everywhere, its full natural result of impoverishment and disaffection; and Bengal, which has been exempted from its action, has alone remained prosperous. I do not propose to argue out this great question here. But I intend to return to it on a future occasion; and it will be sufficient for me now to say, that the value placed by native opinion on a fixed revenue settlement is the cause of the strong agitation actually in progress against the Bengal Rent Bill. This measure, in spite of Lord Ripon's immense popularity, is decidedly unpopular, and native politicians see in it a first blow struck at the prosperity of the only province which has hitherto escaped the universal drain of wealth into the Imperial coffers; nor am I without reason to believe that so it was intended, not by Lord Ripon, but by some of his advisers. At present, however, I only state the fact that a permanent settlement of the land revenue is urgently demanded by all India.[1]

To sum up, Indian economists are in favour, first, of import duties on manufactured goods such as are imposed in Australia and other colonies; secondly, of a shifting of the financial burden as far as possible from the agricultural poor to the commercial rich; and thirdly, of a renunciation by the Government of its indefinite claims upon the land. These views will probably be considered preposterous in England, where we have cut-and-dried principles of economy in contradiction to them. But it is certain that all native opinion is against us, and that our present system is bringing India very near to ruin. Surely, there must be something wrong in a state of things which has produced the spectacle of a Government, after having absorbed to itself the whole land rent of a country, still finding itself constantly in financial shifts. The Government of India, as landlord, does practically nothing for the land. All is squandered and spent on other things; and the people who till the soil are yearly becoming poorer and more hope-

[1] It was, I believe, a maxim of Sir John Strachey's that, in the interests of Finance, the Bengal Settlement must by hook or by crook be rescinded.

less. This I call the agricultural danger, and if it is not one I again ask where the flaw in my reasoning lies. At least it is a reasoning held by ninety-nine out of every hundred educated and intelligent Indians.

Note.—Since this was published, in 1884, some reduction, as already stated, has been made in the iniquitous salt tax; but most of the other economic evils still prevail, some of them in an exaggerated form. No attempt has been made, by the imposition of import duties, to re-create the lost native industries, nor has any permanent settlement of the land revenue been granted, notwithstanding the example of its astonishing success in restoring agricultural prosperity under very similar conditions in Egypt. Famines continue to be attributed by Viceroy after Viceroy, not to their true economic causes, but to the "act of God" in withholding the rain, which in spite of the forest laws is still in periodical default. Imperial expenditure has not been lessened, nor has the burden of personal debt on the ryot's back been relieved. He is still the rack-rented tenant of an absentee state-landlord throughout the greater part of British India.

CHAPTER XIII

RACE HATRED

IF agricultural distress is the major premiss of revolution in India, the growth of political education in the towns is its minor—political education, that is, unaccompanied by any corresponding growth of political power.

With all my belief in Asiatic progress, I confess that before my recent visit to India I was not prepared to find this latter at all so far advanced as in fact it is; and from first to last I remained astonished at the high level at which native intelligence in political science already stands. I had judged it till then by such scraps of Indian newspaper criticism as I had come across, quoted not seldom by English writers in a hostile sense, and I had judged it wrongly. The newspapers of India, at least those edited in English, are neither on a par with our own, nor do they bear an equal relation to the mental powers of those whose views they expound. I mean that, whereas in England an article in the "Times" or in one of the leading magazines, on a given subject, is, as a rule, intellectually superior to the speeches statesmen are delivering on the same subject, in India the oral arguments are always the best.[1] Nor is it too much to say that for conversation of a political character there are few races in the world which can equal those of India, or that it would be difficult from our own House of Commons to choose men capable of sustaining a successful argument with the best educated Indians on any of

[1] The literary calibre of the native Indian press has immensely increased since this was written.

the subjects specially interesting to them. I was throughout struck by this. The native mind is quick, lucid, and, it seemed to me, also eminently judicial; and I found it distinguished by the absence of all such passionate exaggeration as I had been led to expect. Though in some of the public speeches I heard made at Calcutta the flowers of rhetoric were certainly not wanting, I did not find anything but what was substantial in the arguments used, and I was repeatedly conscious of being tempted myself to use stronger language than any which even at private meetings was indulged in by the speakers. It seemed to me that a great deal more might have been said without violating the truth, that evils were often minimized, advantages dwelt on, and that there was a general disposition to understate rather than exaggerate matters in discussion. Often in conversation I have been on the point of protesting against the too naïve confidence of men known as demagogues in the good faith of English political action, against their implicit trust in the virtue of reason and a just cause, and their belief that, when they should have proved their griefs to be well founded, relief would thereupon be given. They seemed intentionally to ignore the selfishness and indifference of party statesmanship in England with regard to India, and to be only too willing, in spite of political deceptions, still to be deceived.

It is indeed remarkable that, considering how much real ground of complaint there is against the present state of things, how just and deep are the causes of personal resentment stirring the minds of men, how galling to them are the everyday incidents of being ruled by an alien race, and how little prospect there is of any speedy change, there should be so few agitators of Indian opinion who speak even in secret of any real rupture with England as a thing to be desired. I hardly met with one on my travels seriously so minded; and all seemed vividly to remember the evils of their past history, and to see in them a warning of possible dangers in the future and a reason for caution in their words and actions. This, I say, was remarkable, and to one who, like myself, was seeking the germs of self-governing power in India, presented itself as a very hopeful sign. Froth, fury, and passionate denunciation I found little of in India. Of logical argument I found much, and of that reasoning from facts which is the best of all reasoning, and which in politics goes by the name of common sense.

While, however, I observed and am able to testify to the extreme moderation of what may be called the responsible leaders of native opinion in their purely political views, I could not fail in my intercourse with the educated of all classes to become aware of the ever-widening gulf of personal dislike which separates these from the individual Englishmen who rule them. The question of race hatred in India is a very delicate one to approach; and I am conscious of accepting no little responsibility in venturing to treat of it at all; and if I have resolved to attempt it, it is that I consider it would be affectation in a writer on India to pass over so marked and growing a feature of modern Indian society, and that there are cases where the truth at any risk should be told, and where facts, however painful and humiliating, are better stated in their nakedness, while they can still be stated calmly, than left to disclose themselves in some violent form at a day when calm judgement shall have become impossible.

It is my distinct impression, from all that I have seen and heard, that the ill-feeling now existing in India between the English there and the indigenous races is one which, if it be not allayed by a more generous treatment, will in a few years make the continued connection between England and India altogether impossible, and that a final rupture of friendly relations will ensue between the two countries, which will be an incalculable misfortune for both, and may possibly be marked by scenes of violence, such as nothing in the past history of either will have equalled. We have seen within our own recollection a complete obliteration of kindly feelings in Ireland, brought about originally by injustice, later by want of understanding. We are seeing the same thing repeated through the same causes to-day in Egypt. And to-morrow we may well find the case of India equally hopeless. I do not believe it to be already so; but the injustice is there, and the people are beginning to be awake and to resent the stupidity of those who, representing England in India, wantonly affront them; and unless the English public at home, with whom as yet the Indian races have no quarrel, becomes awake too to the danger of its own indifference, the same irreparable results of a general race hatred will follow. Only it should be remembered that, whereas Ireland and Egypt are countries comparatively insignificant in extent and population, and for that reason easily overawed by force, India is a vast continent peopled by races ten times more numerous than ourselves, and that the convulsion when it comes will be on a scale altogether out of proportion to our experience, and so the more alarming. Let India once be united, as Ireland and Egypt are, in a common sentiment of hatred for all that is English, and our rule there will *ipso facto* cease. Let it once finally despair of English justice, and English force will be powerless to hold it in subjection. The huge mammal, India's symbol, is a docile beast, and may be ridden by a child. He is sensible, temperate, and easily attached. But ill-treatment he will not bear for ever, and when he is angered in earnest, his vast bulk alone makes him dangerous, and puts it beyond the strength of the strongest to guide him or control.

The account given me by the oldest and best informed of my native acquaintance (and I am not talking here of Bengali demagogues, but of men holding, it may be, or who have held high office under Government, and are deservedly trusted by it), of the gradual estrangement which has come about within their recollection between themselves and the English in India, is most instructive. In the days, they say, of their youth, thirty and forty years ago, though there were always among the Company's officers men who from their abuse of power were disliked and justly feared, the general feeling of the natives towards the English civilian was one of respect and even of affection. The Indian character is affectionate, enthusiastic, and inclined to hero-worship; and the English in early days, from their superior knowledge and strength of character, exercised no little fascination on the native mind. Nearly all of the older men talk with reverence and esteem of certain teachers who instructed them in youth, and of certain early patrons to whom they owed their success in after life; and they willingly acknowledge the influence exercised over themselves and their generation by such individual example. The English official of that day, they affirm, had more power than now, but he exercised it with a greater sense of responsibility, and so of honour, in its discharge. He took pains to know the people; and in fact he knew them well. Except in the very highest ranks of the service he was readily accessible. He lived to a great extent among the people, and according to the customs of the people. He did not disdain to make friends with those of the better class, and occasionally he married among them, or at least contracted semi-matrimonial relations with the women of the land. This may have had its ill consequences in other ways, but it broke down the hedge of caste prejudice between East and West, and gave the official a personal interest in the people, which no mere sense of duty, however elevated, could supply. The Englishman of that day looked upon India not unfrequently as his second home, and, taking the evil with the good, treated it as such. England could only be reached by the Cape route. Travelling was tedious and expensive, the mails few and far between; and many a retired officer had at the end of his service become so wedded to the land of his adoption, that he ended his days in it in preference to embarking on a new expatriation. It is easy to understand from this that the Anglo-Indian official of the Company's days loved India in a way no Queen's official dreams of doing now. Also that, loving it, he served it better than now; and was better loved in return.

Steam communication, however, with England and the increased facility given by it of maintaining home associations, had, even before the death of the Company, begun to effect a change in the way of living of its officers, a change which the Mutiny of 1857 accentuated and finally made complete. Gradually, as a visit to England became easier, leave was more frequently applied for; and the officer, returned from furlough, brought back with him a renewed stock of Western prejudices. He no longer considered himself cut off from the political life of his own country, or occupied himself so exclusively with the politics of India; and he came to look forward to other ways of distinction than those the Indian service offered him. Lastly, the Mutiny itself, with the bitter memories it left behind, put an end to the contracting by Englishmen of native habits and native ties. With the introduction of railways, quick posts, and telegraphic messages, Englishwomen ceased to dread India as a field of marriage; and every official now dreamed of making an English home for himself in the station where he lived. Thus he cared yearly more and more for English news and English interests, and less and less for those of India.

I shall no doubt incur anger by saying it, but it is a fact that the Englishwoman in India during the last thirty years has been the cause of half the bitter feelings there between race and race. It was her presence at Cawnpore and Lucknow that pointed the sword of revenge after the Mutiny, and it is her constantly increasing influence now that widens the gulf of ill-feeling and makes amalgamation daily more impossible. I have over and again noticed this. The English collector, or the English doctor, or the English judge may have the best will in the world to meet their Indian neighbours and official subordinates on equal terms. Their wives will hear of nothing of the sort, and the result is a meaningless interchange of cold civilities.

Nothing in the world can be more dreary than the mixed assemblies of the Indian natives and their Anglo-Indian patrons—inverted Barmecide feasts, where everything is unreal but the meats and drinks, and all the rest is ill-concealed distrust. I have more than once assisted at them, and always with a painful feeling. Englishwomen in India look upon the land of their exile unaffectedly as a house of bondage, on its inhabitants as outside the pale of their humanity, and on the day of their departure home as the only star of hope on their horizon. The feeling may be a natural and an unavoidable one, for it is probable that race prejudices are more deeply rooted everywhere in women than in men, but I affirm that it is most unfortunate, and under the circumstances of growing education in the country, a very great and increasing danger.

The excuse commonly made by the Anglo-Indians for the lack of social cordiality between themselves and well-to-do natives is that the caste regulations of the latter bar real intercourse. A man who will neither eat with you nor drink with you, it is said, nor admit you to his own wife's society, cannot be really intimate in your house. But I confess I cannot see the force of that argument. In my own case I certainly did not find that caste prejudices prevented my forming the most agreeable relations with a number of Indian gentlemen, Brahmins of high caste, and Mohammedans, as well as Parsis and native Christians, nor did I find any who did not seem quite willing to treat me on an equal footing. I found no difference of any insurmountable kind between their ideas and my own; not more, indeed, than would have been the case had they been Spaniards or Italians. The fact of their not breaking bread with me, I am sure, constituted no kind of obstacle to our kindly relations. On the other hand, it is obvious that, as regards the native Christians at least, the rule cannot apply. These have no caste prejudices, yet they are just as much excluded from the pale of English society as the rest.

It will hardly be credited in England, but in this present year of grace, 1884, no hotel-keeper in India dares receive a native guest into his house, not on account of any ill-will of his own, but through fear of losing his custom. When I was at Bombay in the winter I was treated with the greatest kindness and attention by various members of the native community, and by none more so than by Mohammed Ali Rogay, the leading Mohammedan of the city. He had travelled in Europe, dressed in European dress, and had even so far adopted our manners as to subscribe to all the public charities and to drive a four-in-hand. Yet, happening one day to ask him to dine with me at my hotel, it was explained to me that this could not be, at least not in the public room, "lest the English guests should take offence and leave the house."

In Bengal and Northern India things are still worse, and I think it is not too much to say that no native gentleman, whatever his rank, age, or character may be, can visit a place of public resort frequented by Englishmen, especially if he be in native dress, without a certain risk of insult and rough treatment. Railway travelling is notoriously dangerous for them in this respect, and nearly all my native acquaintances had tales to tell of abuse from English fellow-passengers, and of having been turned out of their places by the guards to accommodate these, and now and then of having been personally ill-treated and knocked about. Men of high position, therefore, or self-respect, are obliged, either to secure beforehand special compartments for their use, or to travel third class. The second class they are especially afraid of. I should not make this statement unless I had received it from unimpeachable sources. But I have been assured of its truth among others by two members of the Supreme Legislative Council at Calcutta, who separately narrated to me their experiences. I know also that one of the principal reasons with certain of the leading natives of the Presidency towns who have adopted the European dress has been to escape thereby from chance ill-usage.

A painful incident of this liability to insult occurred last winter in my presence, which, as ocular evidence is always best, I will relate. I had been staying at Patna with the principal Mohammedan nobleman of the city, the Nawab Villayet Ali Khan, a man of somewhat advanced age, and of deservedly high repute, not only with his fellow-citizens, but with our Government, who had made him a Companion of the Star of India for his services. On my departure by the morning train on the 7th January last, he and some thirty more of the leading inhabitants of Patna accompanied me to the station, and after I had entered the railway carriage remained standing on the platform, as orderly and respectable a group of citizens as need be seen. There was neither obstruction, nor noise, nor crowding. But the presence of "natives" on the platform became suddenly distasteful to an English passenger in the adjoining compartment. Thrusting his head out of window he began to abuse them and bid them be off, and when they did not move struck at them with his stick, and threatened the old Nawab especially with it if he came within his reach. I shall never forget the astonishment of the man when I interfered, or his indignation at my venturing to call him to account. It was his affair, not mine. Who was I that I should interpose myself between an Englishman and his natural right? Nor was it till, with great difficulty, I had procured the aid of the police, that he seemed to consider himself other than the aggrieved person. Now I can affirm that there was absolutely no reason for his conduct. He was a middle-aged man of respectable appearance—a surgeon-major, as it turned out, in command of a district in the Punjab; he was travelling with his wife; it was in the morning, when ideas are calmest, and he was otherwise without excuse for excitement. In fact, it was a plain, unmistakable act of class arrogance, such as it has never been my lot to witness in any other Eastern country that I have yet visited. Moreover, it was evident to me that it was no unusual occurrence. The railway officials and the police treated it as a matter of small importance, did their best to screen the offender, and declared themselves incompetent to do more than register my complaint. On the other hand, the Nawab and his friends confessed with shame that, though they were insulted, they were not surprised. It had happened to all of them too often before for them even to feel any special anger.

"We certainly feel insulted," writes one of them to me a day or two later, "but are powerless to take any action on it. We are used to such treatment from almost every Anglo-Indian."

"We account for his conduct," says another, "by supposing that he thought us (the natives) to be nothing less than brutes and wild creatures"; while a third remarks:—

"From this you will see how our ruling race treats us with scorn and contempt. Had we been in English dress, then we would not, perhaps, have been so much hated."

"I beg to assure you," writes a fourth, "that the incident was not" (an only) "one of its kind, but such treatment is becoming general. The alarm and dread with which the Anglo-Indians are regarded cannot be described. Alas! we are hated for no other reason but because we have a dark colour; because we put on a national dress; and because we are a conquered race."

"Allow me to say that it will be difficult for England to hold India long if such a state of feeling is allowed to progress without any check."

And so on through a mass of letters. I have hope now, however, that the Government, before whom I laid this case, is taking it up. The Nawab has lodged a formal complaint with the Collector; Lord Ripon has promised that it shall not be allowed to drop; and my only fear is that, through the procrastination with which all inconvenient complaints are met in India by the subordinate officials, the apology due to the offended gentlemen will be deferred so long that its effect will have been in great measure lost.[1]

Another cause of the bad relations in modern times between the Indians and their English masters has been explained to me to be this:—Under the East India Company the official hierarchy, being the servants of a commercial corporation, were mainly recruited from certain families already connected by ties of service with India, and imbued with traditions of rule which, though far from liberal, were yet on the whole honourable to those who held

[1] The apology was made, a lame one enough and rather tardy; but as Mr. Primrose, Lord Ripon's private secretary, remarks in his letter of August 29, 1884, forwarding me a copy of it, "The mere fact of a European addressing a formal apology to a native gentleman is worth something."

them, and not antagonistic to native sympathies. The officer of the Company looked upon himself as the protector of native India against all comers, his own countrymen as well as others; and it was generally found that, where European planting and native interests clashed, the Collector or magistrate was inclined to favour the latter rather than the former in decisions which might come before him. As a rule he belonged to a rank of life superior to the non-official Anglo-Indian, and the distinction of class was felt. Indeed, it often happened that there was more sympathy of breeding between the Company's servant and the well-born Hindu or Mohammedan gentleman than between the same servant and the English adventurer of the towns or the English indigo-planter of the country districts. With the adoption, however, of open competition for the civil service, another class of official has been introduced into India, who is distinctly of a lower social grade, and who in so far exercises less authority over his trading fellow-countrymen, and, the natives say, is less kind and considerate towards themselves. A young fellow, say the son of an Ulster farmer, is pitchforked by a successful examination into high authority in Bengal. He has no traditions of birth or breeding for the social position he is called to occupy, and is far more likely to hobnob with the commercial English of his district than to adapt himself to the ceremonial of politeness so necessary in Oriental intercourse. He is looked upon by the European planters as one socially their inferior, and by the well-bred native as little better than a barbarian. He is lowered, therefore, I am told, in the social scale, and is far more frequently under the influence of his tag-rag English fellow-countrymen than in former days. I cannot say that I have met with men of this description myself, but I have heard of them frequently, not only from the natives, but from the English too, as a new difficulty of the situation.

What I did notice was, that throughout the agitation on the Ilbert Bill, the planters had a considerable backing in the official world. It was evident that the two societies were united in a way which would have been impossible in old times, in their opposition to the native hopes. This change of class in the members of the Civil Service, and—what I am personally inclined to think more important still—their change of duties, must be considered if we are to estimate the increased irritation between race and race. The modern system of bureaucratic regularity, where all is done according to printed forms and fixed rules, entails on the civilians many hours daily of irksome office work, unknown in early times; and has had the double effect of wearying their zeal and of secluding them still further from the people. Red tape has strangled initiative in collectors, magistrates, and district officers, and has left them no time for personal intercourse with those they govern. "How can we sit gossiping with the natives," say these, "when we can hardly get through our daily work as it is by the greatest economy of time?" A valid excuse, truly. Yet it was exactly by gossip that Lawrence and Nicholson, and Meadows Taylor gained their influence in former days.

I consider myself fortunate in having been at Calcutta at the precise moment when the Ilbert Bill controversy was at its fiercest, not on account of any special interest I took in the Bill itself, but for the instructive display of rival passions and motives it evoked. Lord Ripon has most unjustly been blamed for unnecessarily causing the conflagration. But in truth all the elements of a quarrel were there already in the strained relations just described as existing between Englishmen and natives; and it was an accident that the particular ground occupied by the Ilbert Bill should have been chosen on which to fight the battle of race prejudice. The history of the affair as viewed with natives' eyes was this. When Lord Ripon arrived in India, he found the ill-feeling between the two classes very bitter, and he wisely determined on redressing, as far as in him lay, class disabilities, thus carrying out the liberal doctrines proclaimed over and again for India by his party while out of office. For such a work no man could have been better suited by temperament or conviction. It is hardly sufficiently understood in England how large a part personal integrity plays in acquiring the sympathy of Orientals for their rulers, and how impossible it is to govern them successfully either by the mere mechanical instruments of a system or by individual talents, however great, when these are divorced from principle. The display of ingenuity and tactical resource which imposes on our own political imagination and sways the House of Commons is absolutely valueless in the East; and charlatanism is at once detected and discounted by its acute intelligence. The Englishmen, therefore, who have succeeded most permanently in India have rarely been the most brilliant; and the names which will live there are not those which their English contemporaries have always ranked the highest. Moral qualities go farther; truth, courage, simplicity, disinterestedness, good faith—these command respect, and above all a solid foundation of religious belief. Such qualities the natives of India acknowledged from the first in Lord Ripon, and no amount of mere cleverness could have placed him on the pedestal on which he stands to-day with them—or rather, I should perhaps say, on which he stood until the desertion of the Home Government forced him into an abandonment of his position as a protector of the people.

I am glad to be able to bear testimony to the fact that no Viceroy, Lord Canning possibly excepted, ever enjoyed such popularity as Lord Ripon did in the early part of last winter. Wherever I went in India I heard the same story; from the poor peasants of the south who for the first time had learned the individual name of their ruler; from the high-caste Brahmins of Madras and Bombay; from the Calcutta students; from the Mohammedan divines of Lucknow; from the noblemen of Delhi and Hyderabad—everywhere his praise was in all men's mouths, and moved the people to surprise and gratitude. "He is an honest man," men said, "and one who fears God," and in this consciousness all have seemed willing once more to possess their souls in patience. To say that Lord Ripon has been a failure in India, through any fault of his own, is to say the reverse of a fact patent to the whole native world. He has been the most successful governor India has ever had, because the most loved; and the only sense in which he can be said to have failed is in so far as he has failed to seek the favour of the English ruling class or impose his will on the Home Government.

Of his legislative measures I must speak with less enthusiasm. The spirit in which they were brought forward was Lord Ripon's own; but the drafting of the Bills was the work of others; and they have been doubtless disappointing. Thus, the Local Self-Government Bill, though admirable in idea as marking a first step towards native administration, is in itself a poor thing, and is appreciated as such even by Lord Ripon's most cordial admirers. The powers it grants are too exiguous, the ground it covers is too small, the checks it imposes are too stringent, for the Bill to excite any great enthusiasm with the natives, and it is difficult for an Englishman to peruse its provisions without wonder at its ever having gained the name of an important measure of reform. Put in a few words, the Local Self-Government Bill means that the native communities are to be allowed to mend their own roads, to levy their own water rates, and devise their own sanitation, on the condition and provided that the Commissioner of the district does not think them incapable of doing so. This for the first time after a hundred years of English rule! I know what the natives think of the measure, and how little it fulfils their expectations; but no higher tribute can be paid to Lord Ripon's popularity than that they have been sincerely grateful to him for it.

Thus, too, the Ilbert Bill, of which we have heard so much. It was in itself an infinitesimal measure of relief from native disabilities. It provided that native judges, under certain exceptional conditions, in country districts, should have jurisdiction over Englishmen, a jurisdiction long ago fully granted them in Ceylon with no ill results, and also granted in India in the presidency towns. The only province, as far as I could learn, which would have been at all seriously affected by the Bill was Bengal, where the English planters saw in it a check to their system of managing and mismanaging their coolies. I heard a good deal about this from some Assam planters with whom I sailed on my way out to India, and I know that that is how they regarded it. "It is all nonsense," these told me, "to suppose you can get on without an occasional upset with the niggers, and our English magistrates understand this. But if we had native magistrates we should be constantly getting run in for assault." In other districts, however, where milder manners prevail, there seemed to be no such dread of the Bill; and as to the probability of any real abuse of their position by native judges with Englishwomen, I am certain that the whole thing was purely fictitious. But the agitation against the Bill became dangerous from the fact that it was all along fostered by the Anglo-Indian officials, who chose the Bill as a battlefield on which to contest the principle of Lord Ripon's Liberal policy. In the Local Self-Government Bill they had seen a first blow struck at their monopoly of power, and they seem to have made up their minds to permit no second blow. They were aided by the English lawyers, who recognized in it a menace to their professional advancement; and by the planters for the reasons I have given; and, following the example of the "Times," the whole press of England soon joined in the cry. The natives, too, from first to last, fought the battle as one of principle, though with far more moderation than their assailants.

I was present in Calcutta on the day when the compromise, negotiated by Sir Auckland Colvin, was announced to the public, and I know the effect it produced on native politicians. It was everywhere looked on as a surrender, and a disgraceful one; and there was a moment when it was doubtful whether popular indignation would not vent itself in more than words. But Lord Ripon's personal popularity saved the situation, and moderate counsels prevailed. It was recognized even by the most violent that the pusillanimity of the Home Government, not of the Viceroy, was in fault; and it was felt that, should popular indignation turn now upon Lord Ripon, no Viceroy would ever again dare befriend the people. The compromise, therefore, was accepted with what grace was possible, and bitter feelings were concealed, and the day of indignation postponed.

I consider the attitude of native opinion on this occasion vastly creditable to the political good sense of India, though it would be highly dangerous to trust to it another time. The evil done will certainly reappear, and be repaid upon Lord Ripon's successors. Down to the last year the natives of India, completely as they had lost faith in the official system and in the honest purpose of their covenanted rulers, still looked to the Home Government as an ultimate Court of Appeal, able to defend them if not always willing. The weakness, however, of the Cabinet on this occasion to resist a wholly unjust and unscrupulous attack upon them was now apparent, and I doubt extremely whether they will ever again have confidence in Ministerial professions. The Government was entirely committed to the passing of the Bill, yet it gave way before the clamour of an insignificant section of the public, abetted by the sworn enemies of all reform in India —the Anglo-Indian bureaucracy. The spectacle was not an edifying one, and I know that the natives appreciated it entirely on its merits, and I am much mistaken if they did not also come to the conclusion that the justice of a course was insufficient for its triumph in politics, and that the only path of victory henceforth lay through agitation. If this is so, there is little chance of peace in the future of the sort which governments love.

I do not like to complain of evils without at the same time suggesting remedies, but it is difficult to recommend an immediate remedy for the evils I have been depicting. The ill-feeling which exists between the English in India and the natives is due to causes too deep-seated in the system we have introduced, and until that system is changed, little real good will be effected. I would, however, point out that there is as yet no true hatred of race between Englishmen and Indians, but rather one of class only, and that it is yet within our power in England to change the threatened curse into a blessing. The quarrel in India up to the present moment is with the Anglo-Indians only, not with the English nation; and though recent disappointments have begun to shake their confidence in the Home Government, the natives have not wholly lost their belief in the sympathy of the land where liberty was born. Between the two classes—the English of India and the English of England—they still draw a distinct line, and race hatred in its true sense will not have been reached until this line is obliterated. They say, and truly, that in England such of them as go there find justice, and more than justice, that they are treated as equals, and that they enjoy all civil and social rights. They come back proud of being British subjects, and preserve none but agreeable recollections of the Imperial Island. They do not wish for separation from its Government, and are loyal before all others to its Crown. But the contrast of their subject-life in their own land strikes them all the more painfully on their return, and they are determined to procure reform. "Reform, not Revolution," is their motto, but reform they have made up their minds to have.

With regard to the direction any new change should take, the educated natives argue thus: Purely English Administration, they say, in India has had its day and needs to be superseded. It has wrought much good in the past by the introduction of order and method, by raising the standard of public morality, and by widening the field of public interests. As such it deserves thanks, the thanks of a sick man for his nurse, of a minor for his guardian, of a child for his preceptor. But further than this, India's gratitude cannot go. It cannot be blind to the increasing deficiencies of those who rule it, or forgo for ever the exercise of returning strength and coming maturity. The Anglo-Indian bureaucracy has become too hard a master; it has forgot its position as a servant; it has forgot the trust with which it was charged; it has sought its own interests only, not those of India; it has wasted the wealth of the country on its high living. Like many another servant, it has come to look upon the land as its own, and to order all things in it to its own advantage. Lastly, it has proved itself incapable of sympathy with those whose destinies it is shaping. It neither loves India nor has been able to command its lòve; and by an incapacity of its nature it is now exciting trouble, even where it is most anxious to soothe and to cajole. Meanwhile the sick man is recovering, the child is growing up, the minor is about to come of age. He has learned most of what his tutors had to teach him, and his eyes are open to the good and the evil, the wisdom and the want of wisdom, the strength and the weakness of his guardians. He desires a participation in the management of his own affairs and a share in the responsibility of rule. To speak practically, the Civil Service of India must be so remodelled as to make the gradual replacement of Englishmen by natives in all but the highest posts henceforth a certainty.

It is not proposed, I believe, by any section of

the Indian public to extend present demands farther than this. But, as with all political reformers there is an ideal towards which they look as the goal of their endeavours, so in India the goal of advanced thinkers is complete administrative independence for the various provinces on the model of the Australian colonies. Their thought is that by degrees legislation as well as administration should be vested in native hands. First it may be by an introduction of the elective system into the present councils, and afterwards by something more truly parliamentary. The supreme Imperial Government all wish to preserve, for none are more conscious than the Indians that they are not yet a nation, but an agglomeration of nations so mixed and interblended, and so divided by diversity of tongues and creeds, that they could not stand alone. An Imperial Government and an Imperial army will remain a necessity for India. But they see no reason whatever why the practical management of all provincial matters should not, in a very few years, be vested in their hands. That the present system of finance and the exploitation of India to the profit of Englishmen would have to be abandoned is of course certain. But there is nothing in India itself to make this undesirable.

I refrain here from any attempt to sketch a plan of ultimate self-government for India, but I have argued the matter out with the natives, and I intend in a future chapter to set it forth in detail. Suffice it now to say that a change of some sort is immediately necessary, or at least an assured prospect of change, if worse calamities are to be avoided. The danger I foresee is that, with an immense agricultural population chronically starved, and a town population becoming every day more and more enlightened and more and more enraged at its servitude, time may not be given for the slow growth of opinion in England as to the need of change. I am convinced that if at the present moment any serious disaffection were to arise in the native army, such as occurred in 1857, it would not lead to a revolt only. It would be joined, as the other was not, by the whole people. The agricultural poor would join it because of their misery, the townsmen in spite of themselves, because of their deep resentment against the Anglo-Indians, and the native servants of the Crown because of the checks placed on their advancement. The voice of reason, such as now prevails in the academical discussions of the educated class, would then be drowned in the general noise, and only the sense of anger and revenge remain. I know that many of the most enlightened Indian thinkers dread this, and that their best hope is to make the reality of their grievances, the just causes of their anger, heard in time by the English people. They still trust in the English people if they could only make them hear. But they are beginning to doubt the possibility of attracting their attention, and they are very nearly in despair. Soon they may find it necessary to trust no one in the world but themselves. To-day their motto is "Reform." Let us not drive them to make it "Revolution" to-morrow.

CHAPTER XIV

THE MOHAMMEDAN QUESTION

IT is never well to have travelled from Dan to Beersheba and to record that one has found all barren; and in my present chapter I shall endeavour to paint the brighter side of the India which I saw last winter. The material misery of her peasantry has been enough described, and the bitter feeling of her townsmen educated to a sense of their fallen estate as a conquered people; and it remains to me to show the compensating good which by the mysterious law which rules all human things is being born out of their otherwise unredeemed misfortunes. The apologists of British rule boast that they have given India peace, and peace doubtless is a noble gift; but it has given her far more than this. What really deserves all Indian thanks, and is indeed an inestimable acquisition, because it contains within it the germs of a reconquest of all the rest, is that it has given her liberty of thought. This is a new possession which India never had, and never perhaps would have had, but for English influences, and it is difficult not to see in it a gift undesigned, but which, like the last treasure issuing from Pandora's box, is destined to transform the curse of conquest into the blessing of a wider hope.

I am not one of those who love the East only in its picturesque aspects, and I have no quarrel with Europe because it has caused the East to change. I note, indeed, the destruction of much that was good and noble and of profit in the past by the unthinking and often selfish action of Western methods; but I do not wish the past back in its integrity, or regret the impulse given to a new order there of thought and action. I know that time never really goes back upon its steps, and no one more readily accepts than myself the doctrine that what is gone in human history is irrevocably gone. On the contrary, I see in the connection of East and West a circumstance ultimately of profit to both; and while the beauty of its old world is being fast destroyed, and the ancient order of its institutions subverted, I look forward with unbounded expectation to the new cosmos which shall be constructed from the ruins. I am anxious, indeed, to save what can still be saved of the indigenous plan, and to use in reconstruction something of the same materials; but I see that the new edifice may well be made superior to the old, and I should be altogether rejoiced if it should be my lot to share, however humbly, in the work of its rebuilding.

To speak plainly, the ancient order of Asiatic things, beautiful as it was, had in it the germs of death, for the one reason that it did not change. India especially, in old days, did not change. Conquerors came and went; dynasties rose and perished; and years of peace and war, of plenty and of famine, trod closely on each other's heels, while men were born and lived and died in the same thoughts. It was the natural life, the remnant of a society which still followed the law of instinct rather than of reason; but even in the natural world health must be attended with growth or it will turn into decay. The intellectual growth of India by the middle of last century had long stopped; and there was no sign anywhere, when our English traders first appeared, of a new beginning. Thought had resolved itself into certain formulae from which there seemed no escape; and the brain of the body politic, unused and oppressed with its own mental restrictions, was growing every generation weaker.

We have seen the ultimate result of such inaction in other lands, in Asia Minor, in Persia, and, till within recent memory, in countries nearer home. It was seen everywhere in Europe in the Middle Ages, and seems to be a condition natural to all human societies at a certain stage of their growth. If too long prolonged it would seem they die, leaving their places empty, as in Babylonia, or being absorbed in other more vigorous societies, as the Byzantines were absorbed by the then vigorous Turks. In almost every case the intellectual awakening has been quickened from without, by the presence near it of an intelligence more living than its own and generally hostile, and it may safely be affirmed that the action and reaction of nations on each other's intellectual life is in itself a natural and necessary law of their development. Thus Mediaeval Europe owed the new birth of its thought to the invasion in the eighth century of the cultivated and chivalrous Moors through Spain; and the Catholic Church reformed its lax discipline, not four hundred years ago, in the presence of advancing hosts from Western Asia. Something of the same process, therefore, may be also traced in the counter-wave which has now for the last hundred years and more been driving Europe back in menace to the East. Asia has been awakened by it at last to her danger, and is slowly informing herself with the victorious reason of the West, and assimilating to her needs that intellectual daring which is her adversary's strength. And nowhere more so than in India. After its long sleep the Indian intellect is rising everywhere refreshed, and is attempting each day more boldly to strike out new lines of speculation on the very subjects where it had been most closely and most hopelessly confined.

All this India indubitably owes to England. Nor is there any point on which the intellectual methods of the West have been brought more strongly to bear in Asia than on its creeds. The ancient monotony of religious practice divorced from religious intelligence, is slowly giving place to intrusive questionings which will not be appeased by mere formulae, and men of all faiths are discussing and reasoning where a hundred years ago they only asserted. We have witnessed within the last generation something of this everywhere in Western Asia, but in India it is perhaps still more marked; and it seems certain that, whatever evil may have been there wrought to other interests, the interests of its religions will have been served by our rule, unconsciously, perhaps, and unwillingly, but none the less really. Paradoxical as it may sound, the wholly secular rule of aliens, whose boast it is that they have established no State creed, will be found to have renewed the life of faiths and given them a stronger, because a more intelligent, mode of being. The spiritual believer will be strengthened; and the very pagan will be no longer "suckled in a creed outworn," but in living beliefs which will seek to exercise a moral influcnce on his conduct more and more for good. To speak precisely, what I see will be the outcome of such education as England is giving to the Indian races is a reformation of each of their several religious faiths, leading to purer thought in their followers, and above all to purer practice.

The creeds of India, speaking generally, are four: the Hindu, which under various forms embraces four-fifths of the whole population; the Mohammedan, which is principally powerful in the North of India and Bengal, and which includes a census of fifty millions; the Christian (Roman Catholic), found mainly in the extreme South; and the Parsi.

Of these, Hinduism alone would seem to be a truly indigenous faith, or one wholly in harmony with the instincts of the rural population; and it is impossible for a traveller not to be struck with the tenacity of the ancient superstitions which are its groundwork. Hinduism belongs to an older order of religions than any now practised in the West. It is not a religion at all in our modern sense of being a strict code of morals based upon any revealed or written law; but, like the popular beliefs of ancient Greece and Rome, is rather a mythology resting on traditional reverence for certain objects in certain places. It is essentially national and local. It does not seek to embrace humanity, but is a privilege of the Indian races only; and it cannot be practised in its purity elsewhere than in India. India, according to Brahminical teaching, is a sacred land, and there alone can be the shrines of its gods. There alone man can lead a perfect life, or worship with spiritual profit. Certain localities are specially holy—not, as with the Christians or the Mohammedans, on account of the tombs of holy men, but in themselves as being the chosen homes of the divine powers. All rivers in India thus are sacred, precisely as were groves in ancient Italy, and on their banks the temples of the gods are built and spiritual influences felt.

From an aesthetic point of view nothing can be more seductive to a stranger from the West, or more surprising, than the spectacle of Hindu worship at one of these ancient shrines—the processions of women to some lonely grove by the water-side on holiday afternoons with their offerings of rice and flowers, the old-world music of pipe and tabour, the priests, the incense, the painted statues of the immortal gods, the lighted fire, the joyous sacrifices consumed with laughter by the worshippers. No one can see this without emotion, nor, again, witness the gatherings of tens of thousands clothed in white in the great temples of Southern India for the yearly festivals, and not acknowledge the wonderful continuity of thought which unites modern India with its European kindred of pre-Christian days. The worship of idols here is a reality such as untravelled Englishmen know only from their classics. The temples of Madura and Seringam are more wonderful and imposing in their structure than all the edifices of Europe put together, and the special interest is that they are not dead things. The buyers and the sellers still ply their trade in the porticoes, the birds have their nests beneath the eaves. There are sacred elephants and sacred apes. The priests chaunt still round lighted braziers. The brazen bulls are anointed each festival day with oil, the foreheads of the worshippers with ochre. There is a scent of flowers and incense, and the business of religion goes on continuous from old time, perhaps a little slacker, on account of the increasing poverty of the people, but not less methodically, or as a living part of men's daily existence. When I had seen Madura I felt that I had at last seen a temple of Babylon in all its glory, and understood what the worship of Apis might have been in Egypt. This worship of the gods—not any theological or moral teaching—is the foundation of the Hindu religion, and what is still its distinguishing feature.

At the same time it is beyond a doubt that among the cultivated Brahmins, who have always acknowledged a higher philosophy than that of the people, there is a renewed tendency towards the spiritualization of beliefs. The philosophy of the Vedas is a high one, and presents to the restored activity of thought a standard for reform in intellectual conceptions; and although the Brahminical system is without an absolute written code of morals, it is easily reconcilable with the highest, and akin to all that is best in the Semitic teaching. Nowhere more than among the Hindus is the tradition of domestic virtue a noble one, or the relation of father and child, of husband and wife, acknowledged as a sacred one. The vices, therefore, which ages of intellectual sleep have engendered, are readily recognized as evils now that the intellect is once more awake; and all that is best in the Christian moral code is being instinctively adopted into their system by the enlightened modern Brahmins. This is the common feature of all religious reform. Vicious practice is the concomitant of intellectual sloth, and as that sloth yields to action the practice reforms itself, usually after the model of whatever has roused it from its sleep.

Thus we see the modern Brahmins proclaiming the morality of unselfishness in no other language than that in which Christian divines proclaim it, and making it peculiarly their own. They have the same teaching as these about truth and justice and integrity, and appeal in the same way to conscience as a guide. They choose what is best, and make it harmonize with their own best traditions, and the result is a general elevation of tone in the upper ranks of life which presages a corresponding reform in the lower.

This sometimes shows itself, as must also naturally be, in extravagance. There is a tendency always in such movements to imitate servilely; and so we see in the rising generation of the Hindus a certain advanced party which aims at making itself wholly European. A very few of these have adopted Christianity, but far more have contented themselves with an abandonment of their beliefs in favour of philosophies more or less agnostic. Others, again, without ceasing to be professed Hindus, have contented themselves with throwing off caste restrictions; and a considerable body in Bengal and Northern India have formed themselves into a special sect, known as the Brahmo-Somaj, which would seem to hold doctrines little different from the vaguer forms of Theism. In the South of India, however, which is the stronghold of Brahminism, these extreme innovations have taken little root, and instead there is found only a more reasoned form of the traditional beliefs. Whether the worships of Vishnu and Siva and the rest of the national Indian gods, have a sufficient backbone of practical ethics to undergo a great moral reform without losing in the end something of their vitality as popular beliefs, I am not prepared to say; but I feel certain that distinct moral improvement connected with these worships is in progress, and that the result up to the present has been an increased interest with the leaders of Hindu society in the welfare and social improvement of their religious communities. This shows itself in exertions made to spread education, in anxiety for the better management of religious trusts, in the restoration of temples, sometimes at very large individual cost, and in the rising agitation against child-marriage and in favour of the re-marriage of widows.

Something of the same process may be observed in the case of the Parsis. These would hardly require mention as an Indian sect at all were it not for their very great intelligence and the lead they have recently taken in native political life. They are insignificant in point of population, and very restricted in their locality. Bombay alone of the great cities finds them in large numbers. But their wealth there, their commercial aptitude, and their persistence in availing themselves of every means of education, have placed them in a position of large and growing influence. They are, as is well known, the descendants of the fire-worshippers of Persia, and still hold closely to their traditions. The religion of Zoroaster, originally simple and philosophical, seems, in common with the rest of the religions imported into India, to have become overgrown there with grosser thought and less worthy practice, and to have adopted many of the superstitions peculiar to the Indians. Some of these seem, indeed, to have been forced on the Parsis by the Hindu rulers at the time of their first settlements, and others to be the result of the general decay of knowledge due to political conditions. The Parsis, however, were among the first to take advantage of the intellectual liberty which has been the atmosphere of India since the coming of the English, and being also extremely keen traders they have profited more than others by the commercial *régime* of modern times and have grown rich. Well educated, well mannered, and naturally inclined to good, their religion is now simplifying itself once more, and the tendency of Parsi thought is, even more than the Hindu, towards a spiritualization of theological dogmas and a reform in social practice. Any one who has been with an educated Parsi over their "Towers of Silence" in Bombay must have been struck with the pains at which they are to interpret in a philosophical sense their ancient practice of exposing the dead; or who has discussed social questions, with their desire to improve the condition of their women. Of the Parsis, however, and of the native Christians of Southern India, I will not speak at length. I saw too little of them to learn anything of real value; and the great numerical superiority of the Hindus and Mohammedans entitles them alone to general attention.

My own special attention was naturally most directed to the Mohammedans.

Mohammedanism, as is well known, entered India from two separate sides and under two separate conditions. Its first appearance was on the western seaboard in the shape of Arab traders, who came with the double mission of propagating the faith and making money. These were peaceful preachers, who relied for success not upon the sword but upon the power of persuasion, and the Mohammedanism implanted in this form is still to be found on the west coast, in the Kokhnis of Bombay, the Moplas of Malabar, and the Moormen, or Moors ("os Moros" of the Portuguese) of Ceylon. They are a busy, prosperous people—shopkeepers, pedlars, jewellers, or plying certain handicrafts, and notably that of house-building.

It was extremely interesting to me to find at Colombo the descendants of the ancient Arab settlers of the eighth and ninth centuries still keeping up the commercial tradition of Arabia intact. They number in the whole island of Ceylon about a quarter of a million, and are among the most prosperous of its inhabitants. I found them an old-fashioned community, more occupied with this world than with the next, and only to a very small degree affected by modern thought. Indeed, such change as was to be noticed among them was of as recent growth as the advent in Ceylon of Arabi and his fellow-exiles, whose larger experience of the great outside world of Islam and the prestige of their late championship of the faith had begun to make its impression on their thoughts. Until their arrival no Mohammedan in the island had ever sat down to meat with men of another faith, and very few had sent their children to any secular school. The example, however, of the exiles was beginning to be followed, and I found the Moormen already anxious for wider instruction, and to come into communication with the general body of the faithful. It will be a curious result of Egypt's misfortunes if the persecution of her patriot chiefs shall have brought ideas of religious liberty to the Mohammedans of Southern India; yet it is what seems to be happening. It would be well if these Moormen were more widely spread than they are, for their commercial instincts are a healthy element, and one much needed in the Mohammedan community of India proper.

As I crossed from Ceylon to the mainland and left the coast I first came in contact with the other and more common Mussulman type—the descendants of the northern invaders—men wholly distinct from the busy traders just described, and neither prosperous nor advancing. The Mohammedans of the inland districts of the Madras Presidency are the poorest in India. They represent the extreme wave of Mogul conquest southwards, long ago spent and now receding. They are the descendants, not of preachers and converts, but of the garrisons of the north, and their occupation of government gone, they are fast dying out from want of a means of living. The condition of the small Mohammedan communities of such towns as Tanjore and Trichinopoli is very pitiable. Isolated in a population wholly Hindu, possessed of no traditional industry, without commercial aptitude or knowledge of other service than the sword's, they seem dumbly to await extinction. Their few rich men, owners of landed property, grow daily less and less at their ease, preyed upon as they are by an army of helpless and needy relations. They fall in debt to the Hindu money-lenders, are yearly less able to discharge their liabilities, and bit by bit the civil courts engulf them. Those who have no land are reduced to manual labour of the simplest sort on daily wages. It is a hard but inevitable fate, the fate which rests upon the law, that none shall live who cannot earn his bread. These Mohammedans of Southern India are the extreme exemplification of evils from which the whole community are to some extent suffering. In the south they are few and hopeless, and have almost ceased to struggle. In the north the danger of their condition is rousing them to new activity.

The stronghold of Mohammedan India is the North-West, and there Islam is far from hopeless or disposed to perish. Intellectually the equals, and morally the superiors of their Hindu neighbours, the Mohammedans of the Upper Ganges Valley have not forgotten that till very lately the Administration of India was almost entirely in their hands, and they look upon their declining fortunes as neither deserved nor irremediable. Their historical status is that of descendants of those Tartar and Persian and Afghan conquerors who have at various times invaded Hindustan from the North-West, or of the Hindu converts, principally Rajputs or Pathans, made by these. Their race, indeed, is nowhere pure, except in the case of a few princely and noble families, but the tradition of their origin remains intact, and is at the same time their weakness and their strength—

their strength, inasmuch as it supplies them with a certain standard of honour beneficial to all societies; their weakness, inasmuch as it has given them prejudices against the ordinary means of living open to all the world.

The pride of conquest is the bane of all Mohammedan societies sprung from Northern Asia, and the Mohammedans of India form no exception. The Moguls never condescended to trade, but either settled on the land or took service, civil or military, under government; and their descendants are still swayed by the same proud instincts. Their misfortunes in India came upon them in successive waves. Forced by the Mahratta wars into an alliance with the East India Company, the Mogul Emperors became early dependent on these; and with the gradual absorption of the Delhi Monarchy, the exclusive privilege of rule departed from the Mohammedan caste—not all at once, but by degrees as new regulations were enacted and a new system introduced. The first to suffer were the landowners. By a certain fiscal measure, known as the "resumptions," requiring all holders of lands to show their title deeds, the Mohammedans, who often held by prescription rather than by written grant, lost largely of their estates, and so were reduced to poverty. Next, the military services were in great degree cut off for them by the extinction of the native armies. And, lastly, the Act, changing the official language from Persian and Hindustani to English, took from them their still leading position in the civil employment. The Mohammedans had up to this more than held their own with the Hindus, as Hindustani was their vernacular, and Persian the language of their classics; but in English they were at a distinct disadvantage, for that was already the language of commerce, and so of the educated Hindus. Nor could English be learned except at the secular schools, to which Mohammedans were averse from sending their sons as tending to irreligion. The sources, therefore, of their employment were on every side curtailed, and a growing poverty has been ever since the natural result. The military revolt of 1857, which in Oude and at Delhi assumed a specially Mohammedan aspect, completed their disfavour with the English Government, and with it their material decline.

At the same time, owing to circumstances which I have never heard fully explained, it is an admitted fact that numerically the Mohammedans of Northern India have been and are a rapidly increasing body. This may have been due at times to extensions of British territory, or to conversion among the lower castes of Hindus, or to other causes; but it is certain that, whereas in old calculations the Indian Mohammedans were placed roughly at thirty millions, and more recently by Dr. Hunter at forty millions, they are now by the last census acknowledged to number fifty millions of souls, although the increase of the general population of India has been not at all in like proportion. With regard to their actual position, therefore, we are faced with the unsatisfactory phenomenon in Northern India of a vast community growing yearly more numerous, and at the same time less prosperous; of a community owning the instincts and the traditions of administration excluded yearly more and more from the administration; and of a community which has good grounds for tracing its misfortunes to the unfavourable conditions imposed upon them by the Imperial Government. The Mohammedans of Northern India, there is no denying it, are restless and dissatisfied, and the only question is in what form their repressed energy, fired by misfortune and threatened with despair, is likely to find its vent. It may be in two ways—for their own and the general good, or for their own and the general harm; and I believe that at the present moment it lies largely within the power of those who rule India to guide it to the former and turn it from the latter.

All who are responsible for tranquillity in India must be aware that there are influences at work, both within the country and beyond its borders, adverse to that tranquillity, and that at no time have these been more active than within the last few years, or engaged on ground more carefully prepared to receive them by the unwisdom of English policy. I am not, and have never been, an alarmist about Russian invasion. Viewed as a power hostile to India, Russia is and may for ever remain innocuous, and I should view with equanimity her approach to the Hindu Kush, or even to the actual frontier, were it impossible for her to appear there as a friend. But as a friend I fear her. If our selfish system of government for our own and not for India's good remains unchanged; if we do nothing to secure Indian loyalty; if we refuse to give to the people that assurance of ultimate self-government which shall enable them to await in patience the realization of their hopes; if we continue to treat them as enemies subdued, as slaves to work for us, as men devoid of rights—then it is certain that within a given time all the external world will appear to the Indians under a friendly guise, and Russia as being the nearest, under the most friendly.

Nor can it be denied that under present circumstances the Czar's Government has much to offer which the people of India might be excused for thinking twice before they refused. The Russian, himself an Oriental, would be probably less hateful as a master than our unsympathizing official Englishman. But it is far from certain that it would be at all as a master that he would present himself to Indian hopes. He might well appear as an ally, a liberator from the deadly embrace of our financial system, a friend of liberty, sound economy, and material progress. Who is to say that Russia should not, in exchange for a new commercial pact with herself, offer to establish India in complete Home Rule, and thus outbid us in the popular affection? It would not be hard to persuade India that she would gain by the change, and, Englishman as I am, I am not quite convinced that she would on all points lose by it. In any case, it might well be that men would risk something in the desire of change, knowing that at worst it would not be much worse for them than now.

Nor is there any section of the community to which this kind of argument would apply more strongly than the Mohammedan. The present order of things is distinctly threatening them with ruin, while just outside the frontier, and almost within hand's reach of them, live men of their own race and faith who are still self-ruled. What could be more natural than that they should look to these for support and succour, or to the still stronger Power beyond, if it should present itself as, in any special manner, their religious protector? Our own political unwisdom of the last few years has made this for the first time a possibility; and what was a mere chimera in the last generation is rapidly becoming a practical danger.

Whatever may have been the defects of the old Ottoman alliance, there is no question that it was popular in Mohammedan India, that it symbolized the friendship of England for the outside world of Islam, and that it left to Russia the invidious post of Islam's chief enemy. For this reason the recent Afghan war, in its earlier stages, was condoned, it being understood as an indirect repulse of the Northern Power; and it was not till later that it was looked upon with general disfavour. But the doubtful arrangements of the Berlin Treaty, the discreditable acquisition of Cyprus and the abandonment of Tunis—when these things became slowly to be understood—operated a change in men's minds, and prepared them for still stronger reprobations, when, for the first time, England showed herself distinctly the aggressor in Egypt.

In spite of the illusions of Ministers on the subject, or the subtleties to which they had recourse, it is beyond a doubt that the Mohammedans of India wholly sympathized with Arabi during the war; that they were disgusted with the false issues raised in connection with the Sultan's proclamation of his rebellion; and that for the last two years Russia has ceased to hold with them the position of the most dangerous enemy their faith has to fear. I do not say that as yet the distrust is absolute. No little loyalty still survives for the English Crown as contrasted with the English Ministry; but it is quite certain that the history of Egypt's ruin since the war, and the apparent design of our Government to destroy all that is best and foster all that is least good in Islam, is working on all sides a change. In the decay of Constantinople the Moslem world is looking more than ever for a champion; and if England refuses the office it may well be offered to another Christian Power.

This, I say, is one way in which Mohammedan India may be taught to seek its salvation from accumulating evils. The other—and to my mind the far more hopeful way—it is in the power of our Government still to encourage them to choose. Three years ago I pointed out, in a book entitled "The Future of Islam," the view which Indian Mohammedans took of her Majesty's duties towards them in connection with her assumption of the Mogul title; and, while I was in India last winter, I had the satisfaction of finding my statement of their case fully accepted by those whom it most concerned. The Indian mulvis, Shiah as well as Sunni, held that her Majesty, in making herself Empress of India, had accepted a legal responsibility toward the Mohammedan community which involved a distinct obligation of protection in return for their loyalty, especially in such matters as the administration of their religious trusts, the furtherance of their education, and the arrangements connected with their pilgrimage; and they had even caused a translation of my statement to be published in Hindustani.

With regard to religious trusts, I found everywhere complaint of their being misapplied. It appears that at the time of the *resumptions*, many of these were confiscated on the arbitrary ground of defect in title, and others later on apparently no ground at all but public convenience. The locally notorious case of the Mohsin trust in Bengal has now been in part remedied, but it is worth quoting as a case which the Government has been forced to acknowledge, and it has been cited to me as an example of numerous cases less well known in which similar injustice still exists. In this, a large property was bequeathed by a rich Mohammedan explicitly for pious uses, yet for many years the income held in trust by the Government was devoted, not to any

Mohammedan purpose at all, but to the education of Hindus. This, I say, has been acknowledged; but I have been repeatedly informed that sufficient property is still in Government hands to satisfy, if it were devoted to the uses originally intended, all the pressing needs of Mohammedan education; and I have the authority of Dr. Leitner, Principal of the Lahore Government College, for stating that in the Punjab alone *wakaf* property to the value of many thousand pounds yearly is being officially misapplied.

Of the pilgrimage, I will only say that the need of organization in the shipment of pilgrims is still strongly demanded, and of protection while on their journey. Something has been, indeed, done in the last three years, but exceedingly little; and the Indian Mohammedans regard such protection as a duty of the Imperial Government, made more than ever necessary by the growing abuses connected with the quarantine and other vexatious regulations at Jeddah.

Again, with regard to their education, the case of the Mohammedans is this: Like the Catholics in England, they are extremely attached to their religion, and anxious that their children should inherit in its purity a blessing to which they themselves were born; and they consider that a merely secular education, such as is offered by the State, does not suffice for their need. In no country in the world is the position of a teacher towards his pupil a more powerful one than in India; and the Mohammedans see that at the Government schools and colleges the masters are, almost without exception, English or Hindu. The great mass of the orthodox, therefore, hold aloof from these, and the consequence has been that they find themselves deprived of nearly all State aid in their education, and, for the more rigid, of all public education whatsoever. It is of course cast in their teeth by their opponents that this is mere fanaticism and prejudice; that they refuse to learn English out of disloyalty, and that they desire no progress and no modern instruction. But, whatever may have been the case in former days, I can confidently assert that it is certainly not true now; and I hold the position taken by the Indian mulvis to be an unassailable one in justice, or on any other ground than the theory that all religion is pernicious and should be discouraged by the State. I do not say that the State in India has taken its stand publicly on this ground, but in practice its action with regard to public education affects Mohammedans in no other way. This, therefore, is a point on which the Imperial Government may, if it will, intervene as a protector, and in which its action would be at once appreciated by its Mohammedan subjects, and be recognized by them as a title to their loyalty.

Lastly, I would repeat what I have said elsewhere as to the special nature of the connection between the political and the religious organization of all Moslem societies. Mohammedans look to the government under which they live as a fountain of authority; and they expect that authority to be used; and it is useless to repeat to them that the Government is impartial to all religions and indifferent to their own. Indifference with them is tantamount to neglect of duty; and as such the Mohammedans of India regard the present abstention of the English Government. There are many liberal-minded men among our high officials, and not a few friends of Islam. But the tide of official movement is not in this direction; and the general feeling is indifference. What I mean is that I would have the matter taken up with vigour, as an Imperial duty, and not in Oude only and the North-West, but in every province where the Mohammedans are a numerous community. The advancement of their education, their encouragement in commercial and industrial pursuits, and a faithful protection of their religious interests abroad, will secure to the English Crown the renewed trust of its Mohammedan subjects. The neglect of these things, and a prosecution of the present evil policy of doing harm to Islam, will secure beyond redemption their disloyalty. It is a thing seriously to consider and decide while time is yet given. It soon may be wholly too late, for nothing is more certain than that the Indian Mohammedans, like those elsewhere, are in a crisis of their history; and that, by disregarding their just complaints, we are allowing griefs to grow which will some day overwhelm us with confusion. "England," if I may be allowed to repeat what I said three years ago, "should fulfil the trust she has accepted by developing, not destroying, the existing elements of good in Asia. She cannot destroy Islam nor dissolve her own connection with her. Therefore, in God's name, let her take Islam by the hand and encourage her boldly in the path of virtue." This, in spite of the victory of force in Egypt, is still the only wise and worthy course.[1]

On the whole, the intellectual and religious aspects of India under English rule are what I found there of most hope, and I am glad to think that they could hardly have been witnessed under other domination than our own.

[1] Much of what is here recommended as England's duty towards Islam has within the last two years been taken to heart by our rulers, and adopted as a part of English policy. It is only to be regretted that in India the motive seems to have been the encouragement of Mohammedan loyalty as a counterpoise to the Hindu movement for self-government, 1909.

CHAPTER XV

THE FUTURE OF SELF-GOVERNMENT[1]

BEFORE considering the case for self-government in British India, a few words may be said about the semi-independent Native States.

There is an interest attaching to these Native States which is twofold for the political observer. They present in the first place a picture, instructive if not entirely accurate, of the India of past days, and so serve in some measure as landmarks and records of the changes for good and evil our rule has caused. And secondly, they afford indications of the real capacity for self-government possessed by the indigenous races.

When one has seen a native court, with its old-world etiquettes, its ordered official hierarchies, and its fixed notions, one learns something, which no amount of reading could teach, about the tradition of paternal government long swept away in Madras and Bengal. One recognizes how much there was that was good in the past in the harmonious relations of governors and governed, in the personal connection of princes and peoples, in the tolerance which gave to each caste and creed its recognized position in the social family. One is surprised to find how naturally such adverse elements as the Hindu Brahmin and the Mohammedan nobleman lay down together under a system which precluded class rivalry, and how tolerant opinion was in all the practical details of life. One does not readily imagine from the mere teaching of history the reason which

[1] In reprinting this chapter I have incorporated with it part of another chapter on the Native States.

should place a Mussulman from Lucknow in command of the army of a Rajput prince, or a Hindu statesman in the position of vizier to a Nizam of the Deccan. Yet seeing, one understands these things, and one recognizes in them something of the natural law existing between "the creatures of the flood and field" which makes it impossible "their strife should last." In the traditional life of ancient India there was an astonishing tolerance now changed to intolerance, an astonishing order in face of occasional disorder, and a large material contentment which neither war nor the other insecurities of life permanently affected. It is impossible, too, after having visited a native court, to maintain that the Indian natives are incapable of indigenous government. The fact which proves the contrary exists too palpably before one's eyes. The late Sir Salar Jung was as distinctly a statesman as Lawrence or Dalhousie; and among the Mahrattas there are not a few diwans to be found in office capable of discharging almost any public function.

At the same time it is abundantly clear that in all that constitutes intellectual life the India of old days, as represented in the still independent States, was far more than a century behind the India of our day. Mental culture is at the lowest ebb in the capitals of the native princes. They possess neither schools on any large plan, nor public libraries, nor are books printed in them nor newspapers published. I was astonished to find how in the centre of busy intellectual India large flourishing towns were to be found completely isolated from all the world, absorbed in their own local affairs, and intellectually asleep. At certain of the native courts history is still represented by the reciter of oral traditions, letters by the court poet, and science by professors of astrology; while the general politics of the Empire hardly affect, even in a remote degree, the mass of the unlettered citizens. Last winter's storm over Lord Ripon's internal policy left the native States absolutely unmoved. There is both good and bad in this.

With regard to their material prosperity, as contrasted with British India, I can only speak of what I have seen. The territories of the native princes are for the most part not the most fertile tracts of India; and one cannot avoid a suspicion that their comparative poverty has been the cause of their continued immunity from annexation. Nearly the whole of the rich irrigated ricelands of the peninsula are now British territory; and the estates of the Nizam, and the two great Mahratta princes Holkar and Scindia, comprise a large amount of untilled jungle. These countries possess no seaports or navigable rivers, and their arable tracts are not of the first order of productiveness, while the Rajput princes are lords of districts almost wholly desert. It would be, therefore, misleading to compare the material wealth of the peasantry in any of these States with those of Bengal or the rich lands of the Madras coast, for the conditions of life in them are not the same. But, poor land compared with poor land, I think the comparison would not be unfavourable to the native States. I was certainly struck in passing from the British Deccan below Raichore into the Nizam's Deccan with certain signs of better condition in the latter. Most of the Nizam's villages contain something in the shape of a stone house belonging to the head man. The flocks of goats, alone found in the Madras Presidency, are replaced by flocks of sheep; and one sees here and there a farmer superintending his labourers on horseback, a sight the British Deccan never shows. In the few villages of the Nizam which I entered I found at least this advantage over the others, that there was no debt, while I was assured that the mortality during the great Deccan famine was far less severe in the Nizam's than in her Majesty's territory.

It must not, however, be supposed that in any of the native States the ancient economy of India has been preserved in its integrity. Free trade has not spared them more than the rest. Their traditional industries have equally been ruined, and they suffer equally from the salt monopoly; while in some of them the British system of assessing the land revenue at its utmost rate, and levying the taxes in coin, has been adopted to the advantage of the revenue and the disadvantage of the peasant. On the whole the agricultural condition of the Hyderabad territory seemed to me a little, a very little, better than that of its neighbour, the Madras Deccan, and I believe it is a fact that it is attracting immigrants from across the border. The Rajput State of Ulwar, where I also made some inquiries, was represented to me as being considerably more favourably assessed than British Rajputana.

The best administered districts of India would seem to be those where a native prince has had the good fortune to secure the co-operation of a really good English assessor, allowing him to assess the land, not with a view to immediately increased revenue, but the true profit of the people. Such are to be found in some of the Rajput principalities, where the agricultural class is probably happier, though living on a poor soil, than in any other part of India; for the assessor, freed from the necessity which besets him in British territory of raising a larger revenue than the district can quite afford, and having no personal interest to serve by severity, allows his kindlier instincts to prevail, and becomes —what he might be everywhere in India—a protector of the people. I trust that it is understood by this time that I am far from affirming that Englishmen are incapable of administering India to its profit. What I do say is that selfish interests and the interests of a selfish Government prevent them from so doing under the present system in British territory. Thus it is certain that the Berar province of Hyderabad under British administration has prospered exceedingly; and its prosperity affords precisely that exceptional instance which proves the general rule of impoverishment. What may probably be affirmed without any risk of error is, that the best administered districts of the native States are also the best administered of all India.

With regard to the town population, I found the few independent native capitals which I visited exhibiting signs of well-being in the inhabitants absent in places of the same calibre under British rule. With the exception of Bombay, which is exceptionally flourishing, the native quarter, even in the Presidency towns, has everywhere in British India a squalid look. The "Black Town" of Madras reminds one disagreeably of Westminster and the Seven Dials: and there is extreme native misery concealed behind the grandeur of the European houses in Calcutta. The inland cities are decidedly in decay. Lucknow and Delhi, once such famous capitals, are shrunk to mere shadows of their former selves; and there is a distrustful attitude about their inhabitants which a stranger cannot fail to notice. The faces of the inhabitants everywhere in Northern India are those of men conscious of a presence hostile to them, as in a conquered city. In the capitals of the native States, on the contrary, there is nothing of all this, and the change in the aspect of the natives, as one passes from British to native rule, is most noticeable. The Hyderabadis especially have a well-fed look not commonly found in the inland towns, and are quite the best dressed townsmen of India. There is a bustle and cheerfulness about this city, and a fearless attitude in the crowd, which is a relief to the traveller after the submissive silence of the British populations. Elephants, camels, horsemen—all is movement and life in Hyderabad; and as one passes along one realizes for the first time the idea of India as it was in the days when it was still the centre of the world's wealth and magnificence. That these gay externals may conceal a background of poverty is possible—English officials affirm that they do so; but at least it is better thus than that there should be no gaiety at all, nor other evidence of well-being than in the bungalows of a foreign cantonment.

Nor is the cause of the better condition far to seek. Whatever revenue the native court may raise from the people is spent amongst the people. The money does not leave the country, but circulates there; and, even where the profusion is most irrational, something of the pleasure of the spending remains, and is shared in and enjoyed by all, down to the poorest. In British India the *tamachas* of governors-general and lieutenant-governors interest no one but the aides-de-camp and their friends; and a large portion of the revenue goes clean away every year, to the profit of other lands and other peoples.

Of the administration of justice in the native States I had no opportunity of forming an accurate opinion, but I am willing to believe that it is less satisfactory in these than in British India. The only advantage that I could distinctly recognize in compensation was, what I have already mentioned, the absence of the Civil Courts, which are so loudly complained of in the latter on account of the encouragement they give to usury. It is worth repeating that the only villages I found free from debt in India were in the Nizam's territory. With this exception, it is probable that British justice is better everywhere than "native" justice, and there is certainly not the same check exercised in a native State by public opinion over the doings of magistrates and judges. In all this the native States are far behind the Imperial system, for the despotic form of rule is the only one recognized in any of them, Hindu or Mohammedan, and there is no machinery by which official injustice can be inquired into or controlled. The ideas of liberty are spreading slowly in India, and the native States are hardly yet touched by them.

Having said this much about the native States, in which there is as yet no clamour for reform, I will go on to the question, one quite apart from them, of British India proper.

Unless I have wholly failed to make my reasoning clear, readers of these essays will by this time have understood that, in answer to the question propounded at the outset of this inquiry—namely, whether the connection betwen England and India is of profit to the Indian people; and to the further question whether the Indian people regard it as of profit—I have come to conclusions on the whole favourable to that connection.

My argument, in a few words, has been this: seeking the balance of good and evil, I have found, on the one hand, a vast economic disturbance, caused partly by the selfish commercial policy of the English Government, partly by the no less selfish expenditure of the English official class.

I have found the Indian peasantry poor, in some districts to starvation, deeply in debt, and without the means of improving their position; the wealth accumulated in a few great cities and in a few rich hands; the public revenue spent to a large extent abroad, and by an absentee Government. I have been unable to convince myself that the India of 1885 is not a poorer country, take it altogether, than it was a hundred years ago, when we first began to manage its finances. I believe, in common with all native economists, that its modern system of finance is unsound, that far too large a revenue is raised from the land, and that it is only maintained at its present high figure by drawing on what may be called the capital of the country, namely, the material welfare of the agricultural class—probably, too, the productive power of the soil. I find a large public debt, and foresee further financial difficulties.

Again, I find the ancient organization of society broken up, the interdependence of class and class disturbed, the simple customary law of the East replaced by a complicated jurisprudence imported from the West, increased powers given to the recovery of debt, and consequently increased facilities of litigation and usury. Also great centralization of power in the hands of officers daily more and more automatons and less and less interested in the special districts they administer. In a word, new machinery replacing, on many points disadvantageously, the old. I do not say that all these things are unprofitable, but they are not natural to the country, and are costly out of proportion to their effect of good. India has appeared to me at best in the light of a large estate which has been experimented on by a series of Scotch bailiffs, who have all gone away rich. Everything is very scientific, very trim, and very new, especially the bailiff's own house; but the farms can only be worked now by skilled labourers and at enormous expense; while a huge capital has been sunk, and the accounts won't bear looking into.

On the other side, I have found an end put to the internecine wars of former days, peace established, security for life given, and a settled order of things on which men can count. I have never heard a native of India underrate the advantage of this, nor of the corresponding enfranchisement of the mind from the bondage in which it used to lie. A certain atmosphere of political freedom is necessary for intellectual growth. Where men were liable to fine, imprisonment, and death for their opinions there could be no general advance of ideas, and the want of personal liberty had for centuries held India in mental chains. No one had dared to think more wisely than his fellows, or, doing so, had speedily been stopped by force from teaching it to others. But under English rule, with all its defects, thought has been free, and men who dared to think have kept their heads, so that a generation has sprung up to whom liberty of opinion has seemed natural, and with it has come courage. The Indians in the towns are now highly educated, write books, found newspapers, attend meetings, make tours of public lectures, think, speak, and argue fearlessly, and an immense revival of intellectual and moral energy has been the result. It is not a small thing, again, that the gross licence of the old princely courts has given place to a more healthy life—that crime in high places is no longer common; that sorcery, poisoning, domestic murder, and lives of senseless depravity are disappearing; that the burning of widows has been abolished, and child-marriage is now being agitated against. These things are distinct gains, which no candid Englishman, any more than do the candid natives, would dream of underrating. And, as I have said before, they supply that element of hope which contains in it a germ of redemption from all other evils. This is the "per contra" of gain to be set in the balance against India's loss through England.

It would, therefore, be more than rash for Indian patriotism to condemn the English connection. Nor does it yet condemn it. There is hardly, I believe, an intelligent and single-minded man in the three Presidencies who would view with complacency the prospect of immediate separation for his country from the English Crown. To say nothing of dangers from without, there are dangers from within well recognized by all. The Indians are no single race; they profess no one creed, they speak no one language; highly civilized as portions of their society are, it contains within its borders portions wholly savage. There are tribes in all the hills still armed with spear and shield, and the bulk of the peaceful agricultural population is still in the rudest ignorance. The work of education is not yet complete, or the need of protection passed. All recognize this, and with it the necessity for India still of an armed Imperial rule. Were this withdrawn, it is certain at least that the present civilized political structure could not endure, and it is exceedingly doubtful whether any other could be found to take its place. I do not myself see in what way the issue of a rupture could be made profitable to the Indian nations, nor do I understand that the exchange from English to another foreign rule would improve their condition.

At the same time I recognize that it is impossible the present condition of things should remain unchanged for more than a very few years. For reasons which I have stated, the actual organization of Anglo-Indian government has become hateful to the natives of India, and however much their reason may be on the side of patience, there is a daily increasing danger of its being overpowered by a passionate sentiment evoked by some chance outbreak. Nor do I believe that it will be again possible for England to master a military revolt, which would this time have the sympathy of the whole people. Moreover, even if we should suppose this fear exaggerated and the evil day of revolt put off, there is yet the certainty of a Government by force becoming yearly more costly and more difficult to carry on. It is a mistake to suppose that India has ever yet been governed merely by the English sword. The consent of the people has always underlain the exercise of our power, and were this generally withdrawn it could not be maintained an hour. At present the Indian populations accept English rule as, on the whole, a thing good for them, and give it their support. But they do not like it, and were they once convinced that there was no intention on the part of the English people to do them better justice and give them greater liberty than they have now, they might without actual revolt make all government impossible. It cannot be too emphatically stated that our Indian administration exists on the goodwill of the native employés.

What then, in effect, should that reform be, and towards what ultimate goal should reformers look in shaping their desires and leading the newly awakened thought of India towards a practical end? While I was at Calcutta I attended a series of meetings at which this question was put in all its branches, and at which delegates from all parts of India discussed it fully; and in what I am now going to say I can therefore give, with more or less accuracy, the native Indian view of Indian needs. Many matters of social importance were debated there, many suggestions made of improvements in this and that department of the administration, and the financial and economic difficulties found their separate exponents; but it was easy to remark that, while all looked forward to the realization of their special hopes, none seemed to consider it possible that any real change would be effected as long as what may be called the constitution of the Indian Government remained what it now is. The burden of every argument was, "No reform is possible for us until the Indian Government is itself reformed. It is too conservative, too selfish, too alien to the thoughts and needs of India, to effect anything as at present constituted; and just as in England reformers at the beginning of this century looked first to a reform of Parliament, so must Indian reformers now look first to a reform of the governing body of the country." Constitutional changes are needed as an initial step towards improvement; and it is the strong opinion of all that nothing short of this will either satisfy Indian hopes or ward off Indian troubles.

The Indian Government as at present constituted is a legacy from days when the advantage of the natives of India was not even in name the first object with its rulers. Its direct ancestor, the East India Company, was a foreign trade corporation which had got possession of the land, and treated it as a property to be managed for the exclusive advantage of its members, either in the form of interest on the Company's capital, or of lucrative employment for relatives and friends of the shareholders. The advantage of the natives was not considered, except in so far as their prosperity affected that of the Company; and in early days there was no pretence even of this. India was a rich country, and for many years was held to be an inexhaustible mine of wealth, and was treated without scruple as such. Nor was it till the trial of Warren Hastings that any great scandal arose or any serious check was put to the greediness of all concerned. The directors in London, and their servants in the three Presidencies, had a common object of making money, and the only differences between them were as to the division of profits, while all alike grew rich.

The government of the country was then vested in a Board of Directors sitting at the India House, and delegating their executive powers to a civil service of which they themselves had in most instances been originally members, and whose traditions and instincts they preserved. It was a bureaucracy pure and simple, the most absolute, the closest, and the freest of control that the world has ever seen; for, unlike the bureaucracies of Europe, it was subject neither to the will of a sovereign nor to public opinion in any form. Its selfishness was checked only by the individual good feeling of its members, and any good effected by it to others than these was due to a certain traditional largeness of idea as to the true interests of the Company. It was only on the occasion of the renewal of the Company's charter that any interference could be looked for from the English Parliament and public; and so it continued until the Mutiny.

In 1858, however, the Company as a Company

came to an end. The Board of Directors was abolished, dividends ceased to be paid to owners of Indian stock, and the Government of India was transferred nominally to the English Crown. At that time there was a great talk of reforming the system of administration, and it was publicly announced that India should for the future be governed in no other interest than its own. A royal proclamation gave the natives of British India their full status as British subjects; they were no longer to be disqualified for any function of public trust, and no favour was to be shown to English rather than to native interests in the Imperial policy. The programme was an excellent one, and was received in India with enthusiasm, and caused a real outburst of loyalty to the English Crown which has hardly yet subsided. Its only fault, indeed, has been that it has never been carried out, and that while the Indians have waited patiently the plan has been defeated in detail by vested interests too strong for the vacillating intentions either of the Government which designed the change, or of any that have succeeded it. In spite of all official announcements and statements of policy, and royal proclamations, the principle of Indian government remains what it has always been—that is to say, government in the interests of English trade and English adventure. The more liberal design has faded out of sight.

The explanation of so great a failure I believe is this. When the sovereign power was transferred from the Company to the Crown, it was considered convenient to preserve as far as possible the existing machinery of administration. The East India Company had formed a civil service composed of its own English nominees, whose interests had gradually become part and parcel of the general interest of the concern; and they had obtained rights under covenant which secured them in employment, each for his term of years, and afterwards in pension. These rights the English Government now recognized, and the same covenant was entered into with them as had formerly been granted by the Company, and thus a vested interest in administration was perpetuated which has ever since impeded the course of liberal development.

The only real change introduced in 1858 was to substitute appointment by examination for appointment by nomination; but the composition of the service has remained practically the same, and the English covenanted civilian is still, as he was in the days of the Company, the practical owner of India. His position is that of member of a corporation, irremovable, irresponsible, and amenable to no authority but that of his fellow-members. In him is vested all administrative powers, the disposal of all revenue, and the appointment to all subordinate posts. He is, in fact, the Government, and a Government of the most absolute kind.

But the covenanted Civil Service is also a wholly conservative body. Composed though it may be admitted to be in large part of excellent and honest men—men who do their duty, and sometimes more than their duty—it has nevertheless the necessary vice of all corporations. Its first law is its own interests; its second only those of the Indian people. Nor is it casting a reflection on its members to state this. There has never been found yet a body of men anxious to benefit the world at large at the expense of its own pocket; and the Indian Civil Service, which is no exception to the rule, sees in all reform an economy of its pay, a curtailment of its privileges, and a restriction of its field of adventure. Such a service is of its very nature intolerant of economy and intolerant of change.

When, therefore, I say, in common with all native reformers, that the first reform of all in India must be a reform of its covenanted Civil Service, I am advocating primarily the removal of an obstruction. But the covenanted service is also at the present day an anachronism and an entirely needless expense. Fifty, and forty, and even twenty-five years ago, it may have been necessary to contract on extravagant terms and for life with Englishmen of education, in order to obtain their services in so remote a country as India then was. Such men a generation since were comparatively rare, and the India House, and after it the India Office, may have been right in establishing a special privileged service for its needs, and in granting the covenants it made with them. But modern times have altered all this, and now the supply of capacity is so great that quite as good an article can be obtained without any covenant at all. The commercial companies have all long ago abandoned the old idea, and get their servants for India now as for other parts of the world, in the open market; nor do they find the quality inferior because they enter into no lifelong engagements with them. And so also the Indian Government must do in times to come if it is to keep its head financially above water. It is altogether absurd at the present day to contract with men on the basis of their right to be employed and pensioned at extravagant rates as long as they live. It is not done in the English diplomatic service, whose duties are somewhat similar, nor in any other civil service that I know of. I feel certain that as good Englishmen could be obtained now at a third of the pay, and without any further covenant than the usual one of employment during good behaviour, as are now at the present rates and under the present conditions. If not, it would be far better to dispense with English service altogether, except in the highest grades, and employ natives of the country at the lower rates, which would still be high rates to them. The excessive employment of Englishmen has been a growth of comparatively recent date, and is working harm in every way.

Instead of the covenanted Civil Service, therefore, there would be an uncovenanted service obtained in the open market, and endowed with no more special privileges than our services at home. The members of this would then be under control and, in a true sense of the word, the servants of the State. Now they are its masters.

That they are its masters has been abundantly proved by the success of their efforts to thwart Lord Ripon's policy during the last three years. Lord Ripon came out to India on the full tide of the Midlothian victory, and quite in earnest about carrying out Midlothian ideas; nor has he faltered since. But the net result of his viceroyalty has been almost *nil.* Every measure that he has brought forward has been defeated in detail; and so powerful has the Civil Service been that they have forced the Home Government into an abandonment, step by step, of all its Indian policy. This they have effected in part by open opposition, in part by covert encouragement of the English lay element, in part by working through the English press. When I arrived in India I found Lord Ripon like a schoolboy who has started in a race with his fellows and who has run loyally ahead, unaware as yet that these have stopped, and that all the world is laughing at his useless zeal. The Anglo-Indian bureaucracy had shown itself his master in spite of Midlothian.

But if the covenanted Civil Service is an obstructive and burdensome legacy from the defunct Company, so too is the constitution of the Indian Government in London. In 1858, when the Company came to an end, the India House was replaced by the India Office, and the Board of Directors by the Indian Council: a change which was doubtless intended to signify much, but which in practice has come to signify hardly anything at all. The India Office represents of necessity the traditions of the past, and the Council, which was designed to check it, has proved a more conservative and acquiescent body than even the old Board of Directors, its prototype and model. The reason of this is obvious. The Council, composed as it is almost exclusively of retired civil or military servants, views Indian matters from the point of view only of the Anglo-Indian service. It is even less amenable than this is to the influence of new ideas, and is more completely out of touch with modern native thought. Its experience is always that of a generation back, not of the present day, and it refuses, more persistently even than the younger generation in active service, to admit the idea of change.

Thus the Secretary of State, who is dependent on this blind guide, is in no other position at home than is the Viceroy in India. Ignorant, as a rule, of all things Indian, and dependent for advice on the India Office and his Anglo-Indian Council, he never gets at the truth of things, and blunders blindly on as they direct. It is almost impossible for him, however robust his will, to hold his own as a reformer.

The reforms, therefore, at home and in India which native opinion most strongly and immediately demands are, as regards India, that the active Civil Service should be remodelled, by the abolition of all covenants for lifelong employment, and by the liberal infusion of native blood into the non-covenanted service. It is proposed that as vacancies occur a certain proportion—say a third or a fourth—should be reserved exclusively for men of Indian birth, and that thus by degrees the whole Civil Service, with the exception of the highest posts, should become indigenous. Also, as regards the Government at home, that the Secretary of State for India should have the advice of native as well as Anglo-Indian retired officials on his Council in London. Until this is done they consider that the Government of India will continue to be carried on in the dark, and thus that reform will remain as hitherto, abortive.

It is obvious, however, that such initial changes are a first step only in the direction of reforms infinitely more important. What India really asks for as the goal of her ambitions is self-government—that is to say, that not merely executive but legislative and financial power should be vested in the native hands. At present the legislative authority of each Presidency resides in the Governor in Council, and there is no system whatsoever of popular representation, even of the most limited kind. The Councils are composed wholly of nominees, and, except in very small measure, of English official nominees, and their functions are limited to consultation and advice, for they are without any real power of initiative or even of veto. In each of these Councils a few natives have been given places, but they are in no sense representatives of the people, being, on the contrary, nominees of the Government, chosen specially for their subservience to the ideas of the Governor of the day; and their independence is effectually debarred by the further check that their appointment is for three years only, and reversible at the end of such period by the simple will of the Governor. All the other members—and they form the large majority—are English civil or military officers, who look to appointments on the Councils as the prizes of their service, and who usually represent the quintescence of official ideas. Lord Ripon, indeed, took pains to get together men of a liberal sort in his own supreme Council; but as a rule those who enjoy this position are anxious only to secure reappointment at the end of their three years' term. Thus, instead of representing the ideas current among the native classes from which they spring, they serve merely as an echo or chorus to the Governor, or to the permanent officials who sway the Governor. This is not a healthy condition of things. The remedy should be, as a first condition, that the native councillors should be elected by the various classes of the community, and that their tenure of office should be made independent of the Governor's pleasure. I am convinced that the system would work with good results; and if also the number of councillors were increased and their powers of debate and interpellation enlarged, an excellent basis would be laid for what all Indian reformers look to as the ideal of their hopes, provincial parliaments. That India is unfit for local parliamentary institutions of at least a rudimentary kind I cannot at all admit. Indeed it seems to me that few people would profit more rapidly from a public discussion of public affairs than the temperate conservative Hindus. For a while, indeed, it would doubtless be necessary to retain a large English element in their councils, but the Indian mind educates itself with great rapidity, and in another generation they might probably without danger be entrusted with the sole care of their own domestic legislation, and the sole control of their finances.

At the same time, I would not be understood as advocating for India anything in the shape of an Imperial parliament. Empires and parliaments to my mind have very little in common with each other; and India is far too vast a continent, and inhabited by races far too heterogeneous, to make amalgamation in a single assembly possible for representatives elected on any conceivable system. Possibly in the dim future some such thing might be, but not in the lifetime of any one now living, and any attempts of the sort at present would find for themselves the inevitable fate of the Tower of Babel. The Imperial power should, on the contrary, if it is to be effective, remain in the hands of a single man; and instead of weakening the Viceroy's authority I would rather see it strengthened. But with the provinces and for all provincial affairs, self-government is a growing necessity, and the present age is quite capable of witnessing it in practice.

The crying need of India is economy, and for this the decentralization of finance is the only cure. Each province should have its own budget and its own civil lists, which should be voted annually by the Council of the province. Its civil service should be its own, its police its own, and its public works its own, without any right of interference from Calcutta, or any confusion of provincial with Imperial accounts. At present, from the vastness of the country ruled, and the variety of Imperial services which have their seat at Calcutta or Simla, waste and jobbery receive no adequate check. Places are multiplied, men without local knowledge are employed, and the accounts are confused. Supervision by those who bear the burdens of taxation under such a system is all but impossible, and no one knows precisely how and why the expenses charged in the general budget are incurred. But, were the provincial accounts held strictly separate, and subjected to the inquisition of a local assembly composed of men who, as natives of the province, would know the needs and capabilities of the province, none of the present abuses would have a chance of surviving. With the best will in the world, the heads of departments at Calcutta cannot really control the details of expenditure in Madras or the Punjaub, and as a matter of fact there is everywhere enormous waste and enormous jobbery.

I should like, therefore, to see each province of India entirely self-managed as regards all civil matters, raising its own revenue in its own way, providing for its own needs of internal order, public works, and administration of all kinds, and controlled by the constant supervision of its own provincial assembly. In this way it would be possible to differentiate at once between the various provinces as to their special needs and the composition of their special services. In some the expenditure, and with it the taxation, might be at the outset reduced by the employment almost entirely of native servants; in others the substitution of native for English service would have to be more gradual. In some, large public works might be profitably afforded; in others, economy would have to be the rule. In all there would be an incentive to reduce unnecessary expenditure, seeing that the burden of providing for it would fall directly on the province.

On the other hand it is clear that, as long as India remains under the protection of England, certain charges on the revenue and certain executive and legislative functions would have to remain Imperial. These would be, first, charges and responsibilities in respect of the army and navy; secondly, the diplomatic relations; thirdly, the general debt; and fourthly, the customs.

With regard to the army, there can be no doubt that the charge should be an Imperial one, for though Southern India has little need of troops to preserve order within her borders, she enjoys, in common with the North, that immunity from invasion which the army alone can guarantee, and she should have an equal share of the burden of its cost. To adopt a system of provincial armies would, in my view of the case, be both a mistake of economy, and an injustice to those provinces which lie upon the frontier, as well as a considerable danger from the rivalries they might engender: a mistake of economy, inasmuch as the higher commands would be multiplied, and the less warlike provinces would at an equal cost provide inferior material to the general strength of the empire; an injustice, inasmuch as the North-Western provinces would have to bear nearly the entire burden of defence. Strongly, therefore, as I advocate decentralization in all matters of civil administration, I as strongly advocate centralization in matters military. The Imperial army, according to my ideas, should be under the sole control of the Viceroy, officered, I think, by Englishmen, and composed of the best fighting material to be obtained in India, irrespective of prejudice in favour of this or that recruiting ground. It is manifestly the first condition of an army that it should be efficient, and the second that it should be without political colour, and on both grounds I am inclined to think that Englishmen would prove more useful servants to India in a military capacity than any native class of officers could be. Much as I believe in Indian capacity for civil duties, I accept it as a fact that Englishmen make better commanders of troops, and are worth more even in proportion to their superior pay; while there is no question that they would be exempt, as native officers would not, from religious and caste influences, and thus more reliable as impartial executors of Imperial orders. The Indian Sepoy army, then, as I would see it, should be as distinctly Imperial and English as the civil services should be provincial and native. In saying this I am stating my private opinion only; I believe that native opinion is in favour of native military service. But, as I understand India, the time has not come for that. When India is a nation it will be time enough to think of a national army.

The diplomatic relations, again, of India must of necessity remain Imperial, and their management vested solely in the Viceroy. Indian diplomacy, as at present managed, is a complicated and costly thing; but in the India of the future we may hope this will be much simplified. Two cardinal points of policy might with advantage be observed: the first, to keep wholly apart from foreign intrigues and foreign wars; the second, to keep rigid faith with the still independent native princes within the border. Of foreign wars India has long had enough, and more than enough. The Chinese, the Persian, the Afghan, the Abyssinian, the Egyptian, and now the Soudanese, all these India has been forced to take part in, solely against her interest and her will. Apart from their money loss, there is in these wars a loss of dignity, which the Indian people are beginning to resent. Those who have been educated in the humane literature of Europe find it humiliating that they, a conquered people, should be used as the instrument for conquering others. What quarrel had India with the unfortunate Egyptians? What quarrel has she with the unfortunate Arabs? The educated Indians resent it bitterly, too, that India is made to pay the cost. But these things need no comment. They are but a part of that absolute selfishness which has been the principle of all our past relations with India, and in the new birth of India these too must be changed. The diplomatic relations with the native States have been a tissue of fraud and aggression. In the policy of the future, aggression must be abandoned. There is but one true policy towards the native States; and that is, by giving them the spectacle of a British India more happy than their own to invite their inhabitants to share its advantages. Who can doubt that were India self-governed, prosperous, and happy, the old native principalities would one by one spontaneously be merged in it.

With regard to the Debt, much as we may regret that it was ever incurred, it must remain, I fear, in our new India a charge on the Imperial Government. Its annual interest, like the cost of war and diplomacy, should be apportioned as a fixed charge to each province in proportion to that province's wealth, except in so far as it relates to the guarantees of railways, which might be made a charge on the provinces served by them. It should, however, be a cardinal point of policy that no further debt should be incurred and no further guarantees given for Imperial works. The provinces henceforth should be charged with all works of communication, irrigation, and improvement, the utility of which they will best appreciate.

Remain the Customs. These too must remain an Imperial matter; and it may be hoped that when, in the future, India's interest, not England's, comes to be considered in her government, they may be made to return a fair profit to balance some of the Imperial charges. To India free trade has proved no blessing, and a return to import duties is a first principle of sound finance, which self-governing India will undoubtedly insist on. The majority, I believe, of our English colonies see their advantage in these, and so will India, unless, indeed, some fair equivalent be given. As it is, all the profit is on England's side, on India's all the loss.

Such, very briefly and imperfectly given, is my scheme of self-government for India. That it is one possible—I do not say easy—to realize few will doubt who have marked the wonderful success achieved in a case not very dissimilar nearer our own shores. The Empire of Austria, within the recollection of men of the present generation, was a bureaucratic despotism of the harshest and least sympathetic kind. It had got within its rule, by conquest or inheritance, a half score of nations, owning no ties of birth or language, and united only by a common hatred of their oppressors. The Austrian official of 1847 was a byword of arrogance and self-sufficient pride, and while vaunting to the world the virtues of his own method of rule, was preparing the way for a general revolt against the Empire. Few who watched the history of those days believed that Austria was not doomed to perish, and none that she was destined to achieve the love of her people. Yet we have lived to see this. We have lived to see the Hungarians reconciled, and the very Poles who in their despair had filled Europe for fifty years with their denunciations, thanking Austria for her share in their ruin. If this has been possible through the gift of self-government, all things are possible; and India by the same means of honest government, each province for itself, may become happy and thankful, as the Austrian nations have. One principle keeps these together without force, their loyalty to the wearer of the Imperial crown; and fortunately this is a principle we have in India already framed to our hand. There is no question that the Indian populations are possessed with a strong feeling of personal attachment for her Majesty the Queen, and while they grow yearly more and more estranged from their Anglo-Indian masters they yearly look with more and more hope to England and to her who sits upon the English throne. This is a sentiment of the utmost value, and one which may yet prove the salvation of the Indian Empire, in spite of all the Anglo-Indians can do to wreck it. I look to it in the future as the true bond of union which shall retain for us India, not as our inheritance, for it will not be ours to possess, but as a co-heir to our good fortunes. India will not then be lost to England, but will remain to us a far greater glory than now, because it will have become a monument of what we shall have been able to achieve for the benefit of others, not merely for ourselves.

I dare not, however, dwell too much upon this prospect. I know the huge perils which surround the birth of every new thing in the political world, and I know the unscrupulous rage of vested interests threatened. The interests of the Anglo-Indians stand stoutly in our way, and the interests of an ever more hungry commerce and an ever more pitiless finance. Commerce and finance find their gain in the present system. Manchester must be appeased before India can hope to live, and to stop suddenly the career of Indian extravagance would injure trade in many a North of England town. Debt in India unfortunately means dividends in Lombard Street; and so I dare not hope. I am tempted rather to quote as only too likely to prove true certain desponding words which I once heard uttered by General Gordon when, speaking of the prospect of reform in India, he told me, "You may do what you will. It will be of no use. India will never be reformed until there has been there a new revolt." But what will that revolt be, and how will it leave our power of reformation?[1]

[1] *Note.*—The reader must once more be reminded that this chapter, with the three that precede it, was written full twenty-five years ago. Its scheme of constitutional reform was scoffed at then as fanciful and Utopian. But the Asiatic world has marched on, and English opinion to-day seems to have awakened at last to its recommendations as a coming necessity. Whether the concessions now being elaborated so tardily at the India Office will suffice to allay the bitter feelings aroused by the reactionary policy of a whole past generation since Lord Ripon's time, I forbear to prophesy. It is the common nemesis of alien rule to be too late in its reforms, and, even with the best intentions, to give the thing no longer asked, because its knowledge of the ruled has lagged behind. I deliver no opinion. It must suffice me that I have recorded my full testimony in this volume to a historical understanding of the India I knew in 1883-1884, during the too short rule of its best and wisest Viceroy.

APPENDIX I

THE MOHAMMEDAN UNIVERSITY

SCHEME FOR A UNIVERSITY, FORWARDED TO THE NIZAM, JANUARY 24, 1884

THE lamentable decline, during the last forty years, of the Mohammedan community of India in wealth and social importance, while at the same time it has been numerically an ever-increasing body, makes it a matter of anxious consideration with those who love their religion to consider by what means best to avert the danger attending such a condition of things, and to restore prosperity to the community and its activity as a living and beneficial influence in the progress of the Empire.

It is acknowledged that the evil has been principally brought about by the changed condition of the country. From a ruling and favoured race, the Mohammedan community has become only one of many bodies unfavoured by the State; and the fall from their high station was at the time accompanied by a corresponding collapse of energy; while, later, accidental circumstances, such as the change of the official language from Persian and Urdu to English, still further aggravated their misfortunes.

These, though they may regret them, the Mohammedans now know that it is useless to complain of. They have ceased to look for any reversal of the political settlement of India as a British province; and accepting the fact, they are fully aware that a new departure is necessary for them in correspondence with their new circumstances. Nor is this conviction lessened by the consideration that it would seem to be the tendency of the age to put every year more and more administrative power back into native hands, so that in the future there may be expected to be an ever-increasing competition between the various sections of Indian society for advantage under the imperial rule.

Again, it is no less acknowledged that, in the modern conditions of Indian life, that which principally conduces to the advantage of each community is its superiority in education. The force of natural character is no longer a sufficient element of success, and acquired intelligence is daily asserting itself more strongly as the condition of all participation in public life. Instruction in the arts and sciences of the Western world is at the present day an absolute necessity for high success; and even in the lower walks of life a certain knowledge of these things has become desirable for all perhaps but the lowest class bound to agricultural labour. Certainly no large community, such as is the Mohammedan in India, could hope to hold its own without a general increase of learning; and it is no longer contended by any section of the community that secular knowledge can be dispensed with, or that it is, if rightly directed, at all opposed to the best interests of religion.

On the other hand, it is equally certain that the vast majority of those who profess the faith of Islam look upon that faith as the most precious inheritance bequeathed them by their fathers, and decline to put it in peril for the sake of any worldly advantage. They consider that, in seeking the general good of a Mohammedan community, the first and absolute essential to be considered is the good of the Mohammedan religion; and this is their first thought, too, when the practical question of individual education comes before them. All Mohammedan fathers are desirous that, before everything else, their sons should inherit their own gift of faith in the one true God and the teaching of His apostle.

Thus, then, it happens that, while recognizing fully the necessity there is for worldly knowledge, the mass of respectable Mohammedans have held back, and still hold back, from the purely secular education afforded in Government schools and colleges to Hindus and Christians with themselves. They look with suspicion on the teaching, and with more than suspicion on the teachers. They refuse to believe that any education can be a sound one which is without a religious basis. They see that neither history nor philosophy nor Western literature can be taught by unbelievers in the divine mission of their Prophet without serious risk of undermining their pupils' faith; and they find no institution in India in which these necessary branches of human learning are taught to Mohammedans wholly by Mohammedans. Neither the Indian University, nor the Calcutta Madraseh, nor the Hooghly College, nor even the College of Aligarh entirely fulfil this condition. In the Indian University there is at the present moment no single Mohammedan professor. At the Madraseh, the president and many of the professors are Englishmen; and at Aligarh also the principal is an Englishman, and there are English and Hindu teachers. In none of them is there the certainty that religious influence other than Mohammedan shall not be brought to bear upon the students.

Lastly—and this is the most important consideration of all to the leaders of the Mohammedan community of India—they find in all the Empire, no central school of religious thought such as is to be found in other Mohammedan lands. Although their population is the largest of any now existing in the world, they are without a recognized seat of learning which can claim for them to be the fountain head of orthodox opinion. They have no central body of Ulema, whose teaching and discussion should serve to keep alive the intellectual activity of the religious teachers and so give its tone to the whole mass. They feel this to be the most serious want of all of their situation in presence of the growing intelligence of other religious bodies around them.

In view of all these circumstances, the following resolutions have, therefore, been suggested, and are now put before the Mohammedan community at large:

1. That in each town a Provincial Committee shall be formed, to consider where and under what conditions it will be best to found an educational establishment on a large scale, which shall equally satisfy the religious and the secular wants of the community; and to raise subscriptions for that purpose.

2. That, this being done, a Central Committee shall be convened, the same to be composed of one delegate from each of the Provincial Committees, in order finally to decide the questions raised in the Provincial Committees.

3. That, if possible, his Highness the Nizam of the Deccan be asked to become the patron of a Central Establishment, as being the most powerful Mohammedan prince now reigning in India, and that a humble petition be addressed to his Highness in that sense. The following suggestions also are made:

1. That the educational establishment should take the form of a university, to be called the Deccan (?) University, empowered to grant degrees in religion and in secular knowledge, and to appoint professors in both branches of learning for such as shall repair to its metropolis (say Hyderabad) for their education. It is hoped that his Highness the Nizam may be pleased to grant a building to serve as university hall and lecture-rooms.

2. That, under the university, each province of the Indian Empire, or, if funds suffice, each great city, should erect or purchase at its own cost a building for its own students in the metropolis, the same to be called the college of that province or city, at which lodging (not board or furniture) should be provided at nominal rates to the students. These colleges should be the property of the provinces or cities erecting them, and should be managed by provincial or city trustees appointed by themselves in such manner (subject to the general laws of the university) as they shall themselves think most desirable. Thus each province or city would practically pay for and manage its own education.

3. That an appeal be made to the Mohammedan princes,

noblemen, talukdars, zemindars, and rich merchants to found professorships for the university, the same to bear the name of their founders, and to be vested as religious endowments in the hands of university trustees, the duty of the professors being to give gratuitous public lectures to all students of the university. A donation of Rs. 30,000 shall be considered equivalent to founding a professorship, and shall entitle the donor to have his name perpetually connected with it—this, although it may be hereafter considered necessary to increase the provision out of university funds. Such donors should moreover be granted the title of "Founders" of the university, and should form its special council.

4. That a similar appeal be made to poorer men to found scholarships under the like conditions, except that Rs. 10,000 should be the sum entitling the donor to perpetual remembrance—the said scholarships to be granted in the form of monthly stipends of thirty rupees to such students as, having graduated in religious and secular knowledge in the university, may be chosen by special competition, on the condition that they shall act as schoolmasters in provincial towns and districts. The object of this provision will be to spread religious and secular education throughout the country. The founder of three scholarships to have the same privilege and title as the founder of a professorship.

5. That special provision be made in the scheme for the religious needs of the Shiah as well as of the Sunni communities.

6. That his Highness the Nizam be prayed to grant a perpetual charter regulating the university according to the rules usual in such institutions.

7. That a memorial be at the same time addressed to his Excellency the Viceroy of India, stating the objects of the university, and humbly praying the countenance of the Imperial Government for the scheme.

Hyderabad Deccan,
February 13, 1884.

MY DEAR MR. BLUNT,

I am desired by his Highness to inform you, in reply to your letter of the 24th of January, enclosing a memo. embodying a scheme for the formation of a Mohammedan University, that his Highness cordially approves of your suggestions, and will give every support in his power to any attempt that may be made to carry them out. His Highness had the honour of holding a conversation with his Excellency the Viceroy during his short sojourn here, in the course of which he understood that his Excellency was prepared to countenance and support the scheme.

I am to say that his Highness regards the scheme as one calculated immensely to advance the cause of Mohammedan progress, and that he will be glad if Hyderabad is given the honour, by preference, of becoming the centre of the movement. As, however, the scheme has originated with you, and you have taken the trouble of ascertaining the views of the leading Mohammedans in all parts of India, his Highness would have wished that you had prolonged your stay in this country so as to see it carried out. In any case, if your other engagements give you time to pay another visit to Hyderabad, his Highness will be gratified to have your assistance in the matter. His Highness is glad to say that his Excellency the Viceroy has promised him his.

Believe me, yours very sincerely,

SALAR JUNG.

APPENDIX II

SIR WILLIAM HUNTER TO MR. BLUNT

Calcutta,
6th January, 1884.

DEAR MR. BLUNT,

I have been unable to procure a copy of the "Settlement Handbook." But here is one which I have borrowed. With regard to the Madras settlement, some detailed facts will be found at pp. 668 and 672, among other places.

The rules are: (1) First calculate the actual average produce and actual average value of it, over a period of years. Say the actual gross produce thus ascertained is 100 bushels. (2) Then deduct from the average actual gross produce one-sixth, as an extra allowance for risks of the season; leaving $83\frac{1}{3}$ bushels. (3) Take an average of one-fourth, or 25 per cent., from this reduced gross produce as Government Revenue; this is four eighty-thirds and a half, $= 20\frac{3}{4}$ bushels.

The $20\frac{3}{4}$ bushels are about one-fifth of the actual gross produce (100 bushels), which has already included the risk of seasons, for it is the actual produce yielded, as a matter of fact, on an average of many years and seasons.

The $20\frac{3}{4}$ bushels are about one-half of the *net* produce after allowing for cost of cultivation and all possible risks; and this is probably what your *raiyat* friends meant in Madras.

The actual yield of each class of land is estimated by many experiments, sometimes 1,300 in a single district. The Famine Commissioners, by independent inquiry, came to the conclusion that the average land tax throughout India was only $5\frac{1}{2}$ per cent. of the gross produce; but their calculation included Bengal and the Permanently Settled Districts. I have not been able to examine afresh the evidence on which they based this conclusion; but they were careful men, and by no means favourers of the *status quo*.

I am no favourer of that *status* in many parts of India; and if you care to go into the question I shall be happy to send you my exposure in Council of the heavy burden imposed by our Land Assessments on the Deccan peasant. The speech was telegraphed verbatim to the "Times" fourteen months ago; but, if you did not see it, and care to look at it, I can get you a copy.

I send you the foregoing facts, not to convert you to a system which has grievous defects, but to enable you to deal with that system without running into little inaccuracies which would be laid hold of as vitiating your main argument.

I have been much impressed by your sympathy for the hard lot of the peasant, whether in Egypt or in India, and by your determination to find out the facts for yourself. If at any time you desire to compare the information thus collected with the statistics officially accepted by the Government, I shall be happy to render you any assistance in my power.

Very faithfully yours,
W. W. HUNTER.

APPENDIX III

Major Claude Clerk to Mr. Blunt

9, Albert Hall Mansions, Kensington Gore, S.W.
November 15th, 1904.

Dear Mr. Blunt,

Very many thanks for your "Ideas about India" which you have so kindly sent me. I look forward with pleasure to reading your work, and I know I shall find much in it of the greatest interest to me. Although I have only just glanced at what you then wrote, I can see that all you say is as true now as it was then—the impoverishment of the millions, and the reckless extravagance of their effeminate rulers, living away from the people in their mountain retreats nine months usually out of the twelve. You may put down much of India's woes to the farce of a government whose officials are perched away in the clouds, absorbed in their own amusements, etc., "in the hills," and unmindful of their duty to the people. Lord Curzon has done something to break down this Simla curse of India. Lord Randolph Churchill was a very great loss to India. Had it been fated that his time at the India Office could have been prolonged, he would have set many things to rights there. The hard work he did do there went a long way to break him down, as it did to a good man of the name of Moore he found there, and who died, I think, about the same time as Lord Randolph Churchill. I should like some day, when you are again in England and I alive, to send you a copy of a letter I wrote to Lord Ripon, and of an official report I sent in showing what the state of things was during the last years of the Nizam's minority, affecting as it did his training, etc. I much doubt whether this ever got beyond the Residency.

I had no idea that your knowledge as to what was really going on at Hyderabad had so largely influenced Lord Ripon. You are perfectly right in what you say as to his being put away at Bolarum, removed from the city, etc. I had offered my house but was told there was fear of cholera! That matters went wrong subsequently between the young Salar Jung and his master was no fault of what Lord Ripon did. Foiled in what they had aimed at, the party in power had other sinister objects in view, and with the underhand support of the Residency these they carried out. They, of course, saw that a difference between the Nizam and his young minister opened the road to their designs, especially as the latter—who was throughout in the wrong—was supported by Cordery, which, of course, made matters worse. From the first, when Salar Jung asked me, when here in England, to take up the appointment—which I declined at first and for some weeks—I determined, when I had accepted it, to hold myself entirely aloof from the Simla clique and its ways, of which I was not an admirer. After you left, my summary removal by the party in power was an object to be kept in view. But the first attempt was so clumsy that even Cordery could give it only a half-hearted support. Afterwards they succeeded. My agreement with Salar Jung was to serve ten years, and fifteen if required to do so. The young Nizam, unknown to me, as I was in England on sick leave for three months, had asked to retain my services for the full period, but the Government of India, of course prompted by Cordery, abruptly refused the Nizam's request.

Pray pardon all this personal recollection of what occurred then, but my pen has run on! Your pp. 132, 133, as to the Emir-el-Kabir, the colleague forced by Lord Lytton on Salar Jung, this is what was written of him by Sir George Yule, one of the best men we ever had as Resident at Hyderabad and who retained Salar Jung's friendship to the day of his death:

"In spite of Salar Jung's repeated remonstrances, we have forced upon him as his colleague a man who was notoriously his personal enemy, a man who had heavily bribed others in scandalous intrigues against him, and whose servant had openly tried to murder him." This was the man—the tool—we wanted to work Salar Jung's humiliation to the bitter end. Such had been his iniquitous intrigues in former years that a more honest Government than Lord Lytton's had ordered that he was *never* to be present at any Durbar where English officers were present.

Very truly yours,

CLAUDE CLERK.

9, Albert Hall Mansions,

April 29th, 1905.

I often look at your "Ideas about India," and find always something to interest me and to inform me. Lord Ripon's policy in making the young Salar Jung *Dewan* was of course a risky one. But it was, as you well know, the right course. That it would have been crowned with success there is no doubt whatever—I was behind the scenes throughout—in my mind, had Lord Ripon gone only one step further and changed the Resident. Cordery was bound hand and foot by the action of those with whom he was associated, and they were supporting the very party in the city—which Cordery went so far as to call "our party"—who had determined on the moral ruin of the Nizam during a two years' prolongation of the minority, during which they would have kept the lid of the Treasury open without scruple of any sort or kind. As it was, Lord Ripon had not been gone from Hyderabad for a month before that party, supported through thick and thin by Cordery, had gained the ascendancy. The difference, originally but a trifle, between the Nizam and his Dewan, was skilfully fanned by the bribed members of the Nizam's and the Dewan's entourage, and an open breach between the two was then inevitable. How our Government acted to retain the young Salar Jung in power—when they knew it was too late—is an amusing story, but too long to trouble you with here. But I would like some day when you are again in London to send you my official reports for the last years of the Nizam's minority. These were written by me yearly and submitted to H.H.'s Government and then sent on through the Resident to the Government of India (Foreign Department). I ought to have been called on to explain the statements I had made, or H.H. ought to have been desired to dismiss me on the spot, considering what I had stated. But this only being the truth, the Government of India did neither, fearing the result. My reports were left entirely unnoticed and this after the Government of India's repeated declarations that it, the Government of India, was *the guardian* of H.H. and deeply interested in his education, welfare, etc. But I was much in the way of the party in power, and soon opportunity was found of getting me out of Hyderabad.

Yours very truly,
CLAUDE CLERK.

INDEX

Index

Index